Library of
Davidson College

Library of
Davidson College

# SHAKESPEARE: OUT OF COURT

# Shakespeare: Out of Court

## Dramatizations of Court Society

GRAHAM HOLDERNESS
NICK POTTER and
JOHN TURNER

St. Martin's Press    New York

© Graham Holderness, Nick Potter and John Turner 1990

All rights reserved. For information, write:
Scholarly and Reference Division,
St. Martin's Press, Inc., 175 Fifth Avenue,
New York, N.Y. 10010

First published in the United States of America in 1990

Printed in Hong Kong

ISBN 0-312-04616-2

Library of Congress Cataloging-in-Publication Data
Holderness, Graham.
Shakespeare, out of court : dramatizations of court society /
Graham Holderness, Nick Potter, and John Turner
p.   cm.
ISBN 0-312-04616-2
1. Shakespeare, William, 1564–1616 – Political and social views.
2. Literature and society – Great Britain – History.  3. Courts and courtiers in literature.  4. Social history in literature.  5. Great Britain – Court and courtiers – History.  I. Potter, Nick.
II. Turner, John, 1944–  .  III. Title
PR3024.H65  1990                                                89-70305
822.3'3 –dc20                                                         CIP

Once again, for
Fred and Vera Turner
Ninon, Joel and James Potter
Rachel Phyllis Natasha Holderness

# Contents

| | | |
|---|---|---|
| List of Texts | | ix |
| Acknowledgement | | xi |
| Introduction  *John Turner* | | 1 |
| | PART I: THE COURT AND THE NEW LEARNING<br>*John Turner* | |
| 1 | Prologue: 'Of Studies' and Play | 15 |
| 2 | *Love's Labour's Lost*: The Court at Play | 19 |
| 3 | *Hamlet*: The Court in Transition (I) | 49 |
| | PART II: IDEALIZED COURTS AND DREAMS OF FREEDOM<br>*Nick Potter* | |
| 4 | Wildness and Wilderness: Alternatives to Courtly Life | 83 |
| 5 | *As You Like It*: The Outlaw Court | 86 |
| 6 | *Twelfth Night*: The Court in Transition (II) | 105 |
| 7 | Afterword: 'For the rain it raineth every day' | 122 |
| | PART III: LATE ROMANCES: MAGIC, MAJESTY AND MASQUE<br>*Graham Holderness* | |
| 8 | Introduction: Theatre and Court | 129 |
| 9 | *The Tempest*: Spectacles of Disenchantment | 136 |
| 10 | *The Winter's Tale*: Country into Court | 195 |
| Endgames  *Graham Holderness* | | 236 |
| Notes | | 249 |
| Index | | 263 |

# List of Texts

**Part I  The Court and the New Learning**

Richard David (ed.), *The Arden Shakespeare: Love's Labour's Lost* (Methuen, 1956)

Harold Jenkins (ed.), *The Arden Shakespeare: Hamlet* (Methuen, 1982)

**Part II  Idealized Courts and Dreams of Freedom**

Agnes Latham (ed.), *The Arden Shakespeare: As You Like It* (Methuen, 1975)

J. M. Lothian and T. W. Craik (eds.), *The Arden Shakespeare: Twelfth Night* (Methuen, 1975)

**Part III  Late Romances: Magic, Majesty and Masque**

Stephen Orgel (ed.), *The Oxford Shakespeare: The Tempest* (Oxford University Press, 1987)

J. H. P. Pafford (ed.), *The Arden Shakespeare: The Winter's Tale* (Methuen, 1963)

# Acknowledgement

We should like here to pay our thanks to Ms Jan Greengo for her meticulous preparation of the typescript.

# Introduction
## John Turner

In a poem of 1596, that culminates in praise of the ideal image of Queen Elizabeth and her court as the perfect work of history, we see her as the moon surrounded by a thousand sparkling stars, all moving in measure about her with an orderly variety of change so deft that it baffles the observer's eye and understanding; and when for a moment she lays aside the business of her majesty to watch the revels of her court, she sees a dance 'so full of State, Art, and varietie' that once again the observer's mind is entangled and deceived.[1] The dance is both a particular activity of the court and an emblem of all its activities: an emblem that transforms the multifarious alliances and ruptures of its competitive life into harmonious pattern and fills the awkward distances and lacunae of time and space with plenitude. Penelope – the observer here, gazing into a prophetic glass – is spell-bound; the sublime and benign deception of the dance satisfies both her eye and reason by transcending their powers of apprehension. It sets her mind 'in heaunly thoughts', a response which is presented to the reader as a paradigm: for the just observer must always be drawn in, entangled and – won away from a dangerous, critical aloofness – find his fulfilment in the pattern of the whole. As Coleridge was to argue later, the particular glory of Elizabethan England was that 'the people .... are in order to the state, rather than that the state exists for the sake of the people'.[2] To Sir John Davies writing *Orchestra*, the rituals of the court lay at the centre of this mystery; for it was an institution ordained by God which, if fulfilled in the performance of the queen and her courtiers, would surely fashion the conduct and character of all its observers to the harmony of political obedience.

*Orchestra* had set out to 'represent in liuely show/Our glorious English courts diuine image,/As it should be in this our Golden Age'; but other traditions of courtly representation were directly opposed to such idealism. There was, for instance, the tradition of courtly lament, exemplified in Raleigh's 'Farewell to the Court', where disappointment turned visions like those of Sir John Davies into 'truthles dreames'; the sleeper awoke out of imagined plenitude to find himself 'in a countrey strange without companion', an outsider cast away upon the shores of time and place.³ Alongside such laments were the many traditions of satire: popular verse satire; courtly verse satire, like Wyatt's; popular dramatic satire, that was eventually colonized by the masque and institutionalized in the half-life of the anti-masque; and from the 1590s onward there was also the angry verse and dramatic satire of an urban bourgeois intelligentsia. Here were observers who wrote as though they refused to join the dance and whose discordant writing obstinately desacralized court ritual. To these men the court was a theatre of deception, an institution – whether man-made or man-marred – that imposed falsehood upon all its followers. At worst it was the seat of vice, as Raleigh confirmed from the scaffold: 'And now I intreat you all to join with me in Prayer, that the Great God of Heaven, whom I have grievously offended, being a Man full of Vanity, and have lived a sinful Life, in all sinful Callings, having been a Souldier, a Captain, a Sea–Captain, and a Courtier, which are all places of Wickedness and Vice; that God (I say) would forgive me, and that he would receive me into everlasting Life'.⁴ At best it was no better than a place of seeming where *quedam videntur, et non sunt*;⁵ and all its boasted culture, like that of Marston's Castilio or Jonson's Sir Annual Tilter,⁶ was bought rather than earned, the display of money rather than of genuine personal accomplishment. *Schein not Sein*: the most comprehensive version of this traditional picture of the court as a place of seeming, in which the individual is not realized but derealized, is to be found in the work of La Bruyère, describing the court of Louis XIV at Versailles nearly a century later:

> Dans cent ans le monde subsistera encore en son entier: ce sera le même théâtre et les mêmes décorations, ce ne seront plus les mêmes acteurs. Tout ce qui se réjouit sur une grâce reçue, ou ce qui s'attriste et se désespère sur un refus, tous auront disparu de dessus la scène. Il s'avance déjà sur le théâtre d'autres hommes qui vont jouer dans une même pièce les mêmes rôles; ils s'évanouiront à leur tour; et ceux qui ne sont pas encore, un jour ne seront plus: de nouveaux acteurs ont pris leur place. Quel fonds à faire sur un personnage de comédie!⁷

To the sardonic eyes of La Bruyère, this image of the theatre shows how the monolithic court of the *ancien régime* dwarfs the lives of all those who dance attendance upon it and drains them of significance.[8] But what in retrospect is intriguing about the image in its Elizabethan usage is its great fluidity; for the theatre, like the dance, might image both pomp and pretence, both the graceful adaptability of success and the sycophantic shallowness so self-evident to the satirical eye of failure or contempt. It might sustain equally an ideal or a critical vision, true not only to different attitudes in different people but also to the ambivalence within each individual person attempting to depend upon that least dependable of Tudor and Jacobean institutions, where favour might be won and lost in a moment, the institution of the court.

The subject of this book is Shakespeare's dramatizations of court life, his dramatizations of that aristocratic society and patriarchal order that reached its culmination in the life of the Renaissance court; and it is part of our contention that the theatre provided Shakespeare with not only an appropriate poetic image but also with an appropriate epistemological arena in which both to celebrate and to scrutinize that life as it variously appeared to its various observers. For there was felt to be an affinity between the theatre and the court that nevertheless was far removed from an identity: the two institutions seemed similar enough, and yet were sufficiently distinct, for the one to image the other not only by the *what* but also by the *how* of its representations. The affinity has two aspects that concern us here. In the first place, the theatre raises in a heightened form all those questions surrounding the distinction between reality and illusion that characteristically haunted the court life of the period. It presents person as persona, place as role and success as skilled performance; furthermore, it dresses authority in rhetoric and show and, in so doing, makes it available not only for admiration but also for sceptical analysis. For to think of public life as a stage is at least to entertain the possibility that being may be irretrievably lost beneath layers of seeming, that the self may be known only by the roles it assumes, and that all courtly deeds, as Hamlet found, are 'actions that a man might play' (I.ii.84). Theatre thus proved an ideal site in which to explore the possibilities of honesty in acting out the demands of court life. In the second place, the nature of drama as it developed in Elizabethan and Jacobean England was peculiarly appropriate to explore the sociological tensions of a court world where perpetual motion was maintained, in the words of Norbert Elias, 'by the need for prestige and the tensions which, once they were there, it endlessly renewed by its competitive process'.⁹ For drama at that time seemed to demand conflictual interaction, competition between different characters with different private interests to pursue amidst the social group; and Shakespeare, as we show below in our discussion of *Love's Labour's Lost*, had a clear grasp of the ambiguities structured into the nature of courtly competition – ambiguities disclosed by the remarkable range of meaning that the word itself came to possess in the sixteenth century. His plays were drawn by the very necessities of their form to the central ambiguities and conflicts, the structural fault-lines and *Bruchstellen* of the societies in which they were set; and in their commitment to the excitements of plot, they disclose the fulness of the affinity between theatre and court – for both were arenas in which the demands for an honest morality coexisted uneasily with the need for intrigue. The Elizabethan theatre thus shows itself to be as John Danby described it: 'a new organ of thought'¹⁰ ideally suited to explore the tensions of life at court and to dramatize them in their various interpretative possibilities, relating idealistic and satirical images alike to the facts of social power as they existed at particular moments of their historical evolution.

The causes of the tensions in court life were many. In the first place, there were the internal tensions caused by the multiplicity of the roles demanded of a courtier; for the court was a complex institution, whose diverse functions often placed baffling and sometimes tragically irreconcilable claims upon its followers, both in their work and in their leisure. Its work consisted in the regulation of international affairs in diplomacy, trade and war; in the regulation of national affairs, legal, fiscal, ecclesiastical and administrative, chiefly through its position as the centre of patronage and public appointment; and in its own self-regulation as the king's household, a sprawling economic unit that was also a judicial area in its own right. Its leisure was devoted to pursuits that were in themselves badges of aristocratic distinction and thus not wholly separable from its fundamental work of self-publicity: sporting pursuits such as hunting, jousting, gambling and – perhaps it should be included here – courtly love; and cultural pursuits such as music, masque, dance and all the new learning of the humanist revival. 'Alasse, you will be ungentle gentlemen, if you bee no schollers':¹¹ and yet the claims of all these courtly activities might compete with one another. Love, for instance, might subvert political loyalty; and such conflicts, caused by the multiple and often contradictory demands of court life, will form the chief theme of our opening discussion of *Love's Labour's Lost* below. In the second place, the causes of the tensions within the Renaissance court lay deep in the history of its evolution – in England, deep in the programme of the Tudor pacification. We may agree with Perry Anderson that, from the perspective of the people, the new absolutist states of early modern Europe – and the courts from which they were ruled – were no more than '*a redeployed and recharged apparatus of feudal domination*'.[12] But from the perspective of the aristocracy the development was momentous, since their continued political influence was achieved only at the cost of their military independence. The ebb and flow of the long historical struggle between the English king and his aristocracy, stretching back into the Middle Ages, was of course familiar to Shakespeare, and he dramatized some of its key confrontations in his history plays. What was lost in the course of this struggle seems to have mattered as much to him as what was gained, and the sense of lost (perhaps even of sacrificed) aristocratic glory makes itself felt equally in the heroic poetry of the tragedies and the melancholy of the courtly comedies. The metaphoric patterns of *Love's Labour's Lost*, for instance, show how the competition of courtly life is experienced as a sublimation at once exhilarating and melancholy of lost, more vital military energies. Melancholy here, as so often in later periods, is a measure both of the degree of a civilization and its discontents; the civil war of courtly wits belongs to a safe but shrunken world, where manners have been attained at the price of manliness. Nor was this struggle simply a matter of history to Shakespeare. Its last tragic act was played out in his own life-time, in a form that recapitulated the whole nature of the struggle, and in circumstances that must have interested him deeply if only because they involved the staging of one of his own plays, *Richard II*. For Essex's rebellion against Elizabeth – a defiant attempt at self–vindication before a queen who denied him access on the advice of courtiers whom he considered mere parvenus – was the last in a long line of aristocratic rebellions that were justified by appeal to the aristocratic code of honour, and its failure symbolized the final passing of an age.[13] Indeed, Essex's career and downfall might stand as an emblem, as it was maybe an inspiration, of a story that Shakespeare told again and again and that perfectly expresses his paradoxical reading of historical progress – a story which we may summarize by adopting some words of Yeats, speaking of nobility where Yeats spoke rather of wisdom:

'Shakespeare's myth, it may be, describes a *noble* man who was blind from very *nobility*, and an empty man who thrust him from his place, and saw all that could be seen from very emptiness'.[14] The possibilities of ironic tragedy lie here; and in our chapter on *Hamlet* we offer a reading of the play that traces the failure of its hero's adventure in self-fashioning to his inability to reconcile the demands of the old aristocratic code of honour with those of the new monarchical state in which he finds himself.

In the third place, there were tensions between court and country – longstanding tensions, not simply internal to aristocratic circles, that were increasingly exacerbated by the centripetal pull of the court; for whilst, through his virtual monopoly of the means to prestige, the monarch brought his aristocracy to court and thus secured his dominance over them, at the same time – ironically – he drew them away from the country over which he also needed to establish a full political and cultural control. It was not, therefore, only aristocratic but also popular culture that the Tudor monarchy set out to subdue: if Hal killed Hotspur, he was also directly responsible for the death of Falstaff, overtrumping all his tricks until his final defeat. The processes of the emasculation of popular culture were pursued under Elizabeth by a mixture of outlawry and incorporation; and the sudden efflorescence of pastoral towards the end of her reign may be seen, in functional terms, as part of the tactics of incorporation. There was, however, a paradox at the heart of the pastoral enterprise, which has been recently identified by Louis Montrose:[15] namely, that if, by incorporating into one figure the gentleman and the shepherd, pastoral literature attempts to occlude the tensions between court and country, it may also at the same time by the same manoeuvre draw attention to them in such a way as to heighten them. For typically, whether it is a matter of intention or not, pastoral is a politically equivocal form; and drama in particular, by its very nature, cannot help but give independent form and voice to pastoral life. It may do so in order to mock it; but it may also do so in order to give it dignity. Here too, in Shakespeare's treatment of the struggle between country and court, we shall find the processes of gain and loss paradoxically intertwined. For time after time the plays are drawn down passages which history did not take; the marginalized, the dispossessed and the defeated are given a voice; and the patterns of social conflict are pointed up for our consideration. We shall trace this openness in the closure of the pastoral comedy of *Love's Labour's Lost*, and it will form the chief business in our analyses of *As You Like It* and *Twelfth Night*, in Part II below, as we discuss Shakespeare's historical imagination at work both upon the world before him and the worlds that had been sacrificed to it.

In the fourth place, and lastly here, although 'harmonious relations between court and City were one of the keys to the success and stability of Tudor government',[16] there were of course tensions between them. Indeed, the very frequency of their transactions – in marriage, in business, in parliamentary and courtly affairs – served not only to relax but also to aggravate those tensions by drawing attention to the discrepancies between the supposed stability of the social order and the actual facts of rapid social mobility. The sense of imbalance in wealth, status and power bred ambivalence; and here is the common stuff of Elizabethan and Jacobean drama, both idealizing and satirizing the theatricality of court life, depicting it as glamorous or meretricious not only for the City but also for the wider metropolitan audiences whom the public drama served. Shakespeare, of course, wrote both for city and court; and it is here, upon the site of a set of relationships that may be read as either harmony or friction, that we must interrogate the plays. Accordingly, in Part III, we analyse *The Tempest* and *The Winter's Tale* as representations of court life as performance, representations that would, we believe, yield different meanings to audiences in the different arenas of court and public theatre.

Our common aim, pursued through our different lines of inquiry, has been to tell the changing history of Shakespeare's representations of court life in the light of the changing history of the institution itself. Both are darkening histories, it seems. Even Holofernes, in a play that belongs to the very end of the two most successful decades of Elizabeth's court, expresses outraged decency at the courtly manners of Navarre; and increasingly during the 1590s as Elizabeth's reign fell into 'social, economic and military crisis',[17] with bad harvests, rising inflation and rising unemployment, with the country endangered by invasion and the court by factional struggle, so Shakespeare's depictions of court life changed too. The brilliance that had characterized *Love's Labour's Lost* and the early city-state comedies disappears, or is subjected to the kind of problematization that we find in *Much Ado About Nothing*; and in its place we find increasingly – as in *The Merchant of Venice* and *As You Like It* – a development of the satirico-utopian potential that had always been latent in Shakespeare's comic form. It is

*Hamlet*, however, that marks the real turning-point; for *Hamlet* is Shakespeare's fullest reckoning with the Renaissance, a critique so comprehensive that it deconstructs the two great Renaissance fellow-contraries of platonism and machiavellianism in their antithetical readings of human nature, political power and court culture. The courtly world of Sidney and Spenser is gone forever; and in the problem plays that follow *Hamlet*, by the deliberately fantastic and distasteful nature of their dramatic resolution, Shakespeare exposes key contradictions within the political structures and ideological self-understanding of Renaissance court life. The accession of James, with his Franco-Scottish ideas of royal absolutism, perhaps inspired the critical readings of the feudal court that we find in *King Lear* and *Macbeth*;[18] and as James, partly from personal predilection and partly from political disappointment, came to live an increasingly retired life within an increasingly isolated court, Shakespeare wrote the romances of *The Winter's Tale* and *The Tempest*, where ageing rulers cut off by personal weakness from the life of their court find themselves miraculously restored. For the ironic effect of the programme of the Tudor pacification was to be the gradual cocooning of the king and court in an insulation that helped in the end to create the conditions for the Civil War; and it was out of this process that *The Winter's Tale* and *The Tempest* – by virtue of their status as works for both city and court performance – were able to make their play.

And this brings us at last to our title. *Out of Court*: the phrase in Renaissance England, as David Loades reminds us,[19] was used to describe those royal powers – the power, for example, to interpret the laws of the realm and to see that they were obeyed – which had become detached from the person of the monarch and taken on an institutional life of their own. So the palaces of Whitehall and Westminster had grown to be 'different worlds'.[20] Our interest in this book is with the way that the court itself, by the very fact of dramatic representation upon a public stage, may be said to have gone out of court; for whilst Elizabeth struggled to control the copying and distribution of her own image, she exerted very little censorship upon the many images of royal courts which peopled the Tudor stage and in which the image of her own court might from time to time be read. The theatre was left remarkably free to develop its own ceremonies and rituals, to flourish as an institution which was itself, in Michael Bristol's words, 'the site of experimental institution-making'.[21] The Globe too, built upon the fault-line between the city and the court, was worlds apart from Whitehall.

# Introduction 9

When Danby described Shakespearean drama as 'a new organ of thought', or when C. L. Barber wrote of its role in transforming a 'ceremonial, ritualistic conception of human life' into a 'historical, psychological conception',[22] each was paying tribute to the arena of the public theatre, and to the formal qualities of its drama, in enabling its audience to set the fictional beside the real and thus to celebrate, to interrogate or to challenge the real institutions of their lives. We shall see one example of this process repeatedly below, when we see what happens to the courtly form of the masque when set within the context of a play performed upon a public stage and acted before a stage audience for a real audience to observe. A multivocal conflictual form, juxtaposing social classes with a freedom unknown in real life and drawing its inspiration eclectically from popular and courtly traditions, found itself able to question authority, to problematize virtue and to satirize court life before court and popular audiences alike. If the play could enter the court, the court could also enter the play; and this was something that disgusted both patrician and puritan loyalists, who found in such mingling of kings and clowns a blasphemy against the sanctity of human institutions.

The objections of writers as different as Sir Philip Sidney and Philip Stubbes to this promiscuity of contemporary theatrical forms deserve to be taken seriously, since they remind us of the dangerousness of play within a deference society. Hence Sidney's struggle to restore the unities – 'the laws of poesy', as he called them;[23] the discipline of time and place must be kept up, as surely as the 'mongrel tragi-comedy' must be put down, in order to uphold the law of kinds. Similarly, he argued that the subject-matter of comedy must be subordinated to its highest purpose of 'delightful teaching', lest otherwise we become contaminated by laughter at the sin we should condemn and the unhappiness we should pity. For he saw clearly how comedy equivocates with conscience and how, like tragedy, it touches upon both the ambivalence that lies at the heart of taboo and the 'structural ambiguity'[24] that lies at the heart of social order, subverting those categories upon which our conduct and our social structures rest. Play would not stay in place: if the theatres were situated outside the London city walls, they nevertheless formed a central part of its commercial and cultural life; if the actors were stigmatized as the lowest of the low, they also impersonated and mixed with the highest of the high; and the plays themselves found their most profitable and glamorous materials amidst sexual licence, political insurrection and lawlessness of all kinds. Stubbes too was clear about the danger. The theatre was the forcing-house of the same bawdry and blasphemy that it depicted; the actors were 'painted sepulchres' and 'doble dealing ambodexters'; and 'the arguments of tragedies, is anger, wrath, immunitie, crueltie, iniurie, incest, murther & such like . . . . Of Commedies, the matter and ground is loue, bawdrie, cosenage, flattery, whordome, adulterie . . .'[25] The theatrical self-defence that enters a plea of moral purpose or political education is neatly turned on its head by Stubbes as a usurpation of the word of God which is sufficient alone, and alone sufficient, for our salvation. 'If he be accursed, that calleth light darknes, & darknes light, truth, falsehood, & falshood truth, sweet, sowre, and sowr sweete, than *a fortiori* is he accursed that saith that playes & enterluds be equivalent with Sermons'. Play confounds categories; it usurps time by promoting idleness and place by emptying the churches; and its nature is to spread, contaminatingly – as Shakespeare himself had good cause to know.

> SOME say good *Will* (which I, in sport, do sing)
> Had'st thou not plaid some Kingly parts in sport,
> Thou hadst bin a companion for a *King*;
> And, beene a King among the meaner sort.[26]

Shakespeare's profession as an actor, like the theatre in which it was carried out, clearly threatened social distinction; and so too did the plays that he wrote – for as the wordplay within these four lines entertains a variety of small subversive possibilities that almost disguise the central impossibility grasped by the syntax, so too do the plays entertain those subversive possibilities latent in the tensions that they explore, no matter how impossible their final realization might be.

Out of court and into play: the essays that follow are drawn to the playfulness of the plays that they study, to their paradoxical status as fictions that hold the mirror up to reality. This paradoxical status, it seems to us, has important implications for critical method. One common response, especially amongst critics drawn – as we have been – to the sociological tensions that animate the plays, has been to attempt to iron out the wrinkles of the paradox by fitting the fictions into their contemporary political history and then reading them off as direct ideological interventions in the struggle for social power, conceived either in personal or class terms. Thus, to return to our starting-point, we might see *Orchestra* as the work of a gentleman lawyer who hoped through flattery of those at court to gain the patronage necessary to further his public career; and we might see *Les Caractères* as the work of a bourgeois lawyer presumably disappointed in the same hope. Self-interest here is the skeleton key that unlocks all doors upon the world. Or we might consider Sir John Davies and La Bruyère together, alongside other writers such as Marston, Shakespeare, Donne and Jonson, studying their writings as illustrations of the divided response of an emergent bourgeois intelligentsia towards the aristocracy and judging them by their progressive or reactionary attitudes. Class-struggle here is the key. Both kinds of reading are commonplace in literary and historical analysis; both consider the work of art primarily in terms of the function it performs; and both genuinely cast a light upon the past. But it is our belief that we are dealing with a paradox that should be respected rather than ironed out. Clifford Geertz, in his work upon what he calls the theatre-state in nineteenth-century Bali, has attacked 'the worn coin of European ideological debate'[27] which discusses human art and ritual only to decode the fraudulent mystification practised by power upon the powerless. For him art and ritual are attempts to realize vision, to actualize belief: each is something *sui generis*, not to be translated into other terms without significant loss. Recently, historians have tried to develop Geertz's expressivism with regard to the arts and rituals of early modern Europe,[28] finding in the re-creation of difference the primary task of the historical imagination: the visions and beliefs that animate *Orchestra* and *Les Caractères*, we might say, equally find their validity in the grounds of their artistic expression and must be honoured for what they are. Yet such a relativism tends always to neglect the material origins of the struggle between the courtly idealist and the courtly satirist in the inequalities of the real world. There may have been no dissent in nineteenth-century Bali, but there certainly was in sixteenth-century England, as all its art and ritual testifies; and such dissent most typically read the world in terms of the competition for power. As Geertz remarks elsewhere, 'functionalism lives',[29] and we shall need to shuttle between the discourses of functionalism and expressivism in what follows, as we discuss the fictions that mirror the realities of the Renaissance court in Tudor and Jacobean England.

In the end, Sidney and Stubbes were right: play will not stay in place. That is its vitality, its charm, its danger – especially so in Shakespeare's plays, with the irony and openness of their closures.

It is true that they are material products with a material history of their own, that they are cultural products whose evaluation has a history of its own; but their interest for us is not confined to the light that they cast upon the past. *Hamlet* speaks to us of more than the Renaissance Denmark in which it was set or the late Elizabethan England in which it was written; and this is because it invites us to play across the boundaries of time and space. It brings history itself into play, and does so by the very nature of its fictive method: namely, to mix other times and places with the time and place of the theatre, and to do so in a way that not only transgresses the 'laws of poesy' invoked by Sidney to keep play in its place but that also mixes the impossibilities and the might-have-beens of romance with the historically real. The pleasure of the plays lies here, in accepting their invitation to play; and we have not scrupled, in searching out the sociological tensions within the Renaissance court that set the plays in motion, to play along with them. For it has seemed to us that, as we try to understand them in their history, they also have power to understand us in our present: that is, in a poetry that still helps to constitute our sense of the worthwhile, they provide us with an imagery that still helps to articulate our world to us. *Hamlet* images something to us of what we continue to call revenge. The plays, by their readings in the life of the Renaissance court, become provisional readings in our common destiny; and in our repeated shuttling back and forth between the then and there of the plays and the here and now of their performance, in our attempt to grasp them in their difference, to distinguish the individual from the general and history from destiny, we have been enjoying the area of their greatest vitality. Wordsworth thought that 'upon the accuracy with which similitude in dissimilitude, and dissimilitude in similitude are perceived, depend our taste and our moral feelings'[30] – and, he might have added, our historical sense too. Throughout our study of the Renaissance court, it has also been our own world in its sameness and its difference that we have been reconstructing.

# Part I:
# The Court and the New Learning

*John Turner*

# 1
# Prologue: 'Of Studies' and Play

In his essay 'Of Studies', Bacon is as clear about the complex balance to be struck amongst the various uses of the new learning as he is about the need to maintain it in a productive relationship with the 'real' world of practical experience:

> To spend too much time in studies, is sloth; to use them too much for ornament, is affectation; to make judgement wholly by their rules, is the humour of a scholar: they perfect nature, and are perfected by experience: for natural abilities are like natural plants, that need pruning by study; and studies themselves do give forth directions too much at large, except they be bounded in by experience.[1]

There are moral and political dangers in scholarship which the checks and balances of Bacon's prose work hard to contain. Not only is he aware of the potential conflicts between the various legitimate uses of learning that he lists – the enrichment of leisure, the adornment of conversation, the improvement of business. He is aware too of the conflicts that may arise between the 'private' world of imaginative expectation nourished by study (especially study of the *'feigned history'* of poetry)[2] and the demands of the 'public' world of citizenship (to be studied as *'true history'*). Faced with such dangers, Bacon nevertheless remains sanguine. He locates the nature of civic virtue in a process of perpetual adjustment between 'self' and 'world', 'imagination' and 'reality' – a responsible process of self-fashioning that should ward off disintegration of the self by political disaffection and disintegration of the state by sedition; and, in case scholars fail to recognize their own best interest, he also urges the wise ruler to restrict their number to the number of posts available to them for preferment.[3] It is thus a conservative programme that Bacon offers, an attempt to bring intellectuals and the new learning to heel, to subdue the 'poetry' of subjectivity and to discipline the self to political reality.

The two works to be studied in this section – *Love's Labour's Lost* and *Hamlet* – make their play out of the same two kinds of conflict that Bacon was trying to contain in his essay 'Of Studies'. Comedy and tragedy alike, each makes out of the recent history of Renaissance learning a subversive poetry that turns the sanguine faith of Bacon in human rationality quite inside out – like a cheveril glove, as Feste might say. *Love's Labour's Lost* begins with a court that has, for the purposes of self-ornamentation, declared itself an academy, and in so doing has laid itself open to the charge of affectation – a charge brought home by the arrival of the French princess on business. But, as we shall see, the purpose of the play is not to ridicule the lords' affectation in order to celebrate a complex balance that they themselves have failed to attain: it is rather to make fun out of all their attempts at that same process of adjustment that Bacon was later to recommend. For there is no moral, no point of complex balance within the play. Instead, there is a sequence of demands – made upon lords and ladies alike – that are so various, so changeable, so giddy in pursuit of one another across the stage of public life, that no adjustment can accommodate them. In *Love's Labour's Lost* no mind can take the measure of the world. Condemned by the necessities of courtly life to an endless provisionality that undermines all faith in progressive self-fashioning, the self is laughed out of court; and so too at the end of the play is the court itself, as the perspective established by the final songs enables us to see all those same necessities of courtly life as themselves provisional. Here is no gradual coming to terms between self and world: the vitality and subversiveness of comedy desubstantiates them both.

*Hamlet* similarly problematizes the idea of a rapprochement between self and world – not by exploring the conflictual demands placed upon the followers of the courtly life, as was the case in *Love's Labour's Lost*, but by exploring instead the conflicts between their imaginative expectations of that life and its reality. Hamlet takes his expectations of courtly life seriously, with a hunger for integrity unknown in Navarre; and we feel him right to do so since it is by his concern for truth and justice that Claudius and his court are exposed for what they are. Here is a world that must not be adjusted to. The play presents us with what was to become a typical late Renaissance scenario: the picture of a learned but disaffected intellectual searching painfully for a style with which to confront a corrupt world. The style that he finds the most appropriate is that of the satirist, a self-lacerating style that indeed yokes expectation and experience together but only to hold them in a state of perpetual contradiction. It is a shift that of necessity offers Hamlet no more than a temporary respite, and as he increasingly suffers violence from without and within, the repertoire of his styles begins to fragment and his capacity for personal relationship disintegrates. We shall trace this fragmentation of the self in a corrupt court by exploring Hamlet's failure to integrate three relationships that are crucially important to him, those with his father, with Ophelia and with Claudius – people who each confront him with a different vision of what court life should be. For what *Hamlet* captures about the Renaissance is its sudden proliferation of cultures. It shows how different visions of 'reality' conflict because 'imagination' is inseparably woven into their construction; and in so doing it exposes the inadequacy of Bacon's conservative stance in its neglect of the facts of human subjectivity, as historically shaped at any given time. The new learning, instead of stabilizing the state, might equally well destabilize it. The disaffected intellectual will never be short of ideological grounds upon which to denounce those centres of moral and political authority that he 'should' respect, and at the same time to paint to the self a tragic picture of itself as alienated, marginalized, decentered.[4]

Where Bacon sought to compose ideological conflict, Shakespeare sought an aesthetic shape to draw it out in the historical context that gave it its fullest meaning. *Love's Labour's Lost* and *Hamlet* – themselves a part of the new cultural life of the court that they depict – mirror that life so that their audiences may recognize in the new learning of the Renaissance not only an agent of national pacification but also a field for the extension of courtly competition. Again and again the plays bring the new ideologies of the period – the expressions both of conviction and convenience – to the test of experience; and they do so not only to examine their worth but also to examine the worth of the court itself, the worth of any possible adjustment between them. The new dramatic form, multivocal and conflictual, calls all in doubt. Certainly neither the comedy of *Love's Labour's Lost* nor the tragedy of *Hamlet* will bring an audience to terms with the world; neither will 'buckle and bow the mind unto the nature of things', which Bacon thought the office of reason.[5] Nor, on the other hand, will either quite fulfil the office which he prescribed for poetry, 'submitting the shows of things to the desires of the mind'. It is not a question of submitting; rather, by letting Feigned History play across the face of History, the plays allow imagination and reality to enter into an open and potentially subversive relationship with one another. All things are brought into play, and it is the play that matters, enabling us again and again to open up and explore from different perspectives the relationships between the individual self and the institutions amongst which he or she moves. The utopian spirit is not satisfied in Shakespearean drama, as Bacon might have asked; but it is set free – increasingly from around the turn of the seventeenth century, as we shall see in Part II – to enrich our judgements of the real with all the might-be and the might-have-been of fiction and romance.

# 2
# *Love's Labour's Lost*: The Court at Play

In Act 2 of *Love's Labour's Lost*, Boyet describes Navarre and his court as 'he and his competitors in oath' (II.i.82); and in so doing, he uses a word whose ambiguity perfectly captures the structural tensions at the heart of the court society of the play. For *competitor* had an intriguing double meaning in Renaissance times, as expressive of the aristocratic culture of late feudalism as the double meaning of *owe* had been of an earlier feudal formation.[6] Each word enjoyed a larger range of meaning than it does now under the restrictive relationships of present-day capitalism. For *owe*, which might mean either *owe* or *own*, was true to the characteristic richness – at the same time a dangerous structural ambiguity – of early feudal society as it extended from the king throughout his country: namely, that possession might be considered both as debt and ownership. Similarly *competitor*, which might mean either *partner* or *rival*, was true to the richness – again a dangerous structural ambiguity – of a later feudal society where the aristocracy had been drawn away from their country estates to the court: namely, that courtly competition might be experienced as both friendly collaboration and deadly rivalry in the inescapable pursuit of that goal of all aristocratic enterprise, the enjoyment of prestige.

*Love's Labour's Lost* makes its play out of the ambiguities of that competition. It is a mistake to think of the play as static, formal, ceremonious, without appreciating its fidelity to those tensions and anxieties which in real life were controlled, more or less successfully, precisely by such state, such form, such ceremony. Its seemingly tranquil surface proves on closer inspection to race with the ebb and flow of friendships and rivalries, alliances and ruptures, loyalties and betrayals, gestures of social solidarity and subversive private will, as the courtiers who form the central cast vie for prestige, now competing with and now against one another. All the watchful anxieties of court life are transformed into a comedy which yet remains true to the uncertainties of a life where favour may be won and lost in a moment, and where the various opportunities for prestige – scholarship, sexual courtship, legal or financial administration, the devising of courtly entertainment – fold bewilderingly in upon one another until it is uncertain where prestige may be won at any given time. Small wonder then that Boyet, setting watch upon the King of Navarre, should speak of 'the court of his eye' (II.i.234), or that the eye of all those with power in the play, lords and ladies alike, should be dwelt upon so often by Shakespeare, in this depiction of a world where watchfulness, secretiveness and self-restraint are so necessary. For the rules of the courtly game might always change, subject to the caprice of the prince, the interest of his powerful favourites, the machinations of one's fellow-competitors or, indeed, the demands of the international community to which the prince himself was bound. It was a world where the business and pleasure of both king and court were shadowed by perpetual insecurity; and so, sailing such dangerous seas, as David Starkey says, 'like practised sailors, they had to keep a weather-eye'.[7]

Thus, whilst we may agree that *Love's Labour's Lost* is 'Shakespeare's most courtly play',[8] this is not simply because, as C. L. Barber puts it, 'Shakespeare made a play out of courtly pleasures'.[9] For the courtly pleasures in the play, its masques, pageants and so forth, constitute only part of its larger aim, to hold a mirror up to the nature of court life in all its pleasures and anxieties alike. Barber's festive account of the play, though important, is false to its range. When, for instance, he argues that 'the evolutions in *Love's Labour's Lost* express the Elizabethan feeling for the harmony of a group acting in ceremonious consort',[10] he shows himself deaf to those dissonances in the play which originate in what one historian has called 'the fiercely competitive atmosphere'[11] of the English Renaissance court. Its nine scenes, astonishingly few for a play so long, are alive with the tensions that typify the rhythms of courtly relationships in their most characteristic field of competition, where festive pleasure and the threat of violence were never far apart: conversation. The tongue rivals the eye in importance in *Love's Labour's Lost*. 'Society, saith the text, is the happiness of life' (IV.ii.154–5): Sir Nathaniel's praise of the pleasure that is to be found in conversation needs to be balanced by the counter-awareness of the Princess of France when she observes that 'good wits will be jangling' (II.i.224). Fellowship and rivalry throughout the play run ambiguously into one another in an endless 'civil war of wits' (II.i.225) – where the pun upon *civil* is fully at work. The true successor to *Love's Labour's Lost* in English will be Congreve's *The Way of the World*, equally firmly rooted in another highly competitive aristocratic world whose pleasurable civilities of style are also always on the point of breaking down into civil violence.

The word *competitor* was a sixteenth-century importation from France: if 'continental literature of the court was borrowed, adapted or translated'[12] to describe its English counterpart, so too was continental language. Shakespeare, moreover, turned to a continental event – the establishment by the King of Navarre of an academy to rival the Palace Academy of France[13] – in order to image the new culture of Renaissance humanism which he wished to hold up as mirror before his English courtly and popular audiences. We should think of the court of Navarre in the play, I believe, as one of Weber's 'ideal types', a model to facilitate analysis, self-analysis; in the words of Louis A. Montrose, from what seems to me the best modern essay on *Love's Labour's Lost*, 'a possibly direct relation between the play and a specific historical event is perhaps less important than the event's significance as the concrete example of a general cultural condition that is being refracted in the play's fiction'.[14] Through what Montrose calls 'the humorous court of Navarre', Shakespeare presents an ideal type of cultural activity stripped of its familiar self-justifications and seen instead as merely one further manifestation of the competitive life of the court – as a badge of social distinction rather than as, say, proof of the dignity, rationality or divinity of the human mind.

My purpose here is to explore the competitiveness of court life in its threefold aspect within the play: the competition internal to the court; the competition between the court of Navarre and the court of France, represented here by the Princess and her ladies; and, most interestingly perhaps, the competition between the court of Navarre and the country it rules. As we proceed, we shall see how Shakespeare, transforming court life into comedy, is able to be true to those fellow-contrary feelings of exhilaration and entrapment that are the twin faces of competition; for in the tension between them we find one mechanism of maintaining what Lawrence Stone called the 'delicate and extremely complicated political balance'[15] upon which the court's survival as an institution depended. We shall see too how the play elucidates many of the social and political contradictions involved in the competition of court life, clarifying them increasingly for us throughout the play with all the shapeliness of art until at the end they stand fully exposed in their dangerous contrariety. Finally, we shall see how comedy interprets destiny: how, that is, Shakespeare uses the court as an image of the human condition, caught between necessity and freedom, between a fatalistic entrapment and the joyously improvisational energies upon which we may draw in our competitive struggle to survive.

## THE COURT OF NAVARRE

*Arts-man, preambulate: we will be singled from the barbarous.*
(V.i.73–4)

*Love's Labour's Lost* begins and ends with a contract. In its opening speech, the King of Navarre recapitulates an earlier proclamation in which he had announced the transformation of his court into 'a little academe'. These fashionable Renaissance experiments in international competition were in part quite consciously undertaken by European monarchs in order to pacify their unruly aristocracy at home, to bring them to court and to keep them there under royal supervision. As Peter de la Primaudaye put it in *The French Academie*, itself the product of civil wars in France, philosophy must be encouraged to replace the prevalent militarism as an outlet for the young aristocrat's competitiveness, his 'ielousie of glorie, which by nature is in him, to desire and bring to passe all great matters woorthie to be remembred'.[16] Shakespeare shows by the military metaphors of the king's speech his own awareness of the historical processes of this pacification, this attempted sublimation; and its long parenthesis suggests the king's determination to comprehend all potential dissidence under the single head of his own new academic definition of honour:

> Therefore, brave conquerors – for so you are,
> That war against your own affections
> And the huge army of the world's desires –
> Our late edict shall strongly stand in force:
> Navarre shall be the wonder of the world;

Our court shall be a little academe,
Still and contemplative in living art.

(I.i.8–14)

It is this last line that in the theatre gives us pause; for good drama, of course, is not to be made out of stillness and contemplation. Suddenly within the orotund authority of the royal will we hear the possibilities of hubris and sense the future pattern of the play – a pattern to be fulfilled in Act 5 when the cultural activities of the court revert back to a kind of comic civil war amongst the models of its humanistic enterprise, the 'Nine' Worthies.

The court addressed by the king at the start of the play consists of three young lords, making a total of four in all – a number probably owing less to the four young rhetoricians of *The French Academie* than to Shakespeare's dramatic sense of the appropriate balance between deference and dissidence in response to the royal proclamation. The king himself is alert to the possibilities of dissidence, as we have seen; such groups of single young men, after all, were troublesome in any court, and hence his attempts to enforce their contracts with him by threatening them with shame, disgrace, dishonour. With the first two lords he has no problem, since they confirm their dedication to 'a three years' fast' (I.i.24) with an excess of zeal that perfectly expresses their compliant subordination. 'To love, to wealth, to pomp, I pine and die' (I.i.31): such eagerness, however, arouses our suspicions of hubris once more since, in their commitment to philosophy, they are prepared to renounce even those pleasures that most define their courtly status.

If it is true, as Michael Bristol has argued in *Carnival and Theater*, that the Battle of Carnival and Lent was 'the stylized form of real structural ambiguity and tension'[17] within the recurrent cycles of plebeian culture, we may add that Shakespeare here in *Love's Labour's Lost* is formally imitating that Battle in order to explore the structural ambiguities and tensions of court culture. The court in real life was a centre of diplomacy, government, law, learning, hospitality and entertainment, and we see the court of Navarre operating in each of these different fields at different stages of the play. But at the start the king, in order to compete for prestige more efficiently in the international community, has chosen to specialize; and his courtiers, competing for prestige at home, have chosen to follow him. They commit themselves to what for them has the air of a *fast*. But then, suddenly, they are undone by the arrival of a diplomatic mission of eligible ladies from another court within that international community. Suddenly the rules change; carnival commences. Real life breaks through, we might want to say; and the play tempts us to say it. Pride goes before a fall. Yet such a language will not do: the play does not simply meet hubris with nemesis, replace mistaken choice with true choice, depict the education of four foolish young men into the truths of their own nature and that of the world around them. Rather, in the various phases of its Battle of Carnival and Lent, it becomes the stylized form of a world condemned to endless mutability, endless provisionality, a world of men and women engaged in a perpetual competition for prestige where the rules were always changing, where no-one was in control, and where each wise choice of today might be the ruin of tomorrow. No wonder such a world sustained cosmologies that saw 'returns and vicissitudes'[18] everywhere and taught that *'constancy it selfe is nothing but a languishing and wavering dance'*.[19] The comic pattern in the play that leads from hubris to nemesis serves just such a vision of an infinitely mutable and unreliable universe. Nor can the idea of nature help us. The point of the Battle of Carnival and Lent, once freed from its liturgical celebration of the world of the spirit over that of the flesh, was that neither side could win but that each should learn its 'natural' place. But in *Love's Labour's Lost*, we shall see, the seemingly natural rhythm will prove as dangerous as the seemingly right choice. However, from the anxiety and excitement of the need to compete, there is no escape; and the man in the play who knows this is the same man who remembers that the ladies are about to arrive, Berowne.

As the play begins, Berowne's deference to the king's will in general is accompanied by an attempted deferral of the demands it makes in particular. He dare not sit out the game (I.i.110) and yet must set out the reservations that he feels about it. This is the entrapment characteristic of the courtier's position, and Berowne's speech in acceptance of the king's contract is accordingly just what it needs to be, a masterly exercise in demurral without defiance. Whilst the opening speech of the king had tried to fold all possible dissidence in under the single comprehensive head of his own authority, Berowne by contrast opens up the contract clause by clause in order to spell out the scruples that he feels. His recollection of the ladies' imminent arrival is his trump card, giving him confidence that he is one move ahead in the game; and his pace accordingly is languid, unravelling the strenuousness of Lenten discipline and culminating in the yawn of a spirit wholly at home in the flesh:

> O, these are barren tasks, too hard to keep,
> Not to see ladies, study, fast, not sleep.
> (I.i.47–8)

For Berowne, it seems, to fast, to renounce this for that, is to court barrenness; his pleasure lies rather in the feeling of his liberty, his power, his versatility and improvisational skills in the game he plays.

His tone, of course, is light; it is Berowne who brings life into the play, and he does so by bringing play into life. Aware that his inclinations do not altogether fit his instructions, he asserts and explores the play between them by the play of wit and humour; for one of the chief functions of wit and humour in a deference society is to defer the immediate demands of power, to deflect the will of others at the point of its attack. There is also, of course, the more familiar use of wit and humour for purposes of aggression, to display power and to assert social solidarity without provoking open confrontation; and this we see in the chorus of the lords' rejoinders to Berowne (I.i.94ff). Shakespeare's comedy captures perfectly the mockery of those real-life court conversations into which the endless jostle for personal space and prestige was sublimated. In such competition, fellowship and rivalry, affection and antagonism could hold an uneasy truce; for it trod a careful line between danger and delight, testing the limits of the possible and keeping conflictual energies alive whilst – usually – defusing their violent potential. Berowne's strategy, therefore, that of an aggressive defence, is a *licensed* strategy, not without power, not unlike that of a court jester; the others expect of him a mockery in which their own dissident impulses may be both voiced and argued down. It is a role that Berowne himself is happy with; and yet, despite its dramatic liveliness and openness, it is not a role with normative authority in the play.

At first it may seem otherwise; we are maybe convinced by the string of paradoxes in which Berowne prefers his own idea of learning, nature and common sense to the unnatural academic aspirations of the court. He prefers love to scholarship, a Platonic to an Aristotelian epistemology, the irradiation of the inner faculty to that doubtful illumination of the outer world which is the work of pedantry; and these preferences claim our sympathy, for they alert us to the hubris of the court and the likely direction of the drama to come. Yet despite his mastery and versatility, Berowne's is not the voice of truth. He is speaking with the airiness of the courtier skilled in what David Loades has called 'the commonest of all indoor games'[20] at the Tudor court, the game of courtly love, and the sincerity of his feelings is perfectly masked behind the impermeability of his style. When the rules of the game shift yet again from the sport of love to the real thing, the mastery and versatility of his tone begin to falter.

For there is a paradox at the heart of Berowne's conception of love that he will be unable to resolve – the paradox that love is experienced as both necessity and freedom. We catch a glimpse of the paradox in the differences between the various arguments developed by Berowne to mock the austerity of the king's contract. On the one hand, he attempts to naturalize love, to make it appear a fruit 'in season' (I.i.107) for young men; and the tendency of such an organicist metaphor is 'to treat as fixed and natural things which are historically contingent and for which human agents are responsible'.[21] Love, he urges, is the inescapable necessity of young men; and courtly love is the inescapable necessity of young courtiers. On the other hand, however, he celebrates love over scholarship because, whilst scholarship aims at 'base authority from others' books' (I.i.87), love is self-validating, free and thus subversive of authority. Love is at once liberty and its loss; and through the free play of Berowne's mockery here, we glimpse into the paradoxical necessities of the plot to come.

The material base for this paradoxical understanding of love is partly to be found in the actual conditions of court life, where young people from aristocratic families came to enjoy the one place where they could be free from parental interference in their sexual affairs, but where they immediately found themselves drawn into a game – a game liable at any moment to become deadly serious – from which they were unable to extricate themselves. Courtly love was the necessary condition of their freedom in love. They escaped parental supervision only to fall under the eye of the king in that most public of arenas, the court. So love too served the purposes of the Tudor pacification: and maybe men often felt their loss of freedom so acutely because, whilst the courtship rituals of courtly love conferred a small measure of power and status upon women, they tended always to confirm men in their self-reproachful memories of the military independence that they had surrendered up to the state.

These inglorious glories of love, of course, had their appropriate emblem in courtly literature:

> This wimpled, whining, purblind, wayward boy,
> This signor junior, giant-dwarf, dan Cupid;
> Regent of love rhymes, lord of folded arms,
> The anointed sovereign of sighs and groans,
> Liege of all loiterers and malcontents,
> Dread prince of plackets, king of codpieces,
> Sole imperator and great general
> Of trotting paritors: O my little heart!
> And I to be a corporal of his field,
> And wear his colours like a tumbler's hoop!
> (III.i.174–83)

By this stage of the play, Berowne has passed beyond the airy pleasures of the sport of love, equally to be enjoyed and mocked, into the pleasurable pains of the real thing. He is acting out that most typical of courtly roles, the role of Chaucer's Troilus, now become newly important under the Tudor state: the role of the love-critic subdued by love. The mocker is bemocked. Once again, however, it is not enough to talk of hubris and nemesis, of a comic judgement upon Berowne paralleling that already passed upon the others; for this is no act of final retributive justice but simply a sign that the game has moved on another stage and that the master, for all his spirited struggle, finds himself mastered by the necessities of his court existence. The sense of poetic justice that we do feel ('Serve him right') realizes itself most fully neither as a general moral truth about the universe ('Pride always goes before a fall') nor as a general observation about human nature ('It is natural for young men to fall in love') but as an insight into the particular nature of the courtly world ('Such pride in such a world always courts such a fall'); for love, after all, need not always feel like this, either in Shakespeare or in real life.

It is in the sonorous melancholy of Armado that we sense most clearly the entrapment of court life – a melancholy that is the fellow-contrary of Berowne's buoyant resourcefulness and yet that testifies equally to the exacting demands of the life they live. Armado, like the rest of the court, has sworn to do battle against 'the huge army of the world's desires' but has also found himself undone by Cupid's paradoxes: 'his disgrace is to be called boy, but his glory is to subdue men' (I.ii.169–70). His melancholy expresses in part his sense of what it means to be a lover, a role in which he has unexpectedly found himself cast and which perhaps he tries to copy from the gestures of his page (III.i.9ff.). But more important still is the melancholy dignity that he affects as the mark of the courtier, of courtly *gravitas*. It is this affectation, of course, that exposes him to the ruthless mockery of the rest of the court: the identity of the group is confirmed in the incompetent performers it excludes. Yet for the audience there is a double perspective. Certainly Armado is ridiculous, a clumsy competitor in an arena where failure is not tolerated. Certainly he has a pompous and pedantic immobility beside the quicksilver wit of his young page – a Spanish galleon, perhaps, outmanoeuvred by a lighter English frigate. He is the master whose will is perpetually deflected by his servant, the teacher outwitted by his pupil, the rhetorician undercut by chop-logic; but we do not only see him from the court perspective as an object of ridicule. The very gorgeousness of his melancholy folly is more interesting than that; and so too is the parallel between him and Berowne, built so deeply into the play's structure. Affectation may be mocked; but it is also the tribute paid by anxiety to the power of a cultural ideal, and Armado's melancholy self-importance by its very excess lays bare for the audience the artificiality of the social role that Berowne by his success might otherwise naturalize.

The double function of Armado is seen most clearly in the fact that he is the first of the courtiers to fall in love: the competitor who first drops out of the race draws attention to both the success and the strain of those who go on. If we find him ridiculous, perhaps we shall also find him perverse, the affected man who is so very far out of touch with his own desires that he falls grotesquely in love with a woman of low birth. His self-dissociation is revealed in the way in which he expresses his sense of his falsehood as a knight: he demonizes love, denounces the woman he loves and bewails his own guilt. 'Love is a familar; Love is a devil: there is no evil angel but Love', he says (1.i.162–3); and this is so, he adds, because 'Cupid's butt-shaft is too hard for Hercules' club, and therefore too much odds for a Spaniard's rapier'. His absurdly idealized and rigid self-image as a knight has left him unable to negotiate the transition of role to a lover save by means of the energies that spring from guilt; indeed, his own nature has now become such that he can only love guiltily. In so far as he is ridiculous in this, he performs the function of the scapegoat, attracting to himself the obloquy that we might otherwise heap upon the perjured king and lords. But the dissociation in his nature, which he himself takes seriously and compels us too to take seriously at the end of the play, is not simply ridiculous; it writes large for us the similar difficulties experienced by the king and lords in keeping in touch with their desires – and the scapegoat in this is also the epitome, drawing attention to the guilt which throughout *Love's Labour's Lost* is associated with the play of male sexual desire.

Each of the lords feels acutely the subversiveness of the guilty secret of his passion. At the most obvious narrative level, of course, this is because in view of their contract, their passion will perjure them. Truth to one's word had long been the cornerstone of aristocratic morality; it had been so under the old code of honour, and it remained so when that code was subsumed into the morality of the new nation state. Perjury was thus a central betrayal, even (as Mervyn James reminds us) in cases of error or folly;[22] and nothing could be more mistaken or foolish than the oath with which the play begins. 'He that promiseth to be true to one, and deceiveth him, may be called a traitor, for what is a man but his promise?'[23] These words of Lord Darcy in fact belong to the old code of honour and were spoken in 1536 to justify military confederacy against the crown: here in *Love's Labour's Lost* the same value is set upon promise but now it is love that threatens the crown. Behind the play's narrative preoccupation with perjury, that is, there lies a structural reenactment of the subversiveness of sexual passion. It is not the claims of kinship but of love that make these single young courtiers so dangerous. We must remember the strain that characterized relations between the unmarried Elizabeth and many of her eligible lords and ladies-in-waiting in the last years of her reign – a strain that led some of them, like Sir Walter Raleigh, to the desperate remedy of a secret marriage. Clearly there was no complete immunity for the monarch jealous of power: the same love that successfully kept young people at court under royal supervision also bred in them the dangers of disaffection, drew them away (as it drew Astrophil) from public into private service. Love, we might say, remembering the emblem of Armado, was a *pharmakon* in the processes of the Tudor pacification, both a cure and a poison, the source of guilt and glory alike.

This paradoxical ambiguity was inscribed at the heart of the Elizabethan language and iconography of love, whose pleasurable pains and killing joys could so shake the single state of man that even the most loyal courtier might turn traitor and perjure himself. Armado provides the most obvious epitome in *Love's Labour's Lost*: seduced away from those ancient worthies amongst whom he has hitherto sought his cultural pedigree (though Hercules and Samson themselves may seem at best but ambiguous exemplars), he models himself instead upon King Cophetua who defiantly married a beggar. Berowne too makes a similar point when he notices how in Rosaline's cheek 'several worthies make one dignity' (IV.iii.232). He knows that the eye of the mistress may extinguish that of the sovereign, that Cupid too is an 'anointed sovereign', capable of overthrowing the religion, law and learning through which the new Renaissance states were expounding their legitimacy. He makes his point most clearly when he self-mockingly laments his fall to that 'giant-dwarf, dan Cupid' – a fall which involves not only his aristocratic independence as a young sword-bearing male but also his political loyalty as a subject:

> O! and I forsooth in love!
> I, that have been love's whip;
> A very beadle to a humorous sigh;
> A critic, nay, a night-watch constable,
> A domineering pedant o'er the boy,
> Than whom no mortal so magnificent!
> (III.i.168–73)

Instinctively, Berowne here reaches out to two occupations central to the play in order to define what he has lost – to the constable and the pedant once active within himself, maintaining social order by disciplining the unruly pagan deity of love. Religion, law and learning: each of these three agents of political obedience, embodied dramatically in the three characters who enter at the start of Act 5, Sir Nathaniel, Dull and Holofernes, seems to Berowne to have been betrayed in his love, a love naturally subversive and made more so here by its perjuriousness.

Interestingly too, Berowne here – like Armado in Act 1 – is speaking in soliloquy, which seems subversive in itself; for the business of love is carried on by private intrigue, private letter, perpetually eating away at the sovereign's attempt to control his court by the dispensation of those graces and favours upon which prestige so much depended. But ladies too could dispense graces and favours: the vocabulary of courtly love established them as little sovereigns, powerful within a private sphere of competition that might always subvert the larger frame of the court. So it happens here; and the lords' first meeting with the ladies in Act 2:1 ends in their leaving severally, as court affairs begin to fragment into private affairs. The culmination of this process is reached in the marvellously inventive Act 4:3, the hinge of the whole play, where the lords in succession first spy upon one another's confessions of love and then denounce one another for perjury. This scene, infolded and then unfolded like Chinese boxes, is the climax of the play's concern with the competition of court life and the potential subversiveness of the sexual competition within it. Here for the first time fellowship becomes open rivalry. Suddenly we sense the proximity between watchfulness and spying; between silence and secrecy; between prudence and intrigue; between the compliance of courtly manners and a hypocritical seeming. Suddenly we glimpse a world where advantage is more important than truth and where the possession of another person's secret means power. Not even the common confrontation of their crime can bring the lords any comfort at first. They feel themselves no better than 'pick-purses in love' (IV.iii.205), and the whole honourable court community seems about to disintegrate under the pressure of the desire, guilt, self-interest and revenge which it has fostered. We may even remember *Hamlet* here as Berowne, in a gathering excitement fuelled by guilt, takes on the king in a 'civil war of wits' that threatens total breakdown. Rosaline alone has true *maiestas* (IV.iii.224), he asserts in the course of a traditional battle in preferential praise of one's own mistress; but the blow strikes home at the majesty of the king whom he has already betrayed for love. The comedy is more tense and dangerous here than at any other moment in the play, and it clearly reveals the strains brought into the life of the court by love.

But these strains, of course, do not have tragic consequences in *Love's Labour's Lost*; rather as the family at the end of *The Way of the World* adapts to incorporate the villainies of Fainall and Mrs. Marwood, so here the court adapts to incorporate the stain of its perjury. In each case, the social group is held together by a common interest necessitating its survival: there is nowhere else to run to. What happens here in *Love's Labour's Lost* is that, firstly, as once before, Dumain and Longaville side with the king against Berowne, thereby defusing the danger of their confrontation and driving Berowne back into the safety of his role as licensed jester; secondly, the king dissolves his court as a lenten academy and reconstitutes it as a place of carnival fit for courtly love; and thirdly, Berowne is called upon as a jester to justify this sudden volte-face – which he does in a long piece of 'special pleading,'[24] a string of beautiful sophistical paradoxes, designed to prove to the court that 'it is religion to be thus forsworn' (IV.iii.359). His learning is infinitely adaptable, it seems. His wit, like that of many a Restoration hero after him, lies in his 'being able to call a game a game';[25] but our admiration for the player should not stifle our curiosity concerning the game. Berowne raises the same questions as Dorimant in *The Man of Mode*: what game *is* it that is so patently artificial and yet that its players so persistently naturalize? what is it worth that it demands such sacrifice of time and honesty? and is the man of wit its master or its victim, excelling as he does in a competition which he dare not neglect? For although the king has changed the rules of the game, the inescapability of competition persists, in new roles and in a new international field. The ladies are to be courted and so, in an excitement born of their guilt, the lords freely launch themselves upon the necessities of courtly love as, in their excitement, they conceive it to be.

## THE LADIES FROM FRANCE

*We are wise girls to mock our lovers so.*
(V.ii.58)

The ladies from the French court contrast strongly with the lords of the court of Navarre; for they are sure of themselves from the start and confidently able to establish their priorities amongst the variety of courtly roles demanded of them. They have come to Navarre as a negotiating team to conduct a particularly delicate piece of diplomatic business – to take back again the half that has already been once repaid of a debt owed by France to Navarre and to forfeit instead the possibly overvalued territories in Aquitaine that had been laid in surety against that debt – and they allow nothing to deflect them from their purpose. Lawrence Stone has noted the frequency with which court officials in Elizabethan England 'used their wives as intermediaries'[26] in delicate negotiations, and here we see unmarried daughters used to defuse an otherwise potentially explosive confrontation in international affairs. No doubt the unspoken communication of this specially commissioned envoy was that a royal marriage, if desirable, might be thrown in to cement the deal. So, at least, Boyet implies in the long flattering address to the Princess at the start of Act 2, where he urges her to remember her *worth*, her *value*, and – perhaps making the best of it – describes Aquitaine as a fit 'dowry for a queen' (II.i.8).

Louis Montrose's discussion of this business aspect of the play seems to me admirable. He shows the importance of 'the political strategies lurking behind social rituals' and draws attention to the ambiguities surrounding the 'charming power politics' practised by the ladies: 'while the women may be said to introduce the values of healthy sexuality, common sense, and scorn of pretension into the stilted life of the academe, they also bring the harsher realities of social and political existence'.[27] This ambiguity of response that Montrose finds in himself here is a precise index of the ambiguities of courtly competition with which the play is concerned. For the ladies play the court game sensibly, winningly; they are good competitors, watchfully exploiting their position as female negotiators and *parleying* (II.i.5) with just that mixture of play and aggression which is appropriate to their position. They are, moreover, successful, their request being conceded quite casually, it seems, by a king whose appreciation of the Princess's value proves far to outweigh his fear that France has overvalued Aquitaine. Yet for all their skills, however, the ladies are only enacting the will of a distant patriarchy. We need to add to Montrose's account a recognition that the ladies, although so apparently in control in the play, are nevertheless themselves in the control of the absent King of France. If Boyet urges the Princess to recollect her worth, the king her father knows her price. To be a queen she must first be a pawn. For she too is trapped by the rules of the game at which she excels; and it is by our ambivalence to her skills, and to the skills of her father behind her, that Shakespeare invites us to know this court world.

If the ladies contrast with the lords in their dutiful attention to business, they contrast with them too in the solidarity with which they enjoy the periods of pleasure that lie between business. The competition between them is as rich, tense and potentially unstable as that between the men, but it is better disciplined: they are even prepared to trust one another with an exchange of identities when they disguise themselves to fool the men. Their wit is in full control, avoiding shrewishness and maintaining an important balance between aggression and defence in relation to their own feelings, to one another and to their lovers. It provides a way of keeping faith and of keeping distance, of keeping relationship alive whilst keeping it under control, of generating excitement without disturbing the solidarity upon which they depend. Yet despite the poised balance that characterizes the ladies beside the giddiness of the lords, there are moments when we hear, as with the lords, a counterpoint of melancholy that enables us to reckon up the cost of success in a currency different from that of the King of France. One such moment occurs in the hunting scene at the start of Act 4. Louis Montrose has written of the emblematic importance of this scene to the play: 'The Princess's station for the hunt is a metaphor for her position in the general action. Like the ladies, once they have established themselves in the park, she is the hunter who does not pursue: her victims come to her to be shot'.[28] She is a hunter hunting the hart, the heart and – on her father's behalf at least – the purse; each of these occupations is inseparably bound up with the others and she must have them each in mind when, in her pastoral exchange with the Forester, she expresses sorrow for the game that her station enables her to pursue:

> Thus will I save my credit in the shoot:
> Not wounding, pity would not let me do't;
> If wounding, then it was to show my skill,
> That more for praise than purpose meant to kill.
> And out of question so it is sometimes,
> Glory grows guilty of detested crimes,
> When, for fame's sake, for praise, an outward part,
> We bend to that the working of the heart;
> As I for praise alone now seek to spill
> The poor deer's blood, that my heart means no ill.
> (IV.i.26–35)

As men had been naturalized in terms of their military independence, women are naturalized in terms of their pity; and both sexes find, on coming to court, that their 'natural' qualities are compromised by the artificial exigencies of the competition for prestige. The woman is lost in the lady: the contradictions of court life are inscribed in the self-division of the Princess's heart. She laments the sacrifice of conscience to compliance, and glimpses for a moment the possibility that all the boasted substance of court life may amount to no more than a hollow seeming; but then, of course, the prettiness and poise of her complaint assure us that this is not a trap from which she is concerned to escape.

However, the problems created by the *seemings* of court life are finally forced upon the ladies by the particular nature of their role in the game of courtly love; and these are problems that take us straight to the heart of the dilemma most characteristic of court life. 'Seems, madam? Nay, it is. I know not "seems"'. The problem of distinguishing between appearance and reality that so haunted Hamlet is endemic in a society where success depended upon the flawless and impenetrable veneer of public manner. David Loades has described a related problem for the modern historian trying to decode Tudor love-poetry: 'unless one actually knows the identities of both parties in these lyrical exercises, it is impossible to tell whether the emotions expressed are real or conventional, because genuine lovers used the same clichés'.[29] However naive this distinction between real and conventional in matters of art, the fundamental difficulty of reading the sincerity or insincerity of courtly addresses was real enough; and in real life it was felt with particular intensity by the women, who had most to lose. Hence in part, perhaps, the popularity of romance literature describing the testing of a knight; for love was always ready to bring the court world to the test. Hence the 'trial' (V.ii.795) that concludes *Love's Labour's Lost*, as the ladies seek to fathom the sincerity of their lovers; and hence too, eighty years later, the attempt of Harriet at the end of *The Man of Mode* to crack the smooth veneer of Dorimant's seductiveness in order to test the reality of his feelings and compel him to a real commitment. But Harriet has no more success than awaits the ladies here in Navarre: their lords remain invulnerable behind their style and language, inscrutable even as they submit to their test.

It is Harriet, I think, at the very end of *The Man of Mode*, who catches something of the fundamental melancholy of the woman's lot in court life, something of the butterfly-like brevity of the period of her power, when she turns to her friend Emilia – unknown to them both, one of her many rivals in Dorimant's future plans – and mocks his imperturbably stylish protestations of love: 'This is more dismal than the country, Emilia; pity me who am going to that sad place'. A similar melancholy, we shall see, colours the end of *Love's Labour's Lost*, bound up in part with the passing of the ladies' power. Structurally from the start, with its four young men and its four young women, the play has laid out the inevitability of engagement in the game of courtly love; and within that game the women seem at first sight dominant. They have freedom of choice, and their freedom is defended by a wonderful resourcefulness of wit. They seem even – to speak paradoxically – masterful; for their freedom itself is a paradox, a real possession but only lent to them for a little while by the men who are their masters. To know this fully, we must remember that behind them is the power of the King of France and ahead of them is the power of their husbands, when in time they change their role and dwindle into wives – into country wives, most of them. Shakespeare's love comedies are in fact misnamed; they should rather be called comedies of courtship – for their most characteristic power, the power which they confer upon their heroines, is licensed to them only during the brief festive period of their courtship, and is to be understood with reference to its fellow-contrary, the melancholy realization that comedy – like the plays themselves – will end with marriage.

## COURT AND COUNTRY

*They have been at a great feast of languages, and stolen the scraps.*
(V.i.35–6)

In a long essay on the pastoral and its sudden popularity during the last decades of the sixteenth century, Louis Montrose has argued that it served the double function of occluding and, in a safely encoded form, articulating certain key contradictions within what he calls 'the cultural logic' of late Elizabethan society. These contradictions originated in the differences between the stories that the dominant culture told itself about the nature of the society that it lived in and the actual facts of the matter – stories about the fixity of social class and the right of the powerful to rule, for example, which were false to the facts of social mobility and the widespread competition, both material and ideological, for a right to share the wealth, power and prestige monopolized by the gentry and, more particularly, by the court. It is thus, for Montrose, a central paradox of Renaissance pastoral that, whilst it 'takes the court as its cynosure' and naturalizes the power of its 'sociocultural elite',[30] it also articulates and embodies the fierce nature of the competition to enter that world and succeed in it: for the successful pastoral poet might win preferment by his verses.

*Love's Labour's Lost*, it seems to me, has much of the pastoral about it, and the weave of its plot serves the same double function that Montrose identifies in courtly pastoral: it both disguises and draws out within the world of the play the contradictions between the picture that the court has of itself and the actual facts of the matter. On the one hand, the lords' leisurely outdoor life, with its playfulness, its ready accessibility to its rustic servants and the clownish nature of those servants, all work together to occlude tensions between court and country and to legitimate the power of the gentry. On the other hand, we shall see, Shakespeare uses the conflictual nature of the dramatic form to articulate those tensions, to shape them until at the end of the play they attain the status of contradictions. For *Love's Labour's Lost* is no courtly pastoral: written for public as well as courtly performance, it shows a court gone out of court and, with a sharpness far beyond that of courtly pastoral, it lays bare some central issues in the real-life cultural competition between court and country. The play sustains both a conservative and a subversive reading − a paradox we have already begun to notice in the double function of Armado, who serves both to naturalize and to undermine the power of the court. It is time now to turn to the same paradox as we see it in the double role performed by the country competitors in the play: firstly by Costard and Jaquenetta, and secondly by Sir Nathaniel, Dull and Holofernes, those least digits at the end of the long arm of courtly authority as it reaches out to pacify the countryside.

Costard's role is a richly ambiguous one. On the one hand, he enjoys a likeness of contrariety with Armado: the one in his foolish illiteracy and the other in his foolish pedantry turn together to a woman − to the same woman, Jaquenetta − and in so doing, together they seem to naturalize sexual desire, to forestall future disapproval of the court's perjury and, between their two extremes, to authenticate courtly manners. On the other hand, however, there is also about Costard a sublime and irrepressible insouciance that shames the court in their watchful concern for prestige. If the court consolidate their identity by mocking Costard, he enables us to consolidate ours by mocking the court; for out of the traditional role of the rustic clown, whose unlettered ignorance and unregenerate sexuality should legitimate the austere culture of the court, Shakespeare has created a powerfully attractive emblem of all-that-which-will-not-be-brought-in-under-the-law.

> *King* Did you hear the proclamation?
>
> *Costard* I do confess much of the hearing it, but little of the marking of it.
>
> *King* It was proclaimed a year's imprisonment to be taken with a wench.
>
> *Costard* I was taken with none, sir: I was taken with a demsel.
>
> *King* Well, it was proclaimed damsel.
>
> *Costard* This was no damsel neither, sir: she was a virgin.
>
> *King* It is so varied too, for it was proclaimed virgin.
>
> *Costard* If it were, I deny her virginity: I was taken with a maid.
>
> *King* This maid will not serve your turn, sir.
>
> *Costard* This maid will serve my turn, sir.
>
> (I.i.277–90)

How shall we characterize the Costard of this exchange? Is he foolish? or cunning? or a wise fool? How shall we understand the nature of his resistance, poised as it is between insolence and deference and contained within the form of a very traditional routine? And how will this in turn affect our understanding of the king's determination to preserve him as a fit object of his sport?

Our characterization of Costard must express an appreciation of his circumstances. Arbitrarily, the king has passed a law to suit his courtly pleasure; Costard in the familiar pursuit of his own pleasures has broken that law; and now he must take the consequences in such a way as not to lose all faith in himself. Similar situations in real life foster the anxious expertise of the comedian forestalling disapproval and defusing threat by laughter; but Costard the stage clown seems at first sight – at the start of the play, at least – blessedly free from anxiety. Maybe a naturalistic interpretation would restore that to him today, making him either consciously cunning or unconsciously neurotic in the strategies of his self-defence; or he might be played non-naturalistically as a theatrical being inhabiting a blessed limbo of licensed folly, free from psychological definition and enjoying all those freedoms denied to the socially compliant; or, again non-naturalistically, he might be played in a Brechtian way by an actor able to step out of part and address the audience directly – over the head of the king, as it were. But whatever interpretation we choose, the key must be sought in this initial competitive parley with the king, in the social tensions between court and country that Shakespeare is exploring by 'mingling kings and clowns'.[31]

The mockery by the weak of the strong is different in kind from that by the strong of the weak – a dissymmetry important to the play here, as the relatively powerless disclose those strategies of appeasement and deferral necessary to safeguard their own view of the world and to resist the claims of power upon it. Costard employs the traditional routines of comedy in a traditional way, to resist authority and all its attendant claims of religion, law and learning – religion obliquely by his bawdy joke about Jaquenetta ('This maid will serve my turn, sir'), but law and learning directly by the detailed texture of his replies. His method is parody. Wench, demsel, virgin, maid: in a recognizably legalistic way, cavilling over the definition of terms, he parodies law, and in a recognizably pedantic way, varying the names of things after the best courtly fashion, he parodies the new learning. Words themselves, the agents of authority and the badges of culture, refuse to keep their place for Costard. He is, like Feste, consciously or unconsciously, a 'corrupter of words', a destroyer of distinctions, a reveller in the anarchic delights of nonsense, a man in touch with the vitality released by acts of misnaming. Feste declares the fashionable popularity of word-play in a famous passage from *Twelfth Night*: 'To see this age! – A sentence is but a cheveril glove to a good wit, how quickly the wrong side may be turned outward' (III.i.11–13). But kings and clowns play differently with words. The courtiers in *Love's Labour's Lost* pun as part of their competitive display, in order to deflect the purposes of others and to demonstrate their control of their own: not even words can escape them. But Costard, although he too has much to defend, dare not do so by assertion of mastery; and so his word-play (or his malapropism) tends always towards the subversiveness of nonsense. 'Welcome the sour cup of prosperity!' he says (I.i.304) on learning his punishment for breaking the king's edict. He does not (or he will not) live the world on the king's terms – a refusal embodying an obduracy common in popular culture, where nonsense has always been one resource against the sentences of power. Indeed, Costard's words and his comic routines resonate with traditions of collective resistance; and, as Michael Bristol says, 'these tactics of delay and petty harassment, and the gradual accumulation of small victories, are predicated on a specific vision of history and historical change'.[32] They are predicated upon an apprehension of the encroaching power of the state and of the patient cunning necessary to keep alive a dissenting country culture; and maybe our initial difficulty in characterizing Costard, in imagining an inner life for him, is an indication of how far that state has already encroached. For Costard's inner life has been driven underground, entrapped within a clownishness whose freedoms nevertheless help us to judge the necessities that control the court.

However, there is a paradox about parody that makes itself felt during Costard's exchange with the king and that also reflects an important aspect of the structural tension between country and court: namely, that parody, being imitative, may love the thing that it mocks. The other side to Costard's obstinate illiteracy, which enlivens the play by the miscarriage of letters, is that he also loves to imitate the cultured language of his superiors: words such as remuneration and guerdon draw him irresistibly. He is excited too by his own verbal skills in competition with Boyet in Act 4:1, where his imitativeness is at its height:

> By my soul, a swain! a most simple clown!
> Lord, Lord, how the ladies and I have put him down!
> (IV.i.141–2)

On the one hand, Costard's imitation of court life counteracts his resistance to it, bearing witness to the cultural power of the court to compromise, marginalize and deform the opposition which it creates. But on the other hand, although it is folly in Costard to believe that he may act the courtier's part, his gullibility has its glory too. For if the courtier may play the countryman in his pastorals, the countryman may play the courtier in his desires: the subversiveness of Costard's foolish self-belief ('I'm a better man than him') enacts a fantasy deep in popular culture, with its utopian hunger to possess the good things of the earth. Our laughter is ambiguous, responsive to the indeterminacy of the tensions between country and court that Shakespeare is depicting.

At the end of the play, however, there is no ambiguity. Costard's country pieties are so outraged by the moral levity of the court that he interrupts their entertainment to voice his anxiety for Jaquenetta:

> *Costard* Fellow Hector, she is gone; she is two months on her way.
> *Armado* What meanest thou?

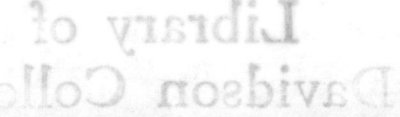

> *Costard* Faith, unless you play the honest Troyan, the poor wench is cast away: she's quick; the child brags in her belly already: 'tis yours.
>
> (V.ii.664–9)

If Costard is clownish in his excitement here, he is dignified in his concern – a concern for which he will even fight the great courtier Don Adriano de Armado if necessary. The seemings of the courtly play in which he has been engrossed cease to matter; and suddenly we glimpse the hostility towards such play that might have animated his earlier words to Jaquenetta: 'Walk aside the true folk, and let the traitors stay' (IV.iii.209). It is the strength of this hostility, as Costard insists that Armado now play honestly, which re-establishes for the last time the deepest rhythm of *Love's Labour's Lost*, pursuing the breakdown of carnival and play into guilt and penitential lenten atonement. What is more, Costard's anger highlights the irresponsibility of the rest of the courtiers as well, as they urge Armado and himself to fight it out. It is a crisis which effectively disperses any lingering pastoral illusion that country and court might exist in harmony. For Jaquenetta in her cheeky flirtatious way – both similar and dissimilar to the more elegant flirtation of the ladies from France – has played the game by traditional country rules, which entitle her not to dishonour but to a husband if she becomes pregnant. The court have their way but the country have theirs, which not all the dissuasions of religion, law and learning can invalidate; and the shape of the play as it moves towards its climax is one that increasingly focusses, out of its earlier ambiguities, the sharpness of the conflict between the two. It is an unequal but real conflict within the play, and it holds the mirror up to crucial tensions within the Tudor state – tensions which were to erupt during the next half century as the monarchy, in its efforts to consolidate its hold over aristocracy and populace alike, succeeded only in creating hostility between them by drawing country peers to court and away from their roots in rural life.

The same tensions belonging to the same historical process are explored from the perspective of another class in the double role performed by Sir Nathaniel and Holofernes within the play. They are both educated men, lowly representatives of the official institutions of the state and men whose patriotism might be expected to be above suspicion. 'You are a good member of the commonwealth', says Sir Nathaniel to his friend (IV.ii.74) – high praise indeed in a play much concerned for political loyalty. We meet them first as they turn complacently away from watching the princess hunt, and the moment emblemizes perfectly the nature of their loyalty: they know their place but love to admire the court, with an admiration fulfilled in imitation. It is, indeed, their imitativeness that makes them at first ridiculous; for in their little country society – a mini-academy, it almost seems, relishing the cultural renaissance of their century – we see an unconscious parody of all that we have already seen at court. We see a society bound together in all the exclusiveness of cultural snobbery; a punctiliously deferential courtesy together with a competitive display of wit; a presumption of prestige swollen into gorgeous vanity; and a pedantic parade of variations played upon the restricted themes of polite conversation. We see, in short, a preoccupation with the dress and address of language so formalistic that it is always in danger of mistaking words for things. This is the peculiar vice of scholarship against which Berowne has always been anxious to safeguard the court: 'every godfather can give a name', he says (I.i.93), arguing that it is not the decoration of the object with names that matters but the illumination of the inner faculty. Yet these arguments themselves, as we have already seen, serve sport and advantage rather than truth; and in this Berowne is no better than Holofernes. Our laughter once again proves ambiguous; for whilst it distinguishes the wit, poetry and versatility of the court above the pretentious vanity of the country, it also levels that distinction in the perception of a commonly competitive humanity.

But Sir Nathaniel and Holofernes are not simply ridiculous; they also have qualities that draw out the limitations of the court. These qualities are at first compounded with the general ridiculousness of their characters; the relish that they take in their pleasures, the warmth that they find in their friendship, their nice determination (in Sir Nathaniel's words) to 'abrogate scurrility' (IV.ii.52) may all of them be mocked. Yet they express a certain sense of decency that is to have its due weight in the play. The courtiers and Costard both enjoy obscenity in their different ways: the former perhaps because it reinforces the solidarity of their privileged social caste and yet keeps them in touch with otherwise dissociated aspects of the self; the latter perhaps because it feels subversive and seems to level social distinction. But the obscenity that we detect in Sir Nathaniel and Holofernes is entirely unintended. They are quite innocent of innuendo; and if their sense of decency is made ridiculous to us by the frequency of their unconscious double entendres, it nevertheless finally enables Holofernes to achieve a powerful dignity when discountenanced by the mockery of the court. 'This is not generous, not gentle, not humble', he objects (V.ii.623); and with justice. Confronted directly with the crudity of courtly manners, these representatives of the minor country gentry and their circle are morally outraged; they have their own standards of educated behaviour and gentility, now rivalling those of the court with which they formerly felt fellowship. Once again the ambiguity of the play's comedy is sharpened into open conflict; and once again that conflict was to prove decisive during the next half century when the king and court had finally forfeited the respect of a significant number of the country gentry.

## CONCLUSION: THE END OF PLAY

*I go woolward for penance.*
(V.ii.701–2)

'Is not a comonty/A Christmas gambol or a tumbling-trick?' asks Christopher Sly at the end of the Induction to *The Taming of the Shrew*. No, he is answered, comedy is 'a kind of history' – a history poised fascinatingly, like the word itself at this period, between fact and fiction, and intended as a mirror, wherein men might see themselves and their place in the world. The history dramatized in *Love's Labour's Lost* holds the mirror up to the competitive life of a representative Renaissance court in all the exhilaration of its power and all the anxiety of its tensions; and it traces those tensions to the unstable mixture of rivalry and fellowship structured into its competition, as it flourished internally between members of the same court, nationally between the court and the country it ruled and internationally between different courts. Life in such courtly circles was an exciting, melancholy affair, an opportunity and a trap from which there was no escape, a round of endless provisionality where the role of the new learning was only to improvise and where the individual's destiny lay lost beyond all individual control. For history perceived from the standpoint of the actor may always be seen as destiny. It is to this question of destiny that I now wish to turn as we consider the patterns of interruption that close the play and sharpen its tensions into final contradiction.

C. L. Barber has seen how these patterns of interrupted play serve to interpret both history and destiny in Shakespeare's plays:

> Shakespeare's plays are full of pageantry and of action patterned in a ritualistic way. But the pageants are regularly interrupted; the rituals are abortive or perverted; or if they succeed, they succeed against odds or in an unexpected fashion. The people in the plays try to organize their lives by pageant and ritual, but the plays are dramatic precisely because the effort fails. This failure drama presents as history and personality; in the largest perspective, as destiny.[33]

But curiously Barber does not allow this insight free play upon the festive comedy which is his chief subject. He allows Shakespearean comedy to be 'conscious of holiday ... in a new way', conscious of the poetry of holiday as 'imagination', conscious even of 'the saturnalian form itself as a paradoxical human need, problem and resource'.[34] But he then disarms his paradox by enfolding it within a reassuring theory of the 'poised two-sidedness'[35] of a drama able to celebrate the seasonable rhythmic alternations between holiday and everyday because these same seasonal rhythms were already widely celebrated in Elizabethan life.

Yet the shapeliness of art need not mirror shapeliness in real life; it may be a shapely patterning of something perceived to be unshapely, disjunctive, in real life. The entertainment of the Nine Worthies at the end of *Love's Labour's Lost* is interrupted by the threat of fighting; the court's mocking delight in that entertainment and its disintegration is itself interrupted by news of the King of France's death; and finally the courtship game between the lords and ladies is interrupted by the test that the ladies impose to coincide with their own enforced period of mourning. These interruptions are all dramatic devices to disrupt the smooth passage of the play; even as they disclose the peculiar tensions of court life, they also problematize the nature and worth of play, indicating disjunctions in real life between the playful and the real that eclipse the harmonious power of art. The lords make a choice that seems responsible, mature: they accept a lenten self-discipline, forsaking play, embracing acquaintance with suffering and death, and thereby seemingly preparing themselves for their 'world-without-end' commitment to the business and 'bargain' of marriage (V.ii.781). But their renunciation of play involves not only themselves but the

## Love's Labour's Lost: The Court at Play

audience. 'Our wooing doth not end like an old play', says Berowne (V.ii.866); the legal term of the ladies' contract, a twelvemonth and a day, is 'too long for a play' (V.ii.870). The smooth passage of the play itself is interrupted, for actors and audience alike; and as the roles of courtly life change giddily again before us, we find ourselves increasingly involved in it as an image of our own. The court of Navarre becomes much more than a precise reflection of a historical institution, that is; it becomes also a problematical emblem of our common human destiny, as we too struggle with the nature and worth of the necessity of play. Carnival and Lent, revelry and responsibility, play and business – and now, theatre and reality – are not simply antitheses; they represent mutually exclusive ways of seeing the world, the boundaries always shifting between them and each able to invalidate and desubstantiate the other. They indicate disjunctions in real life that may be shaped as paradox or contradiction but that none of us perhaps can win into higher synthesis or contain within a seasonable pattern of spring and winter, youth and age, folly and maturity.

Armado emblemizes this disjunction perfectly, the player in the hair-shirt whose sport throughout the play has been split off from a secret penance; he serves to suggest how deeply in *Love's Labour's Lost*, as in all Elizabethan culture, the whole idea of play is tainted with the danger of a highly sexualized licence and a highly politicized subversiveness. He finally feels his guilt so badly that he is driven into the renunciatory, reparative gesture towards Jaquenetta 'to hold the plough for her sweet love three year' (V.ii.875–6); and yet, it seems, the penitential gesture cannot integrate the playful impulse. Armado in this is partly a scapegoat – the fool who cannot find the golden mean – but he is also an epitome of what the Princess calls, paradoxically, the 'dear guiltiness' (V.ii.783) of play. For no-one in *Love's Labour's Lost* can find the golden mean. The lords too, like Armado, suffer in giddy sequence 'gravity's revolt to wantonness' (V.ii.74) and wantonness's chastening back to gravity again; and even the ladies, who struggle so long to separate business from pleasure, find at the last that grief awakens the guilt quiescent at the heart of their play. They apologize after the fashion of courtly lovers by blaming the irresistible charms of the men, and cleverly they find an apology that keeps the play of sexual desire alive whilst apparently disowning it:

If over-boldly we have borne ourselves

> In the converse of breath; your gentleness
> Was guilty of it.
>
> (V.ii.726–8)

Play and penitential guilt: in the court society of *Love's Labour's Lost* these are two extremes beyond integration and thus, as here in the ladies' apology, they are always ready to run into one another. As King James put it, describing the dissolution of the golden mean, 'the two extremities themselues, although they seeme contrarie, yet growing to the height, runne euer both in one'.[36] Or, as Wordsworth wrote two centuries later:

> So meet extremes in this mysterious world,
> And opposites thus melt into each other.[37]

The test that Rosaline sets Berowne – 'to move wild laughter in the throat of death' (V.ii.847) – is one that would meet paradox with paradox; and it is with the paradoxical running together of extremes that the play leaves its audience, as we are suddenly invited to see the mockery with which Berowne has amused us as a 'fault' (V.ii.860), his laughter as 'wild'. The play paradoxically disowns itself, problematizes its own play by frustrating the hopes of a happy ending which it fed. In modern psychoanalytic parlance, the 'failed climax' of its *ludus interruptus* signals a sense of guilty excess in the preceding play.[38] If we are to think of comedy as a mirror held up to history, we are invited to think of it as a flawed one – flawed by the revelry that is, in the most literal sense of the word, its business. *Love's Labour's Lost* ends because it has to end, because it is time to end; but even here in the seasonableness of its conclusion, it remains importantly inconclusive.

This inconclusiveness receives its final shaping in the closing songs with their seasonable debate between Spring and Winter. These songs have been persistently sentimentalized in critical literature. Barber, for instance, sees their vitality as a celebration of the daily goings-on of the country life 'out of which special festive occasions were shaped up', and finds them exactly right to end a festive comedy as 'a last, and full, expression of the controlling feeling for community and season'.[39] Jeremy Hooker too, writing of 'Winter', finds it a celebration of natural order: 'it may seem portentous to say that Tom and Dick and the others are at home in the world, but that is the supreme sense of well-being expressed by the poem'.[40] Even Louis Montrose, who sees the importance of 'indeterminacy' and 'discord' to the play's ending, nevertheless believes that 'the songs wed play to work, love to labor, within the larger cyclical rhythms of a human community that is harmoniously wed to nature'.[41] But such readings as these, anxious to find solace in the harmony between mind and nature which the songs depict, ignore the fact that the same songs also depict a disharmony between them. Nature has two faces as it is seen by the double vision of human nature: alongside the various natural pieties of all the different seasons lies the destiny of an unregenerate human nature, leading to cuckoldry ('cuckoo') and lechery ('to it, to it'). The mockery and merriment with which the play has been full receives here its last impenitent expression in the cries of cuckoo and owl, carrying the threat of betrayal and perjury home to the heart of the marriage vow. If marriage has meant the end of play, play may mean the end of marriage too. Responsibility and revelry, Lent and Carnival, are continually at war, the chances between them often unpredictable, capricious, as trivial and as meaningful as whether or not we hear a double meaning in the cry of a bird. But there is no question of their integration or of a seasonable rhythm between them; for each way of seeing dislimns and desubstantiates the other.

The songs thus provide a fitting end to the play; for if (like pastoral) they are sophisticated celebrations of the simple pieties of rural life, they are also (like nonsense songs, or mock-pastoral perhaps) able to drain those pieties of their meaning and value. They remind us that marriage is a beginning as well as an end; that the ambiguous freedoms of play are a dangerous necessity; and that 'nature' may subvert even the seemingly most 'natural' of human institutions. 'Spring' and 'Winter' are the consummation of a dramatic technique that we have seen at work throughout the play, patterning our understanding of the relationships between Berowne and Armado, the lords and ladies, the court and country: the technique of *doubling*, which establishes a relationship both of similarity and dissimilarity but mystifies the boundary between them. It is a technique that we shall see further developed in *Hamlet*, for it is perfectly suited to the depiction of a court life where each individual exists in a perpetual insecurity of self-comparison with his fellow-competitors. The songs are all activity and exhilaration, or they are all melancholy and emptiness; they share something of the same slippery uncertainties of tone that La Bruyère noted nearly a century later in the play of the French court:

> La vie de la cour est un jeu sérieux, mélancolique, qui applique: il faut arranger ses pièces et ses batteries, avoir un dessein, le suivre, parer celui de son adversaire, hasarder quelquefois, et jouer de caprice; et après toutes ses rêveries et toutes ses mesures, on est échec, quelquefois mat; souvent, avec des pions qu'on ménage bien, on va à dame, et l'on gagne la partie; le plus habile l'emporte, ou le plus heureux.[42]

It is the exhilaration and the entrapment of such a court life that *Love's Labour's Lost* has depicted, and that its closing songs generalize into emblems of the success and disillusion, the freedoms and necessities whose chances make up our common human destiny, as we each of us in our different worlds wrestle with the contradictory requirements of responsibility and revelry.

'The words of Mercury are harsh after the songs of Apollo', the Quarto announces (V.ii.922–3): the necessities of the play-world come to an end, and we are free to turn away to whatever comes next. But if Mercury is 'the presider over roads', we might also remember that he is 'the conductor of departed souls to the Lower World' (*OED*). To what sort of drained world are we dismissed? from what illusory world expelled? The final achievement of *Love's Labour's Lost*, as the carnival comes to an end, is both to reinforce and to blur the boundary-line between playing and reality. We must go, alas, but from what to what? It is a question of mood. In this mysterious marginal moment of the play's ending, we find both renewed vitality and disillusion, both confirmation and frustration of our deepest hopes, both exhilaration and melancholy. We find a paradoxical reading of our common destiny which we are free to take or leave, to receive as a general truth about human life or to break down into a particular truth about court life: we may take the songs either as emblems of man's perennial fate, caught between extremes that melt perplexingly into one another – extremes of revelry and responsibility, of freedom and necessity – or we may leave them to their context within the play. For, as we have seen, the play validates its vision of destiny in its particular historical reading of the book of the Renaissance court, whose uncertain and paradoxical competitiveness – *jeu sérieux, mélancolique, qui applique* – it was the courtier's destiny both to enjoy and endure.

# 3
# *Hamlet*:
# The Court in Transition (I)

Suddenly, unexpectedly, surveying the tragic waste of the Danish court, Horatio can stand it no longer and reaches for the poisoned cup.

> I am more an antique Roman than a Dane.
> Here's yet some liquor left.
> (V.ii.346–7)

It is an extraordinary moment, an attempt at final self-definition by a man aware of the many selves he has to choose amongst. The friend whom Hamlet admired for his stoicism in the face of suffering, a man who seemed 'as one, in suff'ring all, that suffers nothing' (III.ii.66), can suffer no more. The scholar selected to be *spectator ab extra* at the unfolding drama of the Danish court has been so deeply drawn into its goings-on that, like the Cumaean Sybil surveying the waste land of T. S. Eliot's poem, he wants to die. In this most literary of plays, at this most critical of moments, Horatio strikes a classical pose: he will accept the role of the stoic in which he has been cast, the role most commonly opposed to that of the revenger in the revenge tradition to which *Hamlet* belongs,[43] and – faced with a burden too heavy to bear – he will perfect it in honourable suicide.

But what is the burden of suffering that finally breaks Horatio? Its external causes, of course, are obvious: the death of his friend and the slaughter before him. But what are its internal causes? What is Horatio feeling? The various explanations readily offered in various editions of the play seem to me as baffling as the silence of the text itself. What does it add to invoke the names of Mark Antony or Cato and to say that Horatio, like them, prefers death before a life made unworthy by the stain of dishonour or defeat? What dishonour or defeat has Horatio in fact sustained? There is a puzzle here that we need to face, since so much of the drama of *Hamlet* lies in the disjunction that we feel between the language that the characters speak and the inner reality that we imagine for them. Horatio himself cannot help us. He remains essentially inarticulate, his inner life mysterious behind the gesture of his speech; and within a mere twenty lines he has changed role again and reverted back from the antique Roman to the Danish Christian, praying that his friend's spirit, in this play of restless spirits, might be escorted by flights of angels to its final rest.

The key to the tragic events in *Hamlet* lies in the mystery of passion – in what Polonius calls 'a savageness in unreclaimed blood' (II.i.34), a violent contamination of unregenerate passion that spreads from person to person and finally brings even the stoical outsider, Horatio, to the point of suicide. For Horatio, I guess, surveying the slaughter before him, feels such a sense of rage and disgust at life that he can no longer bear to live it. His sense of the sacred is outraged: if this is life, then he must either kill himself or curse it and the Gods who gave it. He has succumbed to what the play elsewhere calls 'ecstasy', a word which literally means 'the state of being beside oneself' and which suggests both the nature and the power of those passionate incursions that usurp the 'sovereignty of reason' (I.iv.73) – incursions against which, to use two terms from contemporary psychoanalysis, *idealization* and *splitting* in the grounds of the self seem to offer the only strategies of self-defence.[44] What is so particularly subversive about the passions at work in *Hamlet*, especially those associated with revenge, is that they are aroused by the breach of what today we should call taboo. They are aroused by betrayal of central trust, by the imagining or doing of those wrongs that wring the soul by striking at the heart of all that it holds most sacred in life; and such betrayal leaves the characters confounded, inarticulate before the strength and mystery of the passions it evokes.

Taboo, Freud reminds us,[45] signifies both holy and unholy, both that which is sacred because it is pure and that which is sacred because it is impure; and *Hamlet*, like the rest of Shakespearean tragedy,[46] is drawn to this central ambiguity structured into the nature of the sacred. Hamlet himself, for instance, from the first moment that he saw how 'the funeral bak'd meats/Did coldly furnish forth the marriage tables' (I.ii.180–1), must have found in the very violence of his outraged pieties a hint – later confirmed, he believes – that he had been divinely set apart to be the 'scourge and minister' (III.iv.177) of all who had offended; whilst Horatio too, outraged at the final unholy slaughter of the court, seems to find in the holy ritual of a stoic's suicide an action commensurate with the sacred violence of the passion that he feels. For, as René Girard remarks, ritual is 'the regular exercise of "good" violence'[47] in the hope to exorcise 'bad' violence. But how shall we decide upon the degree to which Horatio's suicide attempt is determined by the self-violent vindictiveness of disgust and despair or by the determination to rise above them and master them, maybe even to purge the country of their contaminating power? Once again we see how, in King James's words, 'the two extremities themselues, although they seeme contrarie, yet growing to the height, runne euer both in one'.[48] It is an appalling, noble gesture, this ambiguous movement that Horatio makes to drain the poisoned cup to its dregs, but it bears unambiguous testimony to what Girard calls 'the paradoxical nature of violence', namely, the fact that 'evil and the violent measures taken to combat evil are essentially the same'.[49] For it has the taint of ecstasy upon it; and in this it epitomizes the reading of our common destiny that *Hamlet* has to offer us – a destiny in which all action is acting and all language no more than words, words, words, since men and women are at the mercy of mysterious passions that they can neither understand, articulate nor control and that, once aroused, spread from person to person, contaminating even those who resist them.

\*     \*     \*

Hamlet, however, snatches the cup from Horatio's hand and makes a dying request designed perhaps both to save his friend and his own good name:

> If thou didst ever hold me in thy heart,
> Absent thee from felicity awhile,
> And in this harsh world draw thy breath in pain
> To tell my story.
>                         (V.ii.351–4)

'If thou didst ever thy dear father love', urged the Ghost (I.v.23), encouraging Hamlet to succumb to passion: 'if thou didst ever hold me in thy heart', urges Hamlet, encouraging Horatio to resist it. In this play of powerful commandments from the edge of the grave and beyond it, of sacred words uttered in the most holy of marginal conditions, Hamlet's lines open up the kindest possibilities; they leave Horatio with the same choice that they leave us, in our own marginal capacity as *spectatores ab extra*, in the marginal place of the public theatre at the marginal time of the play's end, as we too, like Horatio, find ourselves initiated into the dangers of violence. It is the same choice that was brought delicately into play by the comedy of *Love's Labour's Lost*, fluctuating between exhilaration and melancholy in its depiction of the giddily changing roles of courtly competition: the choice between reading the world as destiny or history. Here in the claustrophobia and confusion of the Danish court, where competition is murderous and the right role mystifyingly hard to find, this choice is structured formally into the meaning of Shakespeare's text. On the one hand, there is the fatalistic possibility: to abandon ourselves to violence, revenge and ecstasy as irresistible necessities of our nature, baleful aspects of a destiny always able to destroy even the best that human culture can devise. Or on the other hand, we may do as Horatio decides to do: we may try to tell the story truly, partly for our own sake, partly for Hamlet's sake, but partly also for the sake of a faith in the power of human rationality to understand, and perhaps also to control, our destiny. So we may keep faith with Hamlet and the new rationalism of Renaissance culture, even in their failure.

In *Love's Labour's Lost*, as we have seen, culture was worn by the court as a badge of their social distinction; philosophical or religious ideas were sported for personal display or class solidarity, whose demands by far outweighed those of sincerity. Here in *Hamlet*, however, culture has an inwardness that belongs to the serious attempts of the mind to measure the world and to define its own appropriate place and conduct within it; and the play shows how the same culture that distinguishes the court may also be turned against it. For whereas Berowne in *Love's Labour's Lost* finally proved himself a dramatic hero by virtue of his brilliant extemporization, his versatile and unprincipled resourcefulness on behalf of the court of Navarre, Hamlet is a hero because – a brilliant extemporizer himself – he sets himself in the name of truth against the unprincipled versatility of Claudius, against the compliance of his court. Hence he tries out the role of satirist, epitomizing all he detests at court in his harsh mockery of Osric:

> A did comply with his dug before a sucked it. Thus has he –
> and many more of the same bevy that I know the drossy age

dotes on – only got the tune of the time and, out of an habit of encounter, a kind of yeasty collection, which carries them through and through the most fanned and winnowed opinions; and do but blow them to their trial, the bubbles are out. (V.ii.184–91)

It is against the seemings and the shows, the essential frivolity and falsity of court life, that Hamlet sets himself. His aim is twofold: to know the world truly and to fashion himself accordingly, realizing himself in an appropriate role. Yet he fails, and his failure is that which Yeats identified three hundred years later in W. E. Henley: 'he never understood how small a fragment of our own nature can be brought to perfect expression, nor that even but with great toil, in a much divided civilization'.[50]

For the business of *Hamlet* lies with a much divided civilization, divided not only by the ferocity of its competition but also by the different ideologies invoked by the competing parties; the play captures perfectly the crisis in moral and political authority that shadowed the exhilarating proliferation of culture and ideology within the new Renaissance states. Perry Anderson's description of the cultural revival of the Italian Renaissance has a broader application than he gave it when he wrote that 'the Renaissance discovered itself with a new, intense consciousness of rupture and loss'.[51] *Hamlet* is the fullest contemporary record that we have of that process of self-discovery through rupture and loss – a loss whose causes lie deep, as Anderson adds, in 'all the obscurity of the *medium aevum*'. For at its simplest level the story of the play is that of a competition between the 'mighty opposites' (V.ii.62) of Claudius and Hamlet, provoked by the appearance of the Ghost out of the obscurity of the Middle Ages and fulfilled only in the tragic symmetry of their mutual destruction. It is a personal competition through which Shakespeare dramatizes the cultural competition between two mighty ideological opposites, two antagonistic conceptions of man and his world, each belonging to the new learning of the Renaissance and each with its own characteristic vision of court life: on the one hand, machiavellianism, politically dominant in the play because inscribed at the heart of the Danish court, and on the other hand, platonic idealism, embryonic in the play because confined to Hamlet's imaginative life and the fantasies of other people about him – an idealism which finds its fullest expression in Elsinore (as in the England of the 1580s and 1590s) only amongst the marginalized, the dispossessed, the relatively powerless who aspire to power or who have lost it. In so competitive a world where factions and ideologies proliferate, in so watchful yet so disturbing a world where passions (like love and revenge) enjoy so ambiguous a status, it proves impossible to integrate the self and find the appropriate role for it to perform. The business of the play lies with the mutual destruction of self-contradictory cultures by competition, with the mystery and mutability of mind and its insufficiency to measure the universe, with the tragic frailty of all those attempts at self-fashioning so dear to the Renaissance; and it is by its detailed, historically specific pursuit of the fragmenting self – 'not the essence, but the passage; not a passage from age to age, or as the people reckon, from seaven yeares to seaven, but from day to day, from minute to minute' – that the play articulates its sense of destiny, creates itself as an emblem of one way in which (to quote Montaigne again) *'every man beareth the whole stampe of humane condition'*.[52]

My aim in what follows – balancing history against destiny – is to trace the failure of Hamlet's self-fashioning by tracing his failure to integrate three of the most important relationships of his life: that with his father, with Ophelia and with Claudius. The cause of his failure lies in the corruption and claustrophobia of Claudius's court, and we shall see how the conflict between the court and its princely satirist brings into play both the best and the worst of Renaissance courtly aspirations, to the destruction of each. But it is with relationship that we must begin, for in *Hamlet*, to borrow some words of Sammy Mountjoy from William Golding's *Free Fall*, 'people are the walls of our room, not philosophies'[53] – and not theologies either. We might say of Shakespeare here what Masud Khan has said of Montaigne in his self-address to La Boétie throughout the *Essais*: 'to transgress against the tradition and establish man's relationship to man as the exclusive and sole referrent of self-experiences was indeed a revolutionary step'.[54] There is no moral or theological frame to organize our intuitions; we must start with the people and their relationships in the history in which we find them. Each of the three relationships discussed below is rendered dramatically by a development of the doubling technique that we saw at work in *Love's Labour's Lost*, and each opens up quite different possibilities of court life and courtiership. The climax, of course, will be the relationship between Hamlet and Claudius, the former of whom tries to integrate the world in the imagined harmony of the divine will and the latter in the desires of his own; it is a relationship

# Hamlet: The Court in Transition (I)

in which both idealism and machiavellianism will be judged and found wanting, each by the agency of the other.

Coming as it does in the troubled last years of Elizabeth's reign, when courtly competition to be well placed after the succession was increasing and the difficulties of Essex were signalling the stifling of an older aristocratic idealism at the hands of new courtly pragmatism, *Hamlet* has a valedictory air about it; written probably in 1600, it is the new century's reckoning with the old, a judgement of the past which also holds a mirror up to the present. Yet, although it shows the best of Renaissance idealism snuffed out by the *realpolitik* of court life, *Hamlet* is not quite all tragic waste. For if a court is a historical institution, it is also an idea in the minds of those who think it. Hamlet, in his satire and the torment of his affliction, keeps alive ideas of goodness, honour and justice that not only survive the waste of Elsinore but also – transformed, no doubt, by the watching audience – survive the aristocratic society that produced them. I shall conclude, therefore, by noticing another aspect of the play that we need to consider alongside its reading of history and destiny: namely, its utopianism. For *Hamlet* keeps faith with the goodness that we know is in the world because we think it but that we do not know how to mix with the world – the goodness that, although real because we in the audience recognize it, belongs to no time and to no place outside the theatre that both brings it into play and extinguishes it.

## HAMLET AND THE GHOST

*This is certain, that a man that studieth revenge keeps his own wounds green, which otherwise would heal and do well.*[55]

*Homo sum; humani nihil a me alienum puto*: I am a man, and think that nothing human is alien to me. Terence's line, so dear to Renaissance humanism,[56] expresses a confidence in the mind's capacity to measure and to integrate its experience that the 'questionable shape' (I.iv.43) of the Ghost at once confounds. For the Ghost is alien; human as we are, we have no way to assess its origins, its nature, its integrity. Instinctively, the characters call it *it*, dreading the power of its unassimilable strangeness, the violence which its ambiguous sacred presence portends – and, indeed, provokes. What is it, after all, 'this thing' (I.i.24)? Is it 'a spirit of health or goblin damn'd'

(I.iv.40)? Is it sorrowful or angry? majestical or guilty? Is it a devil from hell, usurping the bodily form of Hamlet's father and starting offended at the name of heaven because its designs upon Hamlet and the Danish court are evil? or is it a sanctioned visitor from purgatory, come to expose some secret wound in the state for Hamlet to heal? We remain uncertain, even as the Ghost's silence and gestures remain uncertain; and when at last it begins to speak, our difficulties multiply. For if its narration is honest in fact, is it honest in intent? If it comes from purgatory, why are its emotions so unregenerate and its commands so unchristian? The Ghost baffles the language it attracts, and frustrates the beliefs for which it creates the need. Shall we turn to theology – and, if so, to pagan, catholic or protestant theology? – to folk-lore, to superstition or simply to literary convention to place what we see? There is surely something moving, and not a little grotesque, about the amount of scholarly effort that has been expended, in all the anxiety of intellection, upon this theological problem of the Ghost's provenance. 'Tis here; 'tis here; 'tis gone: for as Eleanor Prosser concedes, 'in the fleeting perspective of the dramatic moment, we find only questions'[57] – questions, moreover, that are born in a passionate disturbance which, as Hamlet himself discovers, scholarship is powerless to help.

Of the two incursions that threaten the state in the opening scene, it is that of the Ghost rather than that of Fortinbras that proves the more dangerous. As usual in Shakespearean tragedy, the enemy is within rather than without, subversive not militarily but by the betrayal of trust. The play opens upon the castle battlements at Elsinore, and this imagery of fortification runs throughout the first act. 'Who's there?' 'Nay, answer me. Stand and unfold yourself': from the play's opening exchange between Barnardo and Francisco, the body politic shows itself fortified against Fortinbras in all the clarity of military discipline. But what fortification can afford protection against the Ghost, that glides invisibly through castle walls and penetrates even 'the pales and forts of reason' (I.iv.28)? Against the threat of the Ghost, it seems, all defences, like the 'vain blows' (I.i.151) that the panic-stricken soldiers rain upon it, are both impotent and inflammatory, part of a vicious circle of violence and counter-violence which it is quite out of human control to halt – and then how difficult it becomes to answer Barnardo's question and to meet the challenge of Francisco! For, under the excitation aroused by the Ghost, to identify and to unfold oneself becomes impossible. Like the Sisters in *Macbeth*, the Ghost is subversive because it embodies what we mean when we say of ourselves 'I was beside myself', 'I don't know what came over me', 'I was out of my mind', 'I was a man possessed'. It is an erinnic image of the passion that lies on the far side of taboo and that returns to haunt us when we say 'I could not lie easy in my grave unless –'. It cannot be placed, it cannot be measured, it cannot be integrated, it cannot even be named, as we shall see; for the return of the repressed does not announce itself with a visiting card. Against such a paradoxical power, raised by Claudius's breach of taboo (in which adultery, fratricide, regicide and incest meet), there is no immunity to be won in the categories of moral or theological judgement. Evil is no more helpful a word than hellish: both terms, in their rush to place the Ghost, betray the infection already caught from it.[58] We need to enrich the language of judgement with a language of tragic affliction if we are to begin to articulate something for which the play itself has no language but only an image: namely, the panic sense of horror in which we seemingly irresistibly leap to blot out those tempted irresistibly to acts of central faith-breach.

Let us call this passion – however inadequately – revenge, a passion that may perhaps diversely enter all cultures wherever there is breach of taboo;[59] and then let us say that what the play images for us in the figure of the Ghost is the way that *revenge ghosts us*. Revenge, that is to say, is an affliction that can make us feel like ghosts on the face of the earth, cut off from all the attachments and daily goings-on that keep us sane. The Ghost is an emblem of consciousness almost wholly swallowed up in the memory of injury, a passion frozen into an obsessional state and yet inflamed by the compulsive self-lacerating replay of the history of its own wrongs. 'From wrong to wrong the exasperated spirit proceeds', as Eliot put it, meditating upon one model of purgatory.[60] R.A. Foakes noted how 'the Ghost, who speaks of it as if he had been an onlooker at his own murder, is fascinated by the details of the process of dying, horrible as they are'.[61] This preoccupation with the incursion of poison through the porches of the ears and 'the natural gates and alleys of the body' (I.v.67), alongside its fascination with the ensuing corruption wrought upon the body of the man who had once mystically represented the body politic of Denmark, reminds us that revenge – like the malice embodied in the Sisters of *Macbeth* – fragments and disjoints a world that might otherwise have been seen whole. The Ghost keeps the wounds green that might otherwise have healed and done well. Caught between worlds and unable to find peace in either, it reminds us of the paradoxical nature of revenge as an all-too-human passion that, by its obsessionally narrow intensity of focus, makes us feel inhuman. For an age that had faith in the comprehensive range of the human reason (*humani nihil a me alienum puto*) and yet that was also drawn to all that was paradoxical and anomalous in nature and the intellectual life,[62] the Ghost in *Hamlet* embodies perfectly those strange powers that lurk unsettlingly at the margins of the accepted categories of our theology, morality and of our language itself.

However, if we turn from such psychologization and the temptation to universalize that it brings, turn from images of destiny to the particularities of our social history, we shall find another kind of paradox embodied in the Ghost – the paradox indicated by Bacon when, at the start of the seventeenth century, he called revenge 'a kind of wild justice'. For the play is set in that transitional period within North European feudalism that we now call the Renaissance, when the great aristocratic houses were being brought under the control of a centralized monarchy, and it dramatizes the contradictions between competing traditions of justice that characterized that transition. It is this that makes the play, in Mervyn James's words, 'the classic statement of the problem of choice in a multi-cultural situation'.[63] 'We are sailing with a corpse in the cargo', said Ibsen three centuries later of the failure of a liberal bourgeoisie to shake itself free of its past;[64] and Shakespeare similarly in *Hamlet*, where the corpse returns out of 'all the obscurity of the *medium aevum*', shows how an emergent aristocratic liberalism fails to free itself from vestigial imperatives whose origin lay deep in mediaeval society but which were still powerfully active within Elizabethan court circles. It is through the cultural discontinuities between Old Hamlet and his son, with their different ideologies of revenge, that Shakespeare traces the tragic failure of the new age to be born.

We may epitomize these cultural discontinuities, and the different political structures which they express, by contrasting the two examples of single combat that frame the play: Old Hamlet's duel with Old Fortinbras, described by Horatio at the start of the play, and Hamlet's fencing-match with Laertes at the end. The duel described by Horatio, in such revealingly 'archaic and specialized vocabulary',[65] is in truth no more than a gigantic wager, formalized by chivalric law and fought out between two mediaeval war-lords in a squabble over disputed territory; and yet, because it demanded personal prowess and valour, it is given a certain heroic ring in the play. It was this heroic quality in Old Hamlet that Lawrence recognized when he wrote in *Twilight in Italy* that 'the body politic also will culminate in this divinity of the flesh, this body imbued with glory, invested with divine power and might, the King, the Emperor'.[66] Yet, as Lawrence also recognized, the fastidious presence of the young Hamlet enables us to sense this same heroic age in its antithetical aspect of barbarism too. We sense it in the military dress of the Ghost, no doubt antique in its fashion; we sense it in the heavy drinking of the court, from which Hamlet has long turned in revulsion; and, most particularly, we sense it in the crudity and violent directness of the Ghost's language in its appeal for revenge. For the Ghost, whatever its precise relationship to King Hamlet, is murderously confident in the justice of its demands – demands long since naturalized in the political structures of a kinship society, where loyalty was primarily to family rather than to law and state, where the wife was expected to be faithful in order to preserve the honour of her affinity, and where kindred were expected to avenge affront in order to preserve the honour of their lineage. The violence that the Ghost feels at Claudius's crime is so unmanageable precisely because it strikes home at these central sanctities in the life of the court community that Old Hamlet had known.

It would be wrong, I think, to suggest that the Ghost in its passion is wholly free from contradiction, its consciousness wholly swallowed up in revenge: for the passion of revenge, even in a society committed to the duty of revenge, has always been felt as an affliction, and the Ghost – like Laertes later – is no exception. Its anguish is to be felt in every word that it utters; and it is to be felt too in its profoundly disturbing ambivalence towards Gertrude. Torn between enraged hatred of her lust and chivalric protectiveness towards her soul, it leaves Hamlet caught in a perfect double bind, not knowing how to treat her. Nevertheless, the contradictions in the Ghost's desires are never articulated and are communicated to us only by anxiety. Probably they only serve to fuel its vengefulness against Claudius, paradoxically even to confirm the painful sacredness of its duty; and certainly they lack the strength to deflect its will, fidelity to which – as we saw in *Love's Labour's Lost* – is the true mark of aristocratic distinction.

Yet this aristocratic code, together with the kinship structures that supported it, is clearly in decline in *Hamlet*. Not only do its heroics ring hollow wherever they retain a vestigial life, as in the rant of Laertes; more strikingly still, Claudius has no time for them in the administration of the domestic and foreign affairs of his state – a Denmark now imaged as one of the new nation-states that were evolving throughout Europe, with new forms of internal rule and international diplomacy that quickly professionalized the art of government and restricted it as an expression of merely personal prestige, to be won by military adventure. It is to this new Denmark that Hamlet's fencing-match with Laertes so characteristically belongs. During the sixteenth century, the new Tudor state in England had specifically set out, as Rosalie Colie puts it, 'to gentle the armigerous aristocracy, to disarm them in all kinds of ways';[67] and as military resources were increasingly monopolized by the state, the duel survived, and even flourished for a while, as the cherished symbol of an aristocratic military power that was in fact in terminal decline. For the rapier, to quote Rosalie Colie again, was 'brilliantly and obviously nonfunctional as a practical weapon in an ordnance world'.[68] It provided the perfect emblem of the contradiction in aristocratic life between the desire for autonomous power and the actuality of increasing impotence – a contradiction sufficient to drive men like Essex in real life, as well as Hamlet in the play, into what S. P. Zitner calls 'the self-consciousness and deracination which are the stuff of tragedy'.[69] If aristocratic energies had been channelled by successive monarchs into cultural rather than military competition, that acculturation had had its cost; and in *Hamlet* the refinements that distinguish the son above the father are placed in circumstances where they become progressively disabling – a pattern that reaches its climax in the final fencing-scene, where Hamlet sports with a rapier before the king whom he lacks the will to kill. The afflictive passion of revenge that flowed for the father into the lineal duty of revenge no longer does so for the son. The passion is still there but, despite Hamlet's mastery of the arts of self-vindication, the executive will is not; and although he himself fails to understand the causes of his inactivity, his inhibition suggests a degree of unconscious ambivalence much greater than that found in his father – an ambivalence mirroring the highly charged contradictory attitudes that gathered around the 'wild justice' of revenge in the late Renaissance, when duelling enjoyed its brief but troubled efflorescence in defiance of those processes that were irresistibly stripping the aristocracy of their power.

Such ambivalence, of course, has always gathered around the afflictive passion of revenge. It is to be found in the only surviving source of *Hamlet*, the history of Hamblet that we find in

## Hamlet: The Court in Transition (I)

Belleforest's *Histoires Tragiques*; for Belleforest is unable to reconcile the moral code of the ancient saga tradition upon which he draws – full of tribal celebrations of unscrupulous cunning and implacable vindictiveness – with the official code of his own sixteenth-century Catholic France, that preached patience under affront and submission to the crown as head of the judicature. On the one hand, he argues that a christian should have neither bitter gall nor vengeful desires (*le fiel amer, ni les desirs confits en vengeance*), whilst on the other hand he recommends his history for its aesthetic, sensational revenges (*un nouveau genre de punition*) and its great and gallant deeds (*grandes, et gaillardes occurrences*).[70] But the mystery that is confused in Belleforest is clarified and given shape by Shakespeare's historical imagination, turning the Ghost which he found in the missing source-play, the so-called *Ur-Hamlet*, into an archaic figure able to test Hamlet's new Renaissance idealism with the vestigial desire for blood-revenge. For the Ghost withdraws Hamlet both in time and place, 'desperate with imagination' as he is (I.iv.87), away from the company of men towards 'a more removed ground' (I.iv.61), perhaps toward the sea and cliffs that threaten his reason with madness; and there, in a charged atmosphere of secrecy, inhibiting Hamlet's initial impulse of pity, it dwells with maddening imprecision upon its purgatorial pains and speaks in inflammatory language of poison poured in at the ear and betrayal in the most sacred of trusts. Hamlet is overwhelmed at once, and the test might seem over as soon as it is begun. Nevertheless, when the Ghost leaves, it is wholly characteristic of Hamlet that he should cry out: 'O all you host of heaven! O earth! What else?/And shall I couple hell? O fie!' (I.v.92–3). Despite the full tide of his passion, he still reaches out to find himself in an ideal harmony with the powers of earth and heaven; and it is this new aristocratic sense of the appropriate, more subtle and refined than that of his father, that inhibits his will to revenge. Yet, even here, his ominous coupling of hell with heaven and earth – an excited recognition that there are more things in heaven and earth than he had previously dreamed of – reminds us of the Ghost's power. It has contaminated Hamlet without wholly committing him, leaving him unable either to act upon or to repudiate the passion that he feels and the duty that he acknowledges; and in this way the play refers the mystery of Hamlet's ambivalence to the contradictions within Renaissance culture, demystifying destiny into a matter for historical understanding.

Hamlet and the Ghost: they face one another in Act 1 like split-off parts of the same personality – a reading that the play both suggests and baffles, that this strangely uncategorizable Ghost might be a something in the mind's eye: the son's inner fantasy of his father perhaps, his own 'prophetic soul' (I.v.41). For the deep truth is that Hamlet cannot integrate the violence aroused within him by the Ghost. Nor, more strikingly still, can he even integrate within himself a picture of the man his father was. He sees two fathers in the play, one idealized and one demonized, the one split from the other, Hyperion from the Ghost; and what connection should *we* in the audience see between that form 'where every god did seem to set his seal/To give the world assurance of a man' (III.iv.61–2) and the enraged form of the Ghost? What, indeed, does it even mean to call this Ghost the Ghost of Hamlet's father? It is a name which is no name; for we cannot imagine in what relationship it stands to that hard-drinking hard-fighting warrior-king preoccupied by personal honour which is all that we know of the 'real' King Hamlet. There are times in history, especially transitional times, when the heart of the mystery of the self is hard to pluck out, when it seems (in Conrad's words, from another transitional time) no more than a 'masquerade of something hopelessly unknown';[71] and so it is that the 'reality' of the old King Hamlet has fragmented in the fragmented minds of those who survive him into the Renaissance. A sense of history may only increase the mystery of things. But however we understand the Ghost, it seems clear that it is the negative malign image of his father that haunts Hamlet, as it is the idealized image that offers him protection against the treacheries of Claudius and Gertrude. But the negative image is the stronger; for it embodies vestigial memories of implacable authority from childhood and earlier cultures, primitive desires of hatred, revenge and guilt whose 'strange eruption' (I.i.72) into Hamlet's consciousness brings him close to moral panic. It is his fellow-contrary, the anti-self he cannot integrate; and his failure signifies a more general failure on the part of the emergent court ideology which he shares to integrate the still-present destructive passions and traditions of its own immediate prehistory.

## HAMLET AND OPHELIA

*Thus just as in the heavens the sun, the moon and the stars exhibit to the world, as if in a mirror, a certain likeness of God, so on earth a far truer image of God is provided by those good rulers who love and reverence Him and display to their people the resplendent light of His justice accompanied by a semblance of the divine reason and intellect.*[72]

*Hamlet* articulates with great clarity the polarized nature of those gender roles upon which mediaeval and (with increased idealization) Renaissance society depended – roles which the ladies in the courtship comedy of *Love's Labour's Lost* might temporarily and within measure flout, but whose constraints are lived out here in *Hamlet* to their contradictory and tragic conclusion. The question of gender has a sociological, moral and psychological dimension within the play. We have already noted the difference between the Ghost's design upon Claudius and Gertrude and traced its origin to a feudal formation where men competed uneasily in the world for honour and wealth whilst women formed part of their currency, entitled to chivalric protection in return for their protection of patriarchal honour and wealth at home. Such polarization of sociological role, of course, had its consequences for moral education: a woman must be the chaste unmoving star by which a man might sail abroad on stormy seas, she must safeguard on his behalf the 'feminine' domestic virtues associated with tenderness and pity whilst he evolves his own particular laws and codes elsewhere. It is this precarious complementary relationship – which from another perspective becomes a double standard – that Gertrude disturbs by her desire; and the strength of the taboos that she has breached may be gauged in the violence of the Ghost's revulsion and the greater revulsion of the more idealistic Hamlet. Both in their different ways, torn between revenge and chivalry, betray their ambivalence. 'Leave her to heaven,/And to those thorns that in her bosom lodge' (I.v.86–7), says the Ghost with ambiguous charity; 'I will speak daggers to her, but use none' (III.ii.387), says Hamlet, fighting both to control and to express the rage that now includes not only his mother but his fantasy of all womankind and that threatens his chivalry and his pity alike. Here, focussing upon the inner fantasy rather than the outer object, we can see the psychological consequences of the polarization of gender: namely, the polarization between masculine and feminine in the same mind. We may say, with D. W. Winnicott, that 'it seems possible to use Hamlet's altered attitude to Ophelia and his cruelty to her as a picture of his ruthless rejection of his own female element, now split off and handed over to her, with his unwelcome male element threatening to take over his whole personality. The cruelty to Ophelia can be a measure of his reluctance to abandon his split-off female element'.[73] This further dissociation within the self, this splitting and divorce between self and yet another anti-self, will bring *'the celestial and my soul's idol, the most beautified Ophelia'* (II.ii.109–10) into madness and Hamlet himself to its brink – a madness in which the beautiful Renaissance ideal that they had shared seems destroyed forever.

For Hamlet and Ophelia, it seems, had sustained a dream that we glimpse only in the moment of its fading:

> O, what a noble mind is here o'erthrown!
> The courtier's, soldier's, scholar's, eye, tongue, sword,
> Th' expectancy and rose of the fair state,
> The glass of fashion and the mould of form,
> Th' observed of all observers, quite, quite down!
> And I, of ladies most deject and wretched,
> That suck'd the honey of his music vows,
> Now see that noble and most sovereign reason
> Like sweet bells jangled out of tune and harsh,
> That unmatch'd form and feature of blown youth
> Blasted with ecstasy. O woe is me
> T'have seen what I have seen, see what I see.
> (III.i.152–63)

This generous elegy, pitying and unvindictive in the face of injury, celebrates a familiar idealism of the Renaissance: the picture of a fair nation united in the reason of its prince. As we should expect from a time when political rule was personal, Ophelia in describing the personal virtues of Prince Hamlet is describing a political utopia too. Her words epitomize aspirations new to the world of the play though bygone to its audience, aspirations most typically found amongst those who feel themselves marginal, unrewarded or dispossessed – aspirations best expressed in England in the writings of Spenser and the all-round attainments of Sidney, the courtier, soldier and scholar par excellence. Through her wounded and nostalgic idealization, delivered in words with something of choric authority about them, we glimpse Ophelia's hope to have shared with Hamlet in the platonic idealism of that new age; and we glimpse too the Hamlet-that-might-have-been, a shadowy figure whose power is nevertheless felt throughout the play, not least in the affliction that reminds us of all that he has lost. In praising his reason, and the activities of courtier, soldier and scholar through which that reason was once fulfilled, Ophelia accentuates the cultural differences between the worlds of King Hamlet and his son. For the court life that she half remembers and half imagines for Hamlet is not that of a warlord: it is a vision of harmony, founded in a harmony of vision within the theatre of public life, with Hamlet himself worthy by virtue of his reason to play the leading role, 'th'observed of all observers'. All is open and integrated; the prince is the glass of fashion in which – if we may borrow Castiglione's traditional extension of the image here – his subjects might see reflected the rational harmony not only of Denmark but of all creation.

But Hamlet has been 'blasted with ecstasy', and Ophelia suddenly fears the same for herself: 'O woe is me', she says, 'T'have seen what I have seen, see what I see'. Ominously she fears her own collapse in the collapse of the dream that she dreamed on behalf of the man she loves. Already Hamlet's reason has been usurped; and now as Claudius and Polonius emerge from their hiding-place behind the arras, we see how the open harmonious theatre of public life has shrunk into a closet drama of espionage and counter-espionage. 'In more than one sense is Hamlet "the observed of all observers"', as R. A. Foakes puts it.[74] The realities of Claudius's court are stifling the ideal that Ophelia dreams of; and the tones of her lament are torn between yearning and despair as she wavers between the defensive strategy of further idealization and the horror that she feels at behaviour which she can only bear to contemplate as madness. For she cannot reconcile the two Hamlets that she sees, the one before her and the other in her mind's eye. 'His madness is poor Hamlet's enemy' (V.ii.235), she might have said, pityingly – and self-pityingly too, fearing obscurely the time when she, like him, would be 'divided from herself and her fair judgment' (IV.v.85). For Hamlet admonishes her that blood has the power to overthrow judgment, that (to use another language) in a conflict whose roots lie deep in the clash between old family and new state loyalties in late sixteenth-century aristocratic culture, passion can fragment the unitary visions of the platonic reason.

Ophelia's story – the drowning of the ceremony of innocence – embodies this theme in miniature, as a sub-plot might. Her difficulties begin with the patriarchal family; from her first appearance on stage she is bullied by her brother and father, exercising their male power in parsimonious moralities to urge her to fortify herself against 'the shot and danger of desire' (I.iii.35). Hamlet's love, they say, is the enemy without against whom she must guard her innocence. Laertes in particular is anxious to protect her against what he calls, echoing the language that gathers around the Ghost, 'contagious blastments' (I.iii.42); and in reply, after a little sortie of her own in retaliation, Ophelia can only answer meekly that she will keep his lesson as 'watchman to my heart' (I.iii.46). Polonius's imagery is even clearer than that of his son: she must not sell herself cheaply, she must keep herself intact and refuse to parley with the enemy. If Laertes may drab a little in Paris, Ophelia must remain innocent at Elsinore. The man's innocence, that is to say, is to be left in the care of the woman; and this, of course, allows the man a measure of licence. 'Nymph, in thy orisons/Be all my sins remember'd' (III.i.89–90). No matter how self-mockingly affected we take Hamlet's words to be, they reveal a pattern structured deep in the play: a pattern of the man compelled by honour into deeper and deeper wrong, whilst the woman is compelled by the need to preseve her innocence into deeper and deeper retreat. Hamlet and Ophelia, doubling one another like mirror-images, move further and further apart; the love in which they tried to unify the world brings about its disintegration. Guilt and innocence, revenge and pity, masculine and feminine are increasingly divorced, and the result is common inauthenticity, common ecstasy.

From that first scene with her family onwards, everything that Ophelia holds sacred will be increasingly besmirched by the men around her, until her love becomes an enemy within, generating a treacherous violence like that aroused in Hamlet by the Ghost. Indeed, at the start of Act 2, she sees a ghost of her own: Lord Hamlet

> with a look so piteous in purport
> As if he had been loosed out of hell
> To speak of horrors, he comes before me.
> (II.i.82–4)

These extraordinary last four words capture something of the enormity and the unreality that Ophelia senses in Hamlet's gliding into the sanctuary of her closet, the retreat into which her family have compelled her and which is already beginning to prove ineffective. His appearance and behaviour are as ambiguous and as uncategorizable as those of the Ghost before him. The sheer incomprehensibleness of his presence, his alien unseemliness of dress, his breach of the courtly decorums of eye and tongue, his physical aggression and the pitiableness of his manner all leave Ophelia not knowing what to think or feel. 'Mad for thy love?' asks her father. 'My lord, I do not know' (II.i.85) – and indeed there *is* no knowing, either for Ophelia or for us, since the integrity of communication has broken down between them and the resultant uncertainty is so charged with violence. 'O my lord, my lord, I have been so affrighted' (II.i.75), she cries. For Hamlet has taken a symbolic farewell of her; and in a play full of the sinister invasion of small enclosed spaces, he has taken his farewell in a scene heavy with the metaphor of rape. It is as though he is driven by the vindictive need to degrade still further the innocence which he mistakenly believes to have been degraded already. His disorderly dress, his unsolicited entrance, his forceful detention of Ophelia by the wrist, his rhythmic gestures and deep sigh, and finally his backing away and withdrawal: all are charged with sexual purpose and leave the woman in Ophelia torn between a paradoxical and unmanageable mixture of pity and horror. It is the moment of her initiation into the passion that destroys her.

Hamlet can only hold on to innocence and love by revenging himself upon them. But upon whom is he taking revenge? Ophelia or himself? Did he see innocence or guilt in her face when he bade her farewell? His ambiguous and increasingly violent behaviour at their next meeting (their first on stage) leaves these questions still unanswered. 'Get thee to a nunnery', he shouts (III.i.121); but is the nunnery a convent or a brothel? Is he demanding still further retreat as her only security, or branding her with the universal corruption of mankind? Probably Ophelia hears both meanings as they were intended – as anathematizations, opposites which banish her equally from all possibility of integrated love and drive her deeper into isolation. The end of her isolation is her madness, of which two contradictory things are true: it is the perfection of the innocence into which she has been required to retreat and the perfection of the violence which has so long besieged it. Her betrayal from within is the culmination of her many betrayals from without, of her many enforced denials of the realities of herself and the world. Now at last her spirit is free to come and go as it pleases. Now at last her actions and speech are unbuttoned: she finds a voice for anger and turns to popular culture to find a voice for the treacherous seductiveness of desire. But her new liberty is also a disintegration. She speaks and sings a poetry of doubtful suggestion in which pain at her father's death is chaotically confused with pain at her lover's desertion. The two poles of masculine authority upon which her life has turned have been crushed together; extremes melt together with no commerce between them. She has become a ghost of her former self, another blasted 'rose of May' (IV.v.157), torn like Hamlet himself in his famous meditation upon suicide in Act 3:1 between the desire to leave things patiently to heaven and the desire for blood revenge:

> We must be patient. But I cannot choose but weep to think they would lay him i' th' cold ground. My brother shall know of it. (IV.v.68–70)

And, of course, when she appears to Laertes, the pitiable apparition incites him to revenge: the contagious blastments of ecstasy must run their course.

The manner of Ophelia's death is a wonderful emblem of the dissociation she has suffered: floating and singing, with flowers, upon the surface of the water, until dragged down 'from her melodious lay/To muddy death' (IV.vii.181–2). Is she pure or polluted, innocent or guilty at the last? The play pushes to grotesque limits the failure of its characters to unravel the paradoxes surrounding Ophelia's madness and death. Laertes has no more than an inkling: 'Thought and affliction, passion, hell itself/She turns to favour and to prettiness', he marvels (IV.v.185–6). But he cannot articulate the terrible parodic relationship between the sister he now sees and the sister he had wanted in Act 1:3. His chief wish now, it seems, is to find charm and prettiness in Ophelia and then to expel 'the woman' (IV.vii.188) from himself, assuming instead the hellish ugliness of revenge which his father's unappeased spirit demands 'as 'twere from heaven to earth' (IV.v.213). Grotesquely, he reproduces the old dissociation between man and woman, revenge and pity, guilt and innocence, that has already undone Ophelia. Gertrude's attempt to deal with Ophelia's insanity and death is more grotesque still. Her obituary speech at the end of Act 4, surely no eye-witness account, has the haunted quality of fantasy, as though – despite her formal tone – she were speaking for herself, paying the tribute of guilt to the image of her own lost innocence. For her heart has been cleft 'in twain' by the bitter accusations of her son (III.iv.158); and her consequent inability to see the world whole is beautifully revealed in that moment when, extraordinarily in elegy, her mind flickers amongst the variety of innocent and guilty names by which 'long purples' are known (IV.vii.168–170). Her sentimental farewell to

Ophelia, in celebrating her innocence, is false to the duality of human nature, the ambivalence expressed in her own adultery as well as in Ophelia's madness. But most grotesque of all are the theological disputes that probe the 'doubtful' case of her death (V.i.220) – for she is yet another spirit in the play who, not being 'peace-parted' (V.i.231), lingers on to trouble the living. The two clowns debate at length whether her death was suicide or accident, and ascribe her christian burial to the chance of her high birth, whilst the priest is reluctant to concede even such 'maimed rites' (V.i.212). Is she innocent or guilty? and of what? Ophelia's death in its marginality, like her madness, defies categorization; and yet it serves to disclose the power of a guilty patriarchy which, pressurizing her to preserve her innocence, denies her the involvement in life necessary if she is to work through her ambivalence.

'Sweets to the sweet' (V.i.236): Gertrude's sentimentality is perfectly complemented by the braggadocio of Laertes and Hamlet as they leap into Ophelia's grave – not the first time in the play that men have invaded and fought for possession of 'a plot/Whereon the numbers cannot try the cause' (IV.iv.62–3) and which is not even big enough to bury them. 'I lov'd Ophelia', Hamlet cries competitively (V.i.264), with the melodramatic certainty of a past tense. For it is not only his beloved but his capacity to love that he has lost; and only now, with his revenge upon innocence and love consummated in Ophelia's death, is he free to speak of love at all. More refined and fastidious than his father, as befits the representative of a generation that had idealized the chivalry of the Middle Ages, Hamlet had idealized his love for Ophelia more finely too – maybe at first after the fashion of Sidney and Spenser, certainly later after the fashion of Donne – so that, when disillusion comes, it is accordingly all the more catastrophic. For Hamlet and Ophelia, opposites as they are, it is the same: denied intercourse with their fellow-contrary, the integrity of each is unfashioned and their dream of a new court, a new political order, is tragically destroyed.

## HAMLET AND CLAUDIUS

*Many have dreamed up republics and principalities which have never in truth been known to exist; the gulf between how one should live and how one does live is so wide that a man who neglects what is actually done for what should be done learns the way to self-destruction rather than self-preservation. The fact is that a man who wants to act virtuously in every way necessarily comes to grief among so many who are not virtuous.*[75]

Ophelia's is not the only new Renaissance vision to be diffracted by an old power in *Hamlet*; the same fate awaits the machiavellian vision of Claudius.

> And England, if my love thou hold'st at aught –
> As my great power thereof may give thee sense,
> Since yet thy cicatrice looks raw and red
> After the Danish sword, and thy free awe
> Pays homage to us – thou mayst not coldly set
> Our sovereign process, which imports at full,
> By letters congruing to that effect,
> The present death of Hamlet. Do it, England;
> For like the hectic in my blood he rages,
> And thou must cure me. Till I know 'tis done,
> Howe'er my haps, my joys were ne'er begun.
> (IV.iii.61–71)

Claudius too can speak of love, but he means power; and there is cruel relish in that picture of a land scarred by the Danish sword. Nor is it his own sword that he speaks of, as his brother might have done, but the sword of his armies; for there is nothing of the old heroic warrior or the new Renaissance idealist about Claudius. Royal power for him is grounded not in prowess of arms or in reason but in strategic pressure sustained by military superiority: he knows, with Machiavelli, that 'there is simply no comparison between a man who is unarmed and one who is not'.[76] The convolution of his verse here enacts his faith in the tortuous channels of secret diplomacy and blackmail to achieve his end: namely, to code the world in his own desires. He would like to live out the creed of Cecropia in *Arcadia* 'that there is no wisdom but in including both heaven and earth in oneself; and that love, courtesy, gratefulness, friendship, and all other virtues are rather to be taken on than taken in oneself'.[77] At all times his mind remains obstinately chained to 'my crown, mine own ambition, and my queen' (III.iii.55) – a contraction of consciousness which forms the antithesis to Hamlet's need to act appropriately in the eyes of heaven, earth and hell.

There is, however, a price to be paid by the machiavel for his political adventurism, which the play measures in terms of anxiety: the anxiety which belongs to the tyrant, the bully and the imperialist, the anxiety which is the other face of omnipotent fantasy. 'Do it, England;/For like the hectic in my blood he rages': Shakespeare has transposed the cool prudence of Machiavelli's *The Prince* into the related key of a fearful will-to-power, and in so doing has offered a critical reading of the whole machiavellian enterprise. From his very first appearance Claudius has tried to usurp the common language of reason, nature and manliness (I.ii.87ff.), and thus to hold the state in the grip of his single will; but Hamlet eludes him and leaves him increasingly tormented by hostility from without and fear from within. His security is invaded by sorrows that come 'not single spies,/But in battalions' (IV.v.78–9). Progressively the formal court-scenes of the play disintegrate and slip from his control: the council-meeting of Act 1:2, the play-scene of Act 3:2 and finally, chaotically, the fencing-scene of Act 5:2. His countermeasures become increasingly desperate – green he calls them once (IV.v.83) – and they culminate in the magnificent presumption of his final declaration that the poisoned sword has only hurt him. This is the climax to all the contradictions of will and fear into which he has fallen, and we watch the moment of his greatness flicker troublingly before us; for what on the one hand seems a disturbing but admirable strength of will seems on the other (to borrow some words from *King Lear*) no more than 'an admirable evasion of whoremaster man' (I.ii.132) to disguise from himself and others the real meaning of his defeat and death.

Claudius's firmness of purpose has always been haunted by such a sense of unreality; the anxiety with which he pursues his will desubstantiates the very things he wills. He resembles Macbeth in this: both sexually and politically passionate men, with the avidity that expresses anxiety, both are undone by the essential instability of the will given over to its own good. Claudius's awareness of the unreality of his own desires is suggested in the knowledge that he urges upon Laertes in Act 4:7, that

> love is begun by time.
> And that I see, in passages of proof,
> Time qualifies the spark and fire of it.
> (IV.vii.110–2)

The whole of this speech resonates with a conviction far deeper than the tactics of persuasion demand. Maybe it hints at an awareness of growing estrangement between himself and his wife; certainly it incorporates the knowledge that Gertrude's love has already died back once and been rekindled elsewhere; and the conclusion to which it leads – 'That we would do,/We should do when we would' (IV.vii.117–18) – has the genuine stamp of despair upon it. It is perhaps his own story that he tells, the story of a reckless self-gratification in response to the mutability of desire; and the play passes hard judgement upon him, showing how, under pressure of anxiety, his enterprise loses the name of action and becomes no more than a desperately improvised bungling in a world drained of value.

What Claudius cannot integrate into his vision of the world is his guilt. He is a new man who has committed an old crime, a machiavel whose literary counterpart Hamlet finds in a documentary drama about the Italian Renaissance yet whose breach of the primaeval taboo upon fratricide makes him fear 'the primal eldest curse' (III.iii.37) laid by God upon Cain. It is not so easy as Cecropia implies to take on virtue rather than to take it in, and Claudius from the beginning, behind his mask of temporizing plausibility, knows that his kingship and his court are founded upon a lie. It is all, as Hamlet will never let him forget, seeming – a regime epitomized in the courtiership of Osric, the compliant time-server who remains watchful behind his voluble affability, cultivates surface at the expense of substance and refuses to let honesty stand in the way of opportunity. But Claudius cannot live by seeming: 'O wretched state! O bosom black as death!' he moans (III.iii.67). Michael Long has shown how, increasingly during the play, 'the man who has been habituated to the denial of psychic life seems about to be cracked open or swept away by powers with which he cannot deal';[78] and the ecstasy that overtakes Claudius proclaims a man 'to double business bound' (III.iii.41), unable to integrate his moral sense with his self-interest. Hence the sudden irruption of that soliloquy in Act 3:3, and its curious archaism of language – an irruption no less sudden or strange than the ecstasy that inspired Hamlet's archaic language of revenge some fifty lines earlier (III.ii.379ff). For if Hamlet is an idealist who cannot integrate his violent desires of revenge, Claudius is a machiavel who cannot integrate his violent fears of guilt.

Neither of these two mutually antagonistic Renaissance ideologies is adequate to take the measure of man and his world; and the play traces their mutual invalidation through a common taint of violence differently aroused in each. Hamlet is infected by the horror of Claudius's crime and falls into a vicious circle of revenge that was all too familiar to contemporary moralists. 'Certainly', wrote Bacon, 'in taking revenge, a man is but even with his enemy'.[79] It is 'altogether to be detested', wrote Luis da Granada, 'that thou shouldest revenge another mans maliciousnes with thine owne maliciousnes';[80] and René Girard makes a similar point in a modern way that reminds us how Claudius in turn is reinfected with guilty fear by Hamlet: 'the more a tragic conflict is prolonged, the more likely it is to culminate in a violent mimesis; the resemblance between the combatants grows ever stronger until each presents a mirror image of the other'.[81] Increasingly as Hamlet and Claudius circle and close upon one another, their paradoxical relationship of similitude in dissimilitude develops. Its most memorable instance occurs in Act 3:3 when Hamlet, reversing the roles of Act 3:1 and spying upon the king, tries to kill him as he tries to pray: the good meditative man tries by wrong action to right himself with the world, whilst the bad man who has always been so quick to act tries to do the same by the meditation of prayer. But both turn aside in failure: the former cannot stiffen his sinews (cf. I.v.94–5) whilst the latter cannot soften his (cf. III.iii.71). Neither can reconcile the contradictions within himself; each is 'like a man to double business bound', torn between reparative and retaliatory impulses, and increasingly feeling himself – 'like a whore' (II.ii.581; cf. III.i.51) – inauthentic in action. Increasingly in their difference they come to resemble one another: surely, necessarily, like image and reflection in a glass, they converge upon one another from their opposite positions until they meet in the violent collision that destroys them both.

This dénouement of the play must surely create a divided response. On the one hand, death levels all distinctions in a tragic symmetry of mutual destruction: in Hamlet's words, 'your fat king and your lean beggar is but variable service – two dishes, but to one table' (IV.iii.23–4). Such a response will provoke a sense of poetic justice perhaps, a cathartic recognition of the self-defeating nature of violence, a consolation akin to the melancholy pleasures of fatalism. On the other hand, however, this *union* – 'the central pun of the final scene', Ralph Berry calls it[82] – remains an opposition: neither Hamlet nor Claudius surrenders to the other, neither man can resolve or otherwise negotiate the particular contradictions that beset him. The mighty opposites remain opposed, and therefore self-divided too; and judgments of the distinctions between the two men will therefore be both specific and complex, not fatalistic but part of the way in which we reconstruct our world out of the desolation of tragedy. We have already seen Claudius at the moment of his death, admirable and appalling in his willed determination to disregard both guilt and fear; and now we must turn to Hamlet, still torn at the end between the desire for revenge and the wish to claim relationship with the world. The play pursues this self-division to its furthermost extremes, with that characteristic Shakespearean *jusqu'auboutisme* which undermines all attempts to turn the tragedies into moralities or parables of the educational value of suffering. Such attempts have been common with *Hamlet*. Maynard Mack, for instance, finds a new humility in the Hamlet who returns from England: 'he has now learned, and accepted, the boundaries in which human action, human judgment, are enclosed'.[83] But such readings err on two counts: first, they are narrowly selective in emphasis, focussing (for example) upon the man who declares 'the readiness is all' (V.ii.218) rather than upon the man who fights in Ophelia's grave; and second, in searching for a settled determination of belief in Hamlet, they underestimate his aristocratic concern with attitude, with appropriateness of style to circumstance. If Mack is right in his assertion that *acting* is 'the play's radical metaphor',[84] we should surely add that the Hamlet of Act 5, in the graveyard, in the grave, in conversation with Osric or with Horatio in that fateful moment before the duel, is still trying out the wide range of Renaissance styles that he has at his disposal, still casting around for an attitude adequate to the complex world in which he has lost himself. In this most literary of Shakespeare's plays, where 'morality and sensitivity to language are peculiarly tied up with each other',[85] the hero can never find the simple integrated voice, the one compelling part, that he seeks. He is divided against himself, and it is in our self-division that we in the audience must know him too.

On the one hand, we have to reckon with the increasing violence of his vindictiveness, culminating in the moment when he pours poison down the throat of the dying Claudius: 'Here, thou incestuous, murd'rous, damned Dane,/Drink off this potion' (V.ii.330–1). This is the language of the Ghost, spoken with ugly relish by Hamlet in the sharpness of that aesthetic pleasure which both heightens and legitimates revenge for the revenger himself. Hamlet has at last found his appropriate style, it seems, the 'unrestrained hyperbole that the hero needs to carry him over into the role of revenger';[86] but he has found it only in the moment of his dying. It is an acting style which he has tried already, of course, but which never quite carried him over into action before – or only into the bungled action of Polonius's death. For although his 'excitements' of reason and blood (IV.iv.58) confirm him in the duty of blood-revenge which he learned at his father's court, he clearly also feels a great resistance to it which, remaining unconscious, enrages him against himself. If revenge is always an affliction, it seems especially so to the fastidious Hamlet, coarsening his character and drawing him deeply into impiety. It is wholly characteristic of him that he never looks forward to a Claudius-free future after the completion of his revenge, since to be 'even with his enemy' is so largely to be false with himself. The apposition in the famous soliloquy of Act 3:1 says it all: to suffer in patience the slings and arrows of outrageous fortune is for Hamlet 'to be', whilst to oppose them is 'not to be' – 'to take arms against a sea of troubles' (III.i.59) is, like drawing one's sword against a ghost, a futile gesture inviting destruction. The contradictions in his aristocratic code in this transitional Renaissance period are too great for Hamlet, and Claudius's death proves paradoxically to be in every sense his end; and if the manner and justice of this death satisfy us, we must also regret the revenge that has destroyed Hamlet body and soul, leaving him with those last, ugly, poisonous words against Claudius on his lips.

But these last words to Claudius are not Hamlet's last words of the play; and if on the one hand we must reckon with the vindictive self that is capable of murder, we must also reckon with the reparative self seen when revenge is completed and Hamlet searches for a style appropriate to death. Karen Horney, in an interesting essay on the psychic economy of vindictiveness, has listed the sacrifices it may demand: 'the necessity never to feel weak may involve the whole range of positive feelings toward others or toward life as such: tenderness, affection, sympathy, love, gratitude, joy, enthusiasm. What is left, often, is merely righteous indignation, anger, and highly distilled aesthetic feelings'[87] – an impoverished experience responsible for the factitious excitement and the inner hopelessness which she finds typical of the compulsively vindictive person. Hamlet's positive feelings, however, are never wholly ghosted by revenge. It was characteristic that, when he could not quite kill the praying Claudius whom he hated, he was on his way to see his mother whom in his tormented way he loved.

Furthermore, the poignancy of that scene with Gertrude shows that he has not lost, in his split-off hatred of Claudius, his sense of what is wrong in himself. Always he maintains his wish to live in articulate harmony with the world, to seek out other people and befriend them in the ways appropriate to his class; and so it comes as no surprise that, at the end of the play, having killed Claudius, he remains active in pursuit of relationship. He forgives Laertes, bids his mother farewell, prevents Horatio's suicide, secures his own future reputation and casts his vote for the royal succession. He perhaps ranges more widely too:

> Had I but time – as this fell sergeant, Death,
> Is strict in his arrest – O, I could tell you –
> But let it be.
> (V.ii.341–3)

This glimmering of near-articulation epitomizes Hamlet's alienated, restless spirit throughout the play. 'I cannot live to hear . . . / But I do prophesy . . . ' (V.ii.359–60). His mind reaches out communicatively across time and space to establish the appropriate disposition of things; and only death will silence it. His curiosity and courage in the face of moral danger; his challenge of sham and his solitary faithfulness to truth; his alertness to meanings that reverberate as far as heaven, as hell; his range of mind and comprehensiveness of language; above all, his honesty, his sense of justice and his wish to act rationally and with 'perfect conscience' (V.ii.67) in the open theatre of political life – these are the qualities which command our admiration and which, blasted as they are by ecstasy, continue to assert themselves even in the quality of his affliction. To the very end Hamlet fights against the contamination of the poison that is in him; and yet, torn between the different cultures that claim him, between his idealism and his father's revenge, he too, like Claudius, fails to reconcile the contradictions within himself.

## CONCLUSION: EUROPE AND UTOPIA

*It is a poor centre of a man's actions, himself. It is right earth; for that only stands fast upon his own centre; whereas all things that have affinity with the heavens, move upon the centre of another, which they benefit.*[88]

'The two extremities themselues, although they seem contrarie, yet growing to the height, runne euer both in one': such is the paradoxical vision of *Hamlet*, as the idealist and the machiavel kill one another in a common ecstasy, inspired in the one by revenge and in the other by guilty fear. The two major court ideologies of the European Renaissance, its two most important attempts at self-fashioning, fail. Both are incomplete, partly because they cannot coexist with one another and partly because they cannot stand free of their own past. Claudius in his attempt to live 'upon his own centre' is haunted by the memory of Cain, whilst Hamlet in his wish to live 'upon the centre of another' is haunted by the Ghost of his father: so, driven by the Ghost and the imperative of revenge, away from Ophelia and the fragile possibilities of patience, he embraces his enemy, Claudius, in a conflict that can only end with their mutual destruction. It is a dark mirror indeed that Shakespeare holds up to the cultural aspirations and the political institutions of the Europe of the preceding century. For the contradictions which he explores between its two major ideologies – both unconformably co-present in all early modern courts, though isolated and epitomized here in opposing characters – are sufficient to discredit the court altogether as a centre of moral authority. In consequence, the nature of justice itself becomes problematized and the individual is left particularly exposed to the ambivalence structured into all taboo. To return to the words of Yeats, *Hamlet* is the definitive portrayal of 'how small a fragment of our own nature can be brought to perfect expression, nor that even but with great toil, in a much divided civilization'; or, more simply in the words of John Danby, it shows how much 'the good man needs a community of goodness'.[89] For in a society without integrity, the self disintegrates.

The play itself, moreover, participates in the crisis of authority that it depicts; and we 'that are but mutes or audience' to its acts (V.ii.340) experience it as paradox. It acknowledges nothing or no-one, inside or outside the play, that can satisfy the hunger for justice which it creates. We cannot even rest upon our sense of villain and hero, for how can we help but admire Claudius's finally defiant will or condemn the bloodthirsty imaginings and the aristocratic arrogance of Hamlet? More importantly, how shall we understand the final tragedy? Does it offer an emblem of our common human destiny, doomed always to be victims to our own ambivalence? Is *this* the poisoned cup that it gives us, here in England where Hamlet is told 'the men are as mad as he' (V.i.149–50)? Or is it rather a history of 'carnal, bloody, and unnatural acts' (V.ii.386) that depicts the local failure of sixteenth-century aristocratic cultures to reconcile their contradictions? If we tell it, with Horatio, will the telling exorcise the violence into which we have been initiated? Is it thus a history that can instruct us and hold out hope? Or will it merely confirm the hopelessness of our destiny? The meaning of the play includes a paradoxical range of possibilities that jeopardizes any faith that we might have had in our capacity to take the measure of ourselves and the world in which we find – or lose – ourselves.

Whatever cause for hope or hopelessness we find, however, we shall still want to distinguish between the virtues of Hamlet – patrician though he be in matters of politics and sex – and the merely opportunistic Fortinbras who succeeds him. Goodness counts, even if we can find no place for it; and this is the utopian element of the tragedy, confirmed in us by the scrupulous quest of Hamlet after truth and justice. His aristocratic idealism, imperfect as it is and corrupted as it becomes, is destroyed; but its value has been honoured. *Hamlet* in this sets the pattern for the great tragedies to come: *Othello, Timon of Athens, King Lear, Macbeth, Antony and Cleopatra, Coriolanus* – in each case the contradictions of an aristocratic culture are drawn out in conflict with the meaner world that survives it, but it is the generosity within the corrupted aristocratic view that enables us to judge the meanness of what survives. Something great is lost that was unworthy to live; something mean remains that deserves not to die. If we want an emblem of this paradoxical reading of history, we might find it in the fortunes of the Essex faction at Elizabeth's court: idealistic in the old high-handed way of aristocratic honour, they were yet put down by the pragmatism of Cecil and his followers. The dream, however, should not be scorned because history passes it by; for, whether to our comfort or despair, the dream provides us with another platform from which to view the processes of history. The defeated and the dispossessed have their voices too, and Utopia remains a necessary perspective upon Europe. Nor is it only Shakespeare's tragedies that become progressively utopian from this point on – his comedies too, abandoning their early *commedia dell'arte* idiom and the courtly representation that we find in *Love's Labour's Lost*, turn increasingly to explore their utopian potential. Their concern is increasingly with the self-consciousness of dreams that have no time and place outside the theatre in which they are played but never played out – with dreams of what court life might be, dreams like that of Ophelia in Act 3:1 of *Hamlet*, dreams which, if expelled from the 'envious court' to the woods of *As You Like It*, nevertheless keep faith with the wish that we sometimes have, that things in real life might have turned out differently. It is a wish which, however tragic or nostalgic, keeps us in touch with the goodness and the justice by whose absence we know the world before us.

# Part II:
# Idealized Courts and Dreams of Freedom

*Nick Potter*

# 4
# Wildness and Wilderness: Alternatives to Courtly Life

*As You Like It* (1600) and *Twelfth Night* (1601) belong to a period of crisis for the Elizabethan court.[1] The rivalry between the Cecil and Essex factions issued in the banishment of Essex from court and in the doomed Essex rising of 1601. I want to consider both plays' treatment of an 'antique world' evoked by both and contrasted with 'these times' (both phrases are Orlando's).[2] I want to argue that in *As You Like It* this 'antique world' is identified with values arising from a consideration of 'naturalness' against 'artificiality', and 'authenticity' against flattery and self-interest, and that these values are discovered in Duke Senior and ceremoniously re-installed in the court. In *Twelfth Night* the situation is more complex.

The wilderness of Arden represents a situation in which people can get in touch with the deepest springs of their being, apart from the deceptions and illusions of courtly life. It is a proving ground. Three centuries later, in *Heart of Darkness*, Joseph Conrad was to argue that Western European man would fail the test, but Shakespeare shows Duke Senior emerging strengthened. This wilderness can be seen as a background to human existence, from which we are usually kept, but into which, like Lear later, we may be precipitated.

Its counterpart in human affairs is wildness, and this appears as simultaneously rejuvenating and subversive in those traditional practices subsumed under such headings as 'pastime' or 'revels'. These 'revels' have their roots in much older, collective, responses to wilderness, responses discussed by such recent studies of festivity in relation to Elizabethan and Jacobean theatre as Michael Bristol's *Carnival and Theater* (1985).

What such discussions share is a perspective that looks on festivity from the outside as a mode of the functioning of society. I want to look from the inside, from the point of view of the reveller as it were, and to argue that, taken together, these plays represent a meditation on a deep change in Elizabethan life, a change that only becomes visible in the moment of change itself.[3]

The change I have in mind becomes much more clearly visible as having happened by the seventeenth and eighteenth centuries, and has been charted by J. M. Golby and A. W. Purdue in their *The Civilising of the Crowd* (1984). They describe a process whereby 'popular culture' gradually comes to conform to the cultural norms established by an increasingly successful middle class, and the anarchic figure of Mr. Punch, which they take as emblematic, disappears as respectability and domesticity become established aims. The wildness of Mr. Punch, his stubborn unruliness, simply goes out of fashion.

It is important to ask where it came from in the first place, and I want to suggest that an answer is offered by Friedrich Nietzsche's conception of the Dionysian described by him in *The Birth of Tragedy*. I want further to suggest that this spirit is struggling to be born in Sir Toby. The maypoles which the Puritans had banned during the Interregnum reappeared in 1660 with the Restoration, but dwindled into insignificance under a more relentless pressure than the Puritans could exert, an Apolline dream of respectability, the introduction of which completes the Nietzschean schema I want to offer.

The Dionysian impulse survives on the margins of respectable society, an exhilarating wildness occasionally drawn on to pep up flagging spirits. The originals of these bursts of liveliness are always more complex and demanding than whatever is made of them, such as the Tango as it originated in Rio de Janeiro amongst the outcast, hopeful and hopeless, or the Blues, sung by black Americans disenchanted and disillusioned; painful, self-goading expressions of agony and longing, which find their way into dance-crazes and popular music. In Sir Toby I think we can see the incorporation of an exhausted Dionysian spirit, powerless to be born, into a new compound life made by the influence of a burgeoning middle class on an older, courtly, cultural life. The 'antique world' of these plays is depicted as being in touch with the country, not divided against it but expressing even more deeply than it could itself the deepest meanings of human being in its forms of life, drawing out, refining and intensifying the full range, from the wilderness to the court itself. The court has the right to revelry because only in the refining power of court life can life be expressed most fully. Courtly life is the best life.

The 'antique world', though, both plays acknowledge, is disappearing. They are laments for a lost ideal. Most remarkably, *Twelfth Night* already suggests a mode of dignified acceptance of the new conditions. As the last years of Elizabeth's reign give way to the first years of James's, more anguished Romances suggest a response to a deepening contradiction, as we suggested in *Shakespeare: the Play of History*, between James's attempts to revive a conception of kingship long ruled out by gains in parliamentary power and influence, and that parliamentary power itself. The struggle at Elizabeth's court between Essex and Cecil which, it has been argued, is reflected in *As You Like It*, is the forerunner of this later, deeper, conflict, and may have seemed emblematic of the disappearances of possibilities, ideal visions, from the imaginative life of Elizabethan and Jacobean England, to the mind of a writer, we have already argued, deeply alert to history.

# 5

# *As You Like It*: The Outlaw Court

### PLAY AND RITUAL

It is often an advantage, in order to fill out our sense of a play's 'conditions of possibility', to consider its occasion. In a provocative essay, Leonard Tennenhouse offers a starting point for such a consideration, because he implies that the plays in which he is interested have a function.[4] He explains this function in terms of a display of interactions of power which give the plays an almost ritual quality. Tennenhouse supposes that the transactions of power which he sees encoded in the drama have a kind of illustrative or explanatory function, displaying in order to show, to reveal, and to impress. The plays are almost solemn enactments of particularly tricky moments in the transactions of power within Elizabethan society, serving to offer pictures of the successful negotiations of such moments, but revealing under analysis the sleight of hand by which this has been accomplished. It is not difficult to see how the plays might come to resemble, say, a royal function, such as a Coronation, a social ritual by means of which a meaning is established. Such rituals show what they do. His treatment of the moment in the last act of *The Merchant of Venice* when Portia tells Antonio that three of his 'argosies' are 'safely come to port' is a fair illustration of the method. He argues that this represents a handing back to Antonio of a patriarchal power temporarily usurped by Portia.

Such a view can be pursued to the point at which it can be argued that such moments relieve an anxious compulsion to repeat: that the image of usurpation arouses intense anxiety which such moments relieve. Such relief being of necessity only temporary, the anxiety being structural, it should not surprise that we can find the same kind of moment over and over again in the plays and indeed in other cultural products of the time. In this way it can be said that something is being done by the plays that makes them akin to ritual. This would enable us to think of the plays' 'occasion' as the need repeatedly seeking alleviation. I want to bear such an interpretation in mind while pursuing a different tack.

We have already argued in *Shakespeare: the Play of History* that the plays need to be seen not only as participating in the materiality of history but as being interested in the materiality of history. They are self-conscious: they 'play' history, and we have been keen to exploit the resonances of that word. The movement we are tracing in the dramatizations of courtly life we are looking at is a deepening of those resonant meanings, the complex understanding Shakespeare's poetry seems to centre upon of 'playing'. Our argument involves the effort to see what happens if we think of the plays in this way: to imagine their self-conscious treatment of, and not merely enactment of, the kinds of issue Tennenhouse sees at the centre of the plays' interest. We would want to decentre 'interests' and put in their place 'interest', or, as you might say, 'poetry'. At their heart the plays have poetry itself, the reality of what the imagination makes, placed in a consciousness of the reality of history: 'what might be', or 'what might have been', and 'what is'. In looking at these two plays I want to bring out a scepticism about 'what is' which insidiously suggests that both poetry and reality are but forms of imagination. I want to avoid placing the plays too rigidly in Elizabethan society in terms of 'function' because I think it is important that we are attentive to the plays' consciousness of their own status in that society, for though it is true that 'play' got taken up with the utmost seriousness from time to time and was *used* functionally by the established authorities (or was treated by the established authorities as though it was being so used), this is not the defining characteristic of the relationship of play and society.

The positioning of Burbage's 'Theatre', at the northeast gate of London in 1576, is emblematic. Though the boys' companies such as the choristers gave performances within the City, the theatre with which Shakespeare was associated was not incorporated or established. The company can best be thought of as being on a leash, being 'retainers' in the sense that they were not independent, but that their dependence left them very much at a loose end, to their own devices, much of the time. Though retainers to the Earl of Leicester, they were paid no wages but earned a living from performances for which they charged admission, either in public venues such as the Theatre, or private, such as the Inns of Court, where John Manningham saw *Twelfth Night* in 1602.

This puts the players in a position of considerable ambiguity, able only to act the enactment of harmonies to which they could never quite belong themselves, or to question such harmonies from a position of dependence. The position is not at all unlike that of the licensed Fool, the first of which to appear in Shakespeare's work, Touchstone, is a central figure in *As You Like It*.

These questions are raised by different theories of the occasion of the play, R. B. Sharpe suggesting that it was written to tempt playgoers to the Globe who were drawn by the pastoral plays of Lyly and others that had been revived by the reconstituted boys' companies, and J. H. Walter arguing that it was written for the private marriage of Southampton to Elizabeth Vernon in 1598.[5] Both writers agree that the themes of exile and friends' ingratitude relate to the banishment of the Earl of Essex from the Court. That such different, though equally speculative, views may arise concerning the play's occasion is an eloquent testimony to the curious position of a company such as the Lord Chamberlain's Men. On the one hand they are touting for public business, and, on the other, they are involved in the intimate and ceremonial privacies of the aristocracy, what Leonard Tennenhouse calls 'the community of blood'. They are of the household, but also of the street, as Muriel Bradbrook has described:

> Defying the literary canons of art imposed by the learned poets of the Sidney circle, as the common players grew to resemble craft gilds rather than household servants, so their poets in the course of the 1590s developed craft skills, based on experience.[6]

Such a marginal position may confer possibilities of peculiar insight, and *As You Like It*, I will argue, has an edge which makes it more than something written to occasion, whichever speculation is preferred.

## DUKE SENIOR AND HIS 'MERRY MEN'

The play is remarkable for mixing elements of 'realism', a sense of the hardness and inflexibility of conditions, of the dullness and ordinariness of things, with elements of unashamed fantasy. Duke Frederick's sudden and violent dislike of Rosalind, Oliver's extreme hatred of a brother who, though he has been denied an education, speaks and acts like an accomplished courtier, and, most strikingly, Duke Frederick's offstage conversion, are, I believe, a deliberate flouting of 'reality'. This flouting of 'reality' need not have the effect of making us feel that the play is all fantasy: it may make us think more carefully about those elements in the play not treated in this manner. These elements may not be more 'real', only more 'realistic'. This makes us think of human possibilities that are not those actualized in the particular historical moments in which we exist.

The feeling is caught beautifully in the wrestler Charles's recounting what he has heard of Duke Senior:

> They say he is already in the Forest of Arden, and a many merry men with him; and there they live like the old Robin Hood of England. They say many young gentlemen flock to him every day, and fleet the time carelessly as they did in the golden world. (I.i.114–9)

The unmistakeable note of wistful longing that belongs to the popular fantasy, to what 'they' say, need not be identified with Charles: he is only recounting what he has heard. What he has heard is saturated in the dream of another way of living. This is especially important to note as there was at the time a large body of landless labourers living outside the law in the area of Warwickshire known as Arden.[7] A sort of continuity links these quite different communities in a common enterprise, a utopian 'commonwealth' of a kind. Duke Senior and his 'merry men' enjoy a particular kind of community, deliberately likened to the 'old Robin Hood of England', one in which a charismatic leader secures loyalty to his person without needing or wanting to exercise power, in the sense of a contest of wills. There is room for dissent, as Jacques shows, and, besides a little raillery, Duke Senior shows no desire to bring him to heel, though Jacques' coolly egalitarian style of address to the Duke, an unconsciousness of his being 'the Duke' rather than a deliberate insolence, may seem out of place. The Duke clearly does not feel this. He does not lead because he is the Duke: he is the Duke because he leads. This is far too simplistic to serve as anything other than a convenience, but it illustrates the ideal. Duke Senior's dukeship is a personal quality, not a position conferred by or imposed upon the community he leads in Arden, but confirmed by them.

Robin Hood's community similarly is not 'democratic', but it is unlike the hierarchical and coercive society by which it is outlawed in that the leadership Robin Hood exercises is based in willing consent, like Duke Senior's. This does not make either of them a *primus inter pares*, though, for both situations involve clear distinction between higher and lower status. The lower status is created by the willing subjugation of the one to the other, an act of deliberate abasement, an acceptance of leadership. This is perhaps the essence of loyalty, the free decision to put oneself in bond to something or someone and it is a theme with which the play is much concerned.

The play's opening situation quickly displays the clear, though different, situations in which loyalty is displayed. These are to be the basis of the action in Arden. In the first place Celia follows Rosalind into exile rather than be parted from her, taking the name 'Aliena', 'estranged', though as Agnes Latham points out the name can be pronounced with a stress on the second syllable,[8] and this reveals the word 'lien' which suggests that Celia may be seen as property forfeited by her father as a consequence of his non-payment of a debt, that is, the debt of contrition and restitution he owes to Duke Senior, the repayment of which would be to restore with the appropriate sorrow and remorse what he had taken. This is the way the play sees his wrongdoing: he has not endangered the continuity of an order, as King Lear does in the play which shows some kinship with *As You Like It*: he has taken something which does not belong to him, and it must be repaid. The play does not see this as theft to be punished, but as debt to be repaid.

When Adam declares that he will go into exile with Orlando the latter exclaims:

> O good old man, how well in thee appears
> The constant service of the antique world,
> When service sweat for duty, not for meed.
> (II.iii.56–8)

Adam has *chosen* Orlando: 'Let me be your servant' (l. 46). This theme is extended and developed throughout Rosalind's educating Orlando in her role as Ganymede, by means of which she draws out the love of her 'child's father' for her. I do not mean that Rosalind is to be seen seeking a role wholly analogous to that sought by Adam, any more than it could be said that Celia was seeking such a role. The point is in the similarity of the relationships, which is one of placing an interest perceived by the seeker as 'higher' before more commonplace self-interest.

This can be seen more clearly when it is recognized that Orlando has passed the test when he is able to speak with a curious impersonality out of the depths of his misery, wishing his brother well and acknowledging his own destitution without self-regard or self-dramatization. He is aware of the irony of the situation without wanting to turn it to his emotional advantage. Rosalind is alerted by this tone in his speech:

> Why then tomorrow I cannot serve your turn for Rosalind?
> (V.ii.48–9).

On the face of it this means 'because you will be busy' but it seeks the answer Orlando gives:

> I can live no longer by thinking
> (l. 50)

In a comedy marked by an alert consciousness of rhetoric this line is strikingly unadorned. Orlando has emerged, exhausted, into the truth of his situation, undistracted by the mediating interpretations that have beset him hitherto, the invitations to see himself in terms of roles already developed for him to adopt. His attention no longer diverted to himself, but on his need and therefore on the object of his need (not, that is, on himself needing), Orlando can be trusted by Rosalind. Because he depends upon her, she can depend upon him, and so can her child, the most complete image of helpless dependence in the play. If Orlando is to be Rosalind's child's father, he must be dependable, because though adults may be expected to accept the consequences of their choices, children cannot be said to choose at all.

There is an echo of this in the deepest mystery of the chivalric ideal, that it is more blessed to serve than it is to be served, that lies behind, for example, Le Cid's efforts to create a lord worth serving, or that is encoded in Duncan's vision of deepening debt between a lord and his servant:

> From hence to Inverness
> And bind us further to you.
> (*Macbeth*, I.iv.42–3)

But do they 'fleet the time carelessly' in Arden? Duke Senior's opening speech of Act 2 makes it clear that 'care' is a strong feature in Arden in two senses: in the first place there is discomfort, in the second place, the Duke shows that he and his men are in a position to be acutely attentive to 'being':

> And this our life, exempt from public haunt,
> Finds tongues in trees, books in the running brooks,
> Sermons in stones, and good in everything.
> (II.i.15–17)

They pay the kind of attention we associate with reading books, listening to sermons, to their daily existence (and extract the same kind of benefit from this), thus 'care' in the sense of attentiveness, waiting upon and being attentive to, is present in Arden, is indeed constitutive of life there. To pay attention, to be attentive to, is to be focused upon, while the association with being attendant at, or to, or upon, reminds us that this being focused is not a being poised to act, but a being poised open to receive. It is an exertion and a risk. It is certainly not 'careless', yet it is.

What Charles means by 'care' is what his world means, which is what Eliot describes in 'The Dry Salvages':

> Men's curiosity searches past and future
> And clings to that dimension

and again

> Lying awake, calculating the future,
> Trying to unweave, unwind, unravel,
> And piece together the past and the future.

The sense that Eliot evokes of the past taking shape behind and the future yawning blankly before is shown by that poem to be anxious and untrustful. One implication is that the shapes taken by the past in our imagining are by no means as settled and inevitable as they may appear. The Chronicles and the Tragedies are concerned with worlds in which things take shape and in which our imaginings are the means of our coming to grief, but these two comedies are much more concerned with a sense that things may go a number of ways, and that what has been done may be undone, unwound, unwoven, unravelled, and wound or woven anew.[9] In such a world the court of Duke Senior is not an institution, but a suspended pregnant moment. Its opposite is the 'real' court of Duke Frederick, and this opposition invites its extension towards the 'real' court of Queen Elizabeth.

## THE COURT OF DUKE FREDERICK

Shakespeare returned to the kind of character he created in Duke Frederick in Leontes in *The Winter's Tale* and, perhaps, in *King Lear*. If Duke Senior rules because his followers want him to, because he brings into being their unity, indeed their being what they are, Duke Frederick rules out of power based upon his position as broker in a court life based on competition for place. Orlando's brother Oliver is the very type of the courtier in a situation of this kind. He keeps his most dangerous rival out of court (which engenders the theme of nature and civilization which will be discussed in due course) and bullies and persecutes him. As soon as Charles arrives on stage his demeanour instantly changes and his greeting is that of the eager and anxious courtier:

> What's the new news at the new court?
> (I.i.96–7)

Of course this introduces Charles's account of the story so far, but it also establishes a clear view of courtiership in the play. Novelty is of the essence: being up to date, coupled with the fear of being left behind events which Lear parodies in his vision of life in prison with Cordelia:

> so we'll live,
> And pray, and sing, and tell old tales, and laugh
> At gilded butterflies, and hear poor rogues
> Talk of court news; and we'll talk with them too,
> Who loses and who wins; who's in, who's out;
> And take upon 's the mystery of things,
> As if we were God's spies.
> (*King Lear*, V.iii.11–17)

This mood continues into Oliver's plot to trap Orlando by misrepresenting him to Charles.

Charles is an interesting figure at this stage. He speaks for a certain kind of simple integrity, a kind of honour which is bound up with doing his job well. His concern that Orlando will be hurt emerges from a dilemma into which this integrity places him: he feels bound to fight well and fears that the inexperienced Orlando will be hurt. To take it easy on Orlando would be to compromise his integrity. His concern for Orlando is moving, and introduces a note of honour against which Oliver's scheming and bullying appears especially unpleasant. It is Charles who is given the beautiful, wistful description of Duke Senior's life in the forest as well.

He speaks in this for 'men', for ordinary people who have their sense of dignity and who are not immune from the dream of the golden world but not irresistibly called by it. This is important. The note of longing is real, and yet it is not commanding. It does not vitiate one's life, but casts a light upon it, a play of regret and yearning with which you can yet live quite well enough. This light deepens and extends one's life, dignifying as choice and commitment what might otherwise seem only the way things turned out. To stiffen oneself against regret and longing, to live in spite of it, is to live well, and we feel that Charles lives well. He is an image of a good life.

The theme of honour is picked up in Touchstone's fooling, in particular in the speech with which he comes too close to criticizing Duke Frederick (I.ii.57–79). Honour, we learn, is not associated with Duke Frederick's court. And yet how may this be? How can honour, which is reputation, standing, not be associated with the court, which is its fount? The answer is to be found in the way in which it is possible to speak of a bad king. Monarchy is not an absolute authority but it is controlled by the deposit of tradition in terms of which it defines itself and finds the source of its authority, and from which emerges an idea of kingship to control judgement of actual kings. Duke Frederick is the Duke in name only. In the same movement Touchstone is established, like Charles, as someone who speaks from a sense of what the good life is.

Le Beau adds another layer of meaning in the presentation of the court of Duke Frederick. Like Oliver, he is associated with an obsession with the new. We should be suspecting by now that the discourse of the play is introducing, without stating, the idea of tradition, against which is placed news and novelty, difference for difference's sake, and for distinction's sake. Rosalind, Celia and Touchstone caper round the unfortunate courtier, embarrassing and ridiculing him as he struggles to maintain a faltering and stilted dignity. This dignity contrasts vividly with Charles's dignity. Charles's dignity proceeds from the integrity with which Charles perceives his responsibility to his job. His work calls him to a duty to discharge which is not to become praiseworthy but only to have done one's job. Any standing which proceeds from this proceeds from the dignity of the work done, not from the integrity with which it is done, for that is expected. It is the minimum requirement. To do less is not to do the job. This curious self-effacing anticipates the model of leadership we are shown in the Forest, and which appears again in the loyalty of Adam to Orlando. It is contrasted with Le Beau whose dignity is a dignity of appearance, of bearing, of deportment (one recalls the absurd and appalling Turveydrop in *Bleak House*). Charles's skills are skills to which one submits oneself as to a discipline: Le Beau's are skills which one must exhibit in oneself, which one must become, and thus there is no relationship of submission, no humility. The meaning of one's world is found only in one's exertions within it to create meaning, meaning which is found only in one's exertions. For Charles, the meaning of one's world is found in the tradition to which one submits oneself in loyalty and with the sense that that submission is satisfactory.

Submission to tradition recalls the chivalric ideal, while Le Beau's courtiership indicates the emergence of a courtly aristocracy of talent which will at first infiltrate the court of the hereditary aristocrat, competing for attention, defeating him at his own game of deportment, and eventually will overturn it, ushering in proliferating arenas for display, disintegrating the carefully-nurtured forms the court provided and replacing them with multiplying platforms, stages, spaces on which an expanding series of stardoms will be enacted.[10]

Duke Frederick himself when he appears is no disappointment. Capricious and tyrannical, he is exactly the enthronement of the wilful will made possible by the kind of jostling for position we would expect in a courtly life whose representatives so far have been Oliver and Le Beau. Like Leontes, like Lear, he is a monarch who has been allowed to develop the illusion that he is all-powerful because his court is corrupt and ineffective. His court does not represent the kind of submission to tradition which guarantees the continual presence of the standard by which the monarch is to be judged. His leadership has become absolute power because there is a vacuum where there should be authority. Should we, like Lear, look to 'nature' for authority?

## NATURE AND CIVILIZATION

Therefore if this be civil life and order – to live in cities and towns with so much vice and misorder – meseem man should not be born thereto, but rather to life in the wild forest, there more following the study of virtue, as it is said men did in the golden age wherein man lived according to his natural dignity.

> Reginald Pole, in *Dialogue Between Reginald Pole and Thomas Lupset* by Thomas Starkey, c.1534.[11]

Pole's interlocutor reminds him that the Fall succeeded the Golden Age and that the fault lies not in towns and cities in themselves, but 'in the malice of man, which abuseth and turneth that thing which might be to his wealth and felicity to his own destruction and misery'. Lupset further criticizes 'such as be great, wise and politic men, which fly from office and authority; by whose wisdom the multitude might be contained and kept in good order and civility'. In this way Starkey may be seen to have summarized the main structure of *As You Like It*: a familiar debate between Court and Country resolved by the return to the Court of the good leader establishing the view that it is corrupt leaders that make corrupt institutions and not the other way round.

Such discussions easily separate out into what is essentially human and what is 'added'. Montaigne expresses this view, commenting on the difference between European life and that of recently discovered Brazilian Indians in relation to 'Nature':

> We have so much by invention, surcharged the beauties and riches of her works, that we have altogether overchoked her; yet wherever her purity shineth, she makes our vain, and frivolous enterprises wonderfully ashamed.[12]

This sense of the 'added' arises in the discussion between Rosalind and Celia at I.ii.39–55. The distinction is put by Rosalind:

> Nay now thou goest from Fortune's office to Nature's; Fortune reigns in gifts of the world, not in the lineaments of Nature. (ll. 39–41) [13]

It is here that Orlando's upbringing comes again to mind:

> Yet he's gentle, never schooled and yet learned, full of noble device, of all sorts enchantingly beloved. (I.i.164–6)

and this in spite of the upbringing of which Orlando complains:

> My father charged you in his will to give me good education: you have trained me like a peasant, obscuring and hiding

from me all gentleman-like qualities.
(I.i.66–9)

Orlando is a natural gentleman, in other words. The other side of this appears when the adventurers meet Corin the shepherd, which will be considered separately.

The situation is one to which Shakespeare returns with anguish instead of amusement in *King Lear*, in Lear's puzzled desperation. Lear seizes the idea of 'superfluity' to express his feeling that there is a kind of human being with which he needs to get in touch to be healed, 'unaccommodated man'. What Lear means by 'unaccommodated' is made clear in his argument with Goneril earlier:

> Allow not nature more than nature needs,
> Man's life is cheap as beast's.
> (*King Lear*, II.iv.268–9)

Lear has yet to be persuaded of the virtue of the 'unaccommodated' but has put his finger on a startling paradox. It is possible to understand 'nature needs' to mean whatever is complementary to nature but not part of it without violating the notion that the nature of a thing is what defines it. The case is rather different if we consider Lear's implied 'nature wants', which is 'more than nature needs'. How can nature want more than is complementary to it and remain nature? For it will change with its wants, defining new complements and thus re-defining itself. In what sense may this be a nature, except in the paradoxical sense that its nature is to be without a nature?

Rosalind and Celia do not settle the argument but only set out the terms of a confusion. Orlando the natural gentleman and Corin the gentle shepherd are dramatic reminders of the difficulty of teasing out 'nature' from 'fortune', and yet Duke Senior's opening speech forces us back to the dilemma in which we place ourselves as soon as we try to separate the two. The question is, why should we try to? Montaigne, Reginald Pole, Charles the wrestler, Duke Senior, and Lear, all express the same exasperation: why can we not 'shake the superflux' and find ourselves?

## 'AUTHENTICITY' AND 'SECOND NATURE'

The theme of 'nature' and what we might call a yearning

for 'authenticity' versus 'civilization' is found in the conversation between Touchstone and Corin. Touchstone answers Corin's inquiry 'And how like you this shepherd's life, Master Touchstone' (III.ii.11–12) with a speech described by Agnes Latham as 'nonsense', but which is perhaps not all so:

> Truly shepherd, in respect of itself, it is a good life; but in respect that it is a shepherd's life, it is naught. In respect that it is solitary, I like it very well; but in respect that it is private, it is a very vile life. Now in respect it is in the fields, it pleaseth me well; but in respect it is not in the court, it is tedious. As it is a spare life, look you, it fits my humour well; but as there is no more plenty in it, it goes much against my stomach. (III.ii.13–21)

Touchstone's distinction between 'solitary' and 'private' for example may be suggestive of the difference between being on one's own and being lonely: his distinction between 'in the fields' and 'not in court' is quite substantial, reflecting the tensions between the advantages and disadvantages of what Duke Senior has only praised; the 'spareness' of the life may be a healthy abstemiousness, while there being 'no plenty in it' makes it seem deprived. Is Touchstone not pointing out that a glass may be half full or half empty?

Corin's reply is in true yokel mode, and yet we may suspect that he has his tongue in his cheek, answering Touchstone's display of vocabulary with the ponderous obviousness of country wisdom, as that is pictured by the self-satisfied town, convinced that quality of thought is inseparable from sophistication of expression. Corin's replies to Touchstone's rather cumbersome witticisms are sensible and clear, and Touchstone is led into the declaration that the perfume civet 'is of baser birth than tar, the very uncleanly flux of a cat'.

This is an interesting and ambiguous moment. Touchstone is either an over-enthusiastic *naif*, or else he is pretending to be, and uses Corin's patient interest in courtly life (or his willingness to put up with being told about it) as a 'stalking-horse' to expose the ambiguity of the court as a 'supplement' to nature, a production upon nature, that strives to assert its independence and superiority.

Corin's view is that court and country have their appropriate ways of doing things and he is not interested in asserting the superiority of the one over the other. He answers Touchstone's bullying with a moving statement of his own life:

Sir, I am a true labourer: I earn that I eat, get that I wear; owe no man hate, envy no man's happiness; glad of other men's good, content with my harm; and the greatest of my pride is to see my ewes graze and my lambs suck. (III.ii.71-5)

It is not inappropriate in a scene dominated by Touchstone's showing his familiarity with the procedures of formal disputation ('Instance, briefly; come, instance' l. 50) to point out the careful structure of Corin's speech at this point. He follows classical advice in setting out his speech: he catches the audience's attention in his 'Entrance' (or *'Exordium'*), sets forth the facts of the case (the 'Exposition'), confutes arguments to the contrary (the 'Confirmation': in this case by implication, Corin states that country life is not envious or unhappy, admitting the inference that he means that courtly life is both) and concludes with a dignified *'Peroratio'*. The structure of the central portion is chiasmic, the first point, 'owe no man hate', is answered by the fourth, 'content with my harm', while the second point, 'Envy no man's happiness', is aligned with the third, 'glad of other men's good'.

The effect of these devices is to impress upon the listener a simplicity, clarity, and completeness. Each clause has its own verb and complement (*'Hypozeuxis'*, or to use Puttenham's term, 'Substitute') and thus sets out its meaning without qualification or ambiguity. Its concluding *peroratio* is a powerful statement of generous humility and simplicity. This is such a vivid contrast with the self-regarding mannerism of the Court that it seems to confirm its own unadorned naturalness, its innocence of contrivance and the intent to manipulate. Yet it is, as I have tried to show without too much forcing I hope, rhetorically very subtle.[14]

The difficult question here is, is this subtlety Corin's or Shakespeare's? If it is Shakespeare's then it is a mode of poetry persuasive of simplicity and clarity, which we may take to be an intention of the play, that is that we should at this moment feel for and with 'the country'. We may feel that we have caught him out, as it were, putting a rhetoric in Corin's mouth which does not convince, though it may persuade. Or we may devise an argument from convention to defend him against such a charge, and accuse the accusers of a crass naturalism. If it is Corin's, the question becomes a different and, I think, a more interesting one.

Touchstone has been betrayed into suggesting the 'supplementarity' of the Court, by which I mean what Jacques Derrida means when he points out that many oppositions (such as speaking/writing, nature/culture) appear in discourse so as to suggest that the second of the pair is a belated and corrupt 'supplement' to the first. As Touchstone quizzes Corin he reminds us that the very perfume courtiers use to scent their hands (which Corin has given as a reason why courtiers kiss their hands and country people do not) is derived from an excretion produced by an anal gland of the civet cat. This has the effect of throwing into paradox the court's claims to be more refined than the country. Now it appears that the country is more refined than the court. This impression is confirmed when Corin makes his oration with simple dignity. The anxiety about rhetoric expressed by Socrates in the *Gorgias*, that there is no necessary connection between being persuaded and what is true or good, is eased by our feeling under no compulsion to question whether or not Corin means what he says. Rhetoric here is merely the shape words take when the truth is told.

The paradoxical effect here is that the artificial appears natural. This should alert us to these words, and their playfulness. Something may appear natural and be otherwise. Indeed, the point of saying that it appears natural is to express wonder that it is not. This does not mean that it is artificial, because that word usually means that it is inferior in some way (this impression is confirmed by, for example, Huysmans' *À Rebours*, because Des Esseintes chooses the artificial deliberately as an act of differentiation against 'nature', even to the paradoxical extent of cultivating flowers which look artificial). What is meant is perhaps best caught by the phrase 'second nature'. This is something in between the natural and the artificial, not natural, because it is acquired, not artificial because it is so completely a part of the person, not consciously contrived, but unthinkingly possessed. This second contrast allows us to see Duke Frederick's court as artificial because it is characterized by a watchfulness about what is to be 'put on', either for the purposes of concealment and safety or else for the purposes of display. In Corin's case, rhetorical subtlety I believe should be seen as 'second nature' if we adjudge it his, as I believe we should, because then the play makes a more interesting kind of sense.

If we return to an earlier moment in the play, Corin talks plainly of himself again, at the moment when he meets Rosalind and Celia as Ganymede and Aliena:

> I am shepherd to another man,

> And do not shear the fleeces that I graze.
> My master is of churlish disposition,
> And little recks to find the way to heaven
> By doing deeds of hospitality.
>                             (II.iv.76–80)

Agnes Latham in a note on the exchange that precedes Corin's speech decribes the movement from prose to verse, and notes that:

> It is true that Corin appears to be steadily attempting verse, but he fails to impose it on the scene until Rosalind addresses him in a complete and courteous pentameter at l. 67 to which he replies in kind.[15]

She describes the dialogue between Rosalind and Corin as 'a stately verse-exchange'. Corin has just been attempting to comfort Silvius, whose verse is very uneven, and who is revealed by Corin to be the intending purchaser of the household that employs Corin himself. Silvius will thus be Corin's master. Yet Rosalind's description of them as 'A young man and an old in solemn talk' (l. 18) suggests a relationship of youth to experienced age, a father-son or parallel relationship. This is borne out by our sense of Corin's verse, even though he replies to Touchstone's description of himself and Rosalind and Celia as Corin's 'betters' by saying 'Else they are very wretched' (l. 66). Agnes Latham chooses the right word to describe Corin's verse: it is 'stately'. It is like Rosalind's when she is not being witty. The social relationships we might expect are being subverted by the poetry. The poetry is supplying another world in which relationships are governed by a courtesy you do not find at court and by a naturalness you do not find in nature.

Touchstone is not wrong to point to the less attractive side of country life, and the experience of the two groups who arrive in Arden is at first uncomfortable. It is the courtesy of the Duke's outlaws and the propertyless shepherd that relieves the distress in which they find themselves 'in a state of nature'. It is not 'Nature' that the play opposes to courtly life, but 'second nature'. It is here that the authenticity asserted by Duke Senior, the absence of which is lamented in Jacques's famous speech, the integration, it might be said, of a person and *persona*, so distinct in courtly life, is to be found, and here that the proper equilibrium of Nature and Fortune is to be discovered.

There is, that is, no 'superflux' to be shaken. Lear has mistaken the corruption of refinement for refinement itself. At the end of *As You Like It* Hymen descends and a Masque celebrates the healing and harmonizing of the social world before the courtly characters return to court. The vision supplied by the poetry of the play is one in which good masters head hierarchies composed of positions each of which has its proper dignity. There is no inferiority in being a shepherd in such a world, and no superiority in being a Duke. The gentle shepherd, the natural gentleman, the outlaw Duke, are all intelligible oxymorons in the world of the play's poetry which takes dramatic shape in the masque, by means of which the immanent is manifested.

However, it is to be noted, as Malcolm Evans has,[16] that this scene contains some unstable conditionals: 'If there be truth in sight, you are my daughter'; 'If there be truth in sight, you are my Rosalind'; 'If truth holds true contents' (V.iv.117–18, 129). The play has shown us that sight can deceive, and Hymen's words are most ambiguous.

Through this chink it is possible to glimpse a counter-cursive movement in the play, working to destabilize and to unravel exactly the settled harmony towards which the play is tending at this point, at least on the surface.[17] The surface movement expresses the Apolline view of the festival's place in an accomplished order. The counter-cursive movement expresses the restlessness and dissatisfaction of what I have called the individual reveller. In the tension between the two the play's meaning and significance lie.

## CONCLUSION: 'IF TRUTH HOLDS TRUE CONTENTS'

The essence of compromise is that nobody gets what they want. A tension, and a struggle, can be averted by a distribution of the focus of the tension that appears not to advantage any of the competitors. Thus in their interaction with each other these competitors' feathers can be smoothed. This may be to say no more than that they are, if not happy in themselves, at least not so unhappy that they feel that they have to do something about it.

It is this feeling I want to suggest is the experience of the individual reveller, who, though taken up by the revels, is never quite taken in by them. In the offstage conversion of Duke Frederick and the almost miraculous transformation of Oliver, Shakespeare pushes credibility into incredibility, inviting us to suspect a deliberate exposure of illusion, perhaps even a disgust with its comforts, and he gives us a spokesperson in Jacques.

Throughout the play Jacques has been presented to us as a moralizer and a melancholic, for whom Duke Senior and his men feel a kind of affectionate tolerance, and whom they find amusing and diverting, but who is fundamentally unsound. His great speech on the shallowness of human life is shouldered aside by the entrance of Orlando with Adam, a dramatic denial of his premise. We are encouraged to see that Jacques enjoys his melancholy too much. There is an unpleasant assumption of superiority in his dealings with Touchstone. We are not surprised to see him decline the invitation to return to court.

However he remains an unresolved element, leaving them 'for other than for dancing measures' (V.iv.192).[18] These 'measures' are to be found in the 'religious life' to which Duke Frederick has been converted 'from his enterprise and from the world'. They are not a confirmation of Jacques' self-indulgent melancholy and cynicism, but suggest that his sense of the world is seriously held, if in need of discipline, and that it is this sense of the world that feelingly persuades him what he is. Further these 'measures' are 'other' than dancing measures: they are images of another kind of orderliness, serious rather than frivolous perhaps, or contemplative rather than celebratory, at least.

This has the effect of leaving Jacques' critical commentary in the air, as Corin's replies to Touchstone do not deny his points, but offer us another way of looking at things. These doubts, or doublenesses, are left unresolved. The gathering Apolline smoothness is forced to offer no more than *détente* to these elements: it cannot resolve them into itself. For society the crisis is over: for the individual reveller it has merely sunk below the horizon of action. Discontented with Hymen's truths, Jacques strikes an oddly naturalistic note, looking beyond the epilogue, when he says to the Duke

> To see no pastime, I. What you would have
> I'll stay to know at your abandon'd cave.
> (V.iv.194–5)

The play is not over when it is over. There is something yet to be done. Such exophoric reference is a deliberate unsettling of the harmony proposed by the masque.

The conservative tendency of the play is to suggest the naturalness of the social (and sexual) order and the truth and happiness that are to be found in conformity to it. The counter-cursive tendency is to suggest discontent and restlessness: the unsatisfactoriness of composition and the urgency of desire. In such a light Corin's humility would appear a difficult balance and a considerable achievement: Duke Senior's willingness to make the best of adversity would be seen to have been won out of arduous struggle, a struggle in which he found his meaning; Jacques's melancholy would be revealed as a fatal incapacity to find such equilibrium; Rosalind and Orlando's love would seem a perilous mutual trusting.

It would be to break faith with the play to say that either of these tendencies were *true*. The point is that the play's 'as you like it' is by no means as casual as it might seem, and the comedy not nearly as breezy as many excellent pieces of criticism have persuasively argued that it is.[19] We must practise to be Jacques to the play, while never losing sight of the play's questionings of Jacques. The point, if drawn out, would seem to be that the truth is to be found in trust, of each other, or of existence itself, and the play acknowledges just how daunting it may be to have to give it.

This complex ending leaves us in doubt about its central affirmation, that the good has been re-installed in the courtly heart of society, that the purgative lessons of the wilderness have restored to refinement a salutary humility, that, in short, court life is susceptible of reform and renewal. There is a sceptical current that fastens on the experience of the individual in the composing revels and draws out and gives voice to the unconvinced.[20] This current deepens to produce *Twelfth Night*, a subtle, poignant revel for the year of Essex's final, hopeless and romantic act of defiance.

# 6

# *Twelfth Night*: The Court in Transition (II)

*If music be the food of love, play on.*
(I.i.1)

What comes to light in *Twelfth Night* is a further aspect of the 'antique world' to which Orlando refers in *As you Like It*. As it celebrates and explores courtly life, the play shows that life in change, losing touch with some of its deepest sources, cautiously welcoming new kinds of attitude and behaviour.

The Apolline illusion performed by *As You Like It* is the smooth passage of the outlaw court into the official Court, the kind of restitution dreamed of in the popular Romance of Robin Hood. Jacques' self-exclusion from the composing revels exposes the Apolline illusion as a dream, much as the dreamer threatened with waking by, for example, thirst, is soothed by dream images of drinking which, however, cannot quench the thirst she feels, because they are only dream images. Nonetheless, her waking is postponed. The dream is forced to acknowledge the problem, and contains images of that problem, but puts off its urgency, or attempts to, by ever more extravagant images of its solution which are however powerless to effect that solution.

Freud recounts a nursemaid's dream in which the girl took her charge to urinate and the stream took on such proportions that at last an ocean liner could be seen sailing on it. She awakened to the child's anguished cries. The breaking in of reality in *As You Like It* is not so much in the foreground, but it is nonetheless there, and unresolved by the revels. This, I have argued, is internal to the revels, figuring the dissatisfaction of the reveller with the revels themselves, the excess of desire over dream form.

In *Twelfth Night* both dream and desire are the deliberate subject of the play. In Orsino's sick passion, Olivia's grief and Sir Toby's revelling, these themes are brought more to the surface of the play, because they are the material played, the real life of Illyria, into which Viola and Sebastian are thrown. A pattern emerges in this way, which links Feste, the Clown who wanders between both households, both Olivia's Clown and a free agent (much like the Lord Chamberlain's Men themselves) and Viola and Sebastian, on either side of the group of dreamers, Feste as wistfully, and even mournfully conscious of the dream, Viola and Sebastian as having to live on their wits in the world of the dreamers.

It is speculative, but not perhaps merely fanciful, to see a parallel between this situation and the charged atmosphere of Elizabeth's court in the year of the failed Essex rebellion, 1601, though the themes that R. B. Sharpe and J. H. Walter saw in *As You Like It* as reflections of the banishment of Essex have no direct correspondence in *Twelfth Night* unless we take Orsino's hopeless love for Olivia as a heavily-coded figure for Essex's decline in Elizabeth's regard. I want to stress the atmosphere of enchanted languor which characterizes dream in *Twelfth Night*, and the sterility and listlessness that hangs over the whole world of Illyria, and to contrast this with the vigour and agility of Viola, who enters this world through no choice of her own. It is anachronistic to press the image of shipwreck as an existentialist understanding *avant la lettre* only if it is assumed that the perspectives of the existentialists were discovered wholly originally by those writers themselves. Viola is thrown into a situation of which she must make some sense for herself if she is to survive, at least this is the way she sees things, and I will return to this point. She ends by making things make sense, though not by her own will. She is a catalyst.

She is the new element which the world of Illyria must take in if it is to break through into new life, however changed that life will be. She is, perhaps, if not the Cecil faction itself, then at least something similar enough for such a comparison to come to mind. An old dream has to wake up to new conditions if it is not utterly to die. *Twelfth Night* points these new realities in two figures: Viola and Malvolio. It is not stretching the play to say that the choice is one or the other. Orsino and Olivia are too self-absorbed to do anything about Malvolio, and the dilapidated Dionysian can only bluster as the new reality weaves its dream about him and the others. It is, of course, all dreaming. Words such as 'reality' and 'waking up' need to be used, but it is all dream, a waking from one dream into another, equally attractive, equally unsatisfying, and the wandering clown's sweet sad songs are an unrelenting commentary reminding us that desire seeks shapes which it always passes beyond. These are the deep resonances of 'What You Will'.

\*         \*         \*

> *So full of shapes is fancy,*
> *That it alone is high fantastical.*
>                                   (I.i.14–15)

Courtly life in *Twelfth Night* is exhausted, played out, and this is shown at several key points: in Feste's songs, in the revelling of the ageing rowdies, and above all in the impasse of Orsino's passion for Olivia to which we are introduced in the opening speech:

> If music be the food of love, play on,
> Give me excess of it, that, surfeiting,
> The appetite may sicken, and so die.
> That strain again, it had a dying fall:
> O, it came o'er my ear like the sweet sound
> That breathes upon a bank of violets,
> Stealing and giving odour. Enough, no more;
> 'Tis not so sweet now as it was before.
> O spirit of love, how quick and fresh art thou
> That notwithstanding thy capacity
> Receiveth as the sea, nought enters there,
> Of what validity and pitch soe'er,
> But falls into abatement and low price,
> Even in a minute! So full of shapes is fancy,
> That it alone is high fantastical.
>                                   (I.i.1–15)

This key speech winds its languid way through a narcotic imagery of gluttony and lethargy, inducing a sense of surrender and drowsiness, a richness, even an over-richness, conveyed by the imagery of the perfume of flowers.

Two other key themes emerge in this scene. One is a persistent and vividly imagined mood of death, not at all uncommon in Elizabethan love poetry, but here part of a pattern that works steadily against the important phrase 'quick and fresh', and making any suggestion of growth and life seem morbidly ingrowing and cloying. Then there is a mood of dissatisfaction and restlessness, but enervated and lethargic. Orsino's invocation of excess and surfeit notwithstanding, too much is not enough. The only course of action is to pursue the shapes fancy offers and desire chases, correlatives of the unattainable, inevitably unsatisfying because *like* the object of desire, and therefore not the object itself:

> Away before me to sweet beds of flowers!
> Love-thoughts lie rich when canopied with bowers.
> (I.i.40–41)

The other main business of the scene is to introduce Olivia, and it is important to note that the word 'fresh' is used in Valentine's description of her self-imposed enclosure:

> The element itself, till seven years' heat,
> Shall not behold her face at ample view;
> But like a cloistress she will veiled walk,
> And water once a day her chamber round
> With eye-offending brine: all this to season
> A brother's dead love, which she would keep fresh
> And lasting, in her sad remembrance.
> (I.i.26–32)

The word is being used here in a context which almost forces a sense of irony, in the way that it would to talk of Miss Havisham keeping her wedding day 'fresh' in her mind in her ghastly room. The brother's love is a 'dead' love: 'a dead brother's love' would make a different point. 'Brine' and 'season' suggest preserving, even pickling, which is at least grotesque, if not ridiculous. The scene charges the word with implications of growth which is suffocating, and of keeping from natural decay what should be left, while the word itself reminds us of the spacious and the open, which is exactly what we do not find in this claustrophobic atmosphere of emotional intensity.

The next scene is in striking contrast. With the memory of morbid intensity strong in our minds, we hear that the country is called Illyria, a name with complex suggestions of negation, illness, and song. Viola picks up a bitter pun:

> And what should I do in Illyria?

> My brother he is in Elysium.
> (I.ii.3–4)

But she does not dwell on this. Straightaway she asks the sailors:

> Perchance he is not drown'd: what think you, sailors?

All through the scene Viola moves quickly between reflections on her own situation and questions designed to help her get her bearings. She wants to know what the situation is. 'Who governs here?', 'What is his name?', 'What's she?' The narrative function for the audience is secondary to our getting to know Viola. She is looking for cover. She thinks first of Olivia, but Olivia will not even admit the Duke. In that case the Duke is the only alternative. There are no hints here. When Viola asks if Orsino is still a bachelor it is romantic to think that she is attracted to him. She needs to know how things stand so that she can orientate herself:

> O that I serv'd that lady,
> And might not be deliver'd to the world,
> Till I had made mine own occasion mellow,
> What my estate is.
> (I.ii.41–44)

This is difficult. The Arden editors gloss 'be publicly made known . . . in my true station ('estate') until I considered that the time was ripe'.[21] This, and other hints, may be taken to suggest that Viola's 'station' is at least such that the Duke will not be marrying beneath his station, while at the same time keeping her actual station very vaguely defined. The hints are not helpful. When Olivia asks Caesario directly what his parentage is, Viola replies:

> Above my fortunes, yet my state is well:
> I am a gentleman.
> (I.v.282–3)

Leaving aside the point that Viola is not a gentle*man*, the station itself was not well defined in Elizabethan society, and yet was exact. Conrad Russell comments:

> Probably the real test of a claim to gentility was the attitude of the established gentlemen in the county. If a man kept a good table, dressed like a gentleman, hunted with the other gentlemen, and received letters from J. Ps addressed to him as 'gent.', then, for all practical purposes, he was a gentleman.[22]

Viola is not helping us, nor is her casual reference to her father at I.ii.28 any help. Is it that her 'estate' does not matter? If so, why does she wish to preserve it from disclosure? It can be answered with some convincingness that such details do not bother Shakespeare in the Comedies, but it is surely mere carelessness to leave such an issue unclear. It would have been an easy detail to clear up one way or another: either to invent such an 'estate', or else to find some other reason for her wishing to conceal her identity. There is such a reason, as Antonio explains: the two countries have been at war. Further, nothing is made of Viola's 'estate' in the sense of social position. On the other hand, her 'condition', as a woman on her own in a foreign country with which her own has recently been at war, supplies fully sufficient cause for her concern, her disguise. Less than this was a good enough reason for Rosalind to think disguise prudent in *As You Like It*.[23]

I suggest that the matter of her social position is left unclear to encourage as wide as possible an identification by different audiences with Viola, without offending against a sense of the Duke's 'estate'. Unlike *Love's Labour's Lost* in which we are invited to be spectators as people who are not like us exercise their wit and gallantry, the courtly skills of conversation, in *Twelfth Night* I think that such as John Manningham and his fellows at the Middle Temple who saw the play in 1602 could see in Viola something of themselves.[24]

Like Rosalind in the epilogue to *As You Like It*, Viola is a teasing representation of the convergence of opposites, a man-woman like that strange figure from earlier revels, the Teaser, or the Hobby-horse or Dragon, the man-beast, disquieting unions of the dissimilar, which represent the imagination's power over difference, which, at least in the case of the Middle Temple performance, meant a male imagination.[25] This explains such 'male' jokes as Viola's: 'Pray God defend me! A little thing would make me tell them how much I lack of a man' (III.iv.307–9), which reappears in Feste's closing song, 'A foolish thing was but a toy', as at least one level of its meaning. The presentation of woman as 'lacking' suggests a male imagination though of course this could not in itself argue exclusivity. The point I think is that Viola, crossing boundaries in herself, is a figure of the widest kind of flexibility. Leonard Tennenhouse is probably correct in seeing in the comedy the figure of a transfer of power that is extremely risky. Michael Bristol, drawing on Victor Turner's work, reminds us that carnival often occurs at such moments of

## Twelfth Night: The Court in Transition (II)

risky transition, and it may be fairly said that comedy in figuring carnival depicts the happy resolution of such confusion.[26]

We can put it this way. No revolution is merely a matter of bringing about a single desired goal. A whole range of new possibilities are thrown up: what was thought to be necessary becomes merely possible. Transition and movement of any kind involve both the exciting vision of new possibilities (to which Olivia responds when Caesario comes calling) and the fearful anticipation of new possibilities, of the collapse of all that has been understood. Anyone who would risk social change must be prepared to negotiate such spreading instability. The comedy is a 'safe' image of such radical uncertainty, because it is play, but it is also 'unsafe' because it is an image, because it invites the imagination to entertain it as a possibility.[27]

The socially mobile Elizabethan aspired to join a kind of life the existence of which that very aspiration threatened. As Leonard Tennenhouse puts it, appealing to the resonances of 'blood':

> Shakespearean comedy thus materializes the double bind which organizes many of the cultural products of Elizabeth's reign. This double bind sets the imperative to seek membership in the community of blood against the imperative to keep the community pure. (p. 62)

We may intensify the paradox by pointing out that it is the purity of the 'community of blood' (in Tennenhouse's terminology) which makes it desirable to enter and so pollute.

A further important point that Tennenhouse makes is that power, when it is transferred from the man to the woman (as he argues that it is when Orsino becomes obsessed with Olivia) takes less violent forms. The power exercised by Olivia, or by Viola, is not physically violent and does not have to be to be exerted:

> The more Olivia withholds herself, the more Orsino desires her, and thus he invests her with the power that should normally be his. (p. 64)

Olivia is not, of course, withholding herself: she does not desire Orsino. The whole effect described by Tennenhouse takes place within the charmed circle of male desire. The woman is the occasion, but the transfer of power, in this instance, takes place effectively without her. The transfer, that is, is a commerce between Orsino and the image of Olivia he has in his desiring imagination, which she has unwittingly provided, and which she unwittingly sustains.

Much more importantly, Viola is helpless in the threatened duel, to which Sir Toby is egging on both her and Sir Andrew. This provokes the 'little thing' joke, to which Feste's song surely alludes. That so much should depend on so little is the paradox such considerations evoke. In terms of Tennenhouse's schema the deliberate pollution of the community of blood is being courted and, at the same time, denied. This flat contradiction is part of the meaning of Viola's disguise, the impossibility of a paradox that is nonetheless taking place. There is nothing mysterious about this: the play is all at the level of appearances. What is not seen to be done is, in a sense, not done. But it is serious, for Illyria will die unless this sleight of hand is concluded. The impasse of sexual initiative, conventionally male, seduced into a blind alley of its own making, can only be released by a woman becoming a man, entering Orsino's affections as a man and then revealing herself as a woman, a woman moreover whose membership of the community of blood is at least unconfirmed. Only in these ways can the community be regenerated, though it must not be seen to be done, and that is the gamble, as it were, the subtlety of skill and the exhilaration of 'play' in that further sense. The community of blood can only be preserved by being polluted: the kind of life which is the outward sign of the purity Tennenhouse stresses can only be preserved if the reality of which it is the appearance is compromised. This is a much deeper resonance of the idea of mobility.

\*     \*     \*

   Viola   *What else may hap to time I will commit.*
                            (I.ii.60)

The activity and initiative of male sexuality is replaced by the activity and initiative of Viola. It is she who interpolates the composite figure of Viola(Caesario)Sebastian into the stultified and morbid life of Illyria. The impasse that lies at the heart of Illyria is opened only when it is precipitated as a paradox in a person:

   *Olivia*  Stay:
  I prithee tell me what thou think'st of me.
     *Viola*  That you do think you are not what you are.

> *Olivia* If I think so, I think the same of you.
> *Viola* Then think you right; I am not what I am.
> (III.i.139–43)

Viola's way of putting it is unusual. If she means 'you think you are in love with me but you are not' then surely the order of the sentence should be reversed? The Arden editors suggest that Viola means 'You are forgetting your station', which makes more sense of Olivia's reply, allowing her to imply that she may be forgetting herself, but Viola is concealing him(her)self. Viola then confirms this suspicion, though meaning that she is a woman, *not* that she is nobly born.

Olivia has already suspected noble birth importantly on the grounds of appearance:

> Thy tongue, thy face, thy limbs, actions, and spirit
> Do give thee five-fold blazon
> (I.v.296–7).

Viola later laments the propensity of women to be taken in by appearances:

> How easy is it for the proper false
> In women's waxen hearts to set their forms!
> Alas, our frailty is the cause, not we,
> For such as we are made of, such we be.
> (II.ii.28–31)

Taken together with her reply to Olivia's question concerning her parentage, this suggests a concentricity of contexts for one's being: first 'fortunes', one's circumstances from time to time; secondly 'state', which might be thought of as either 'dignity' or 'honour', 'standing' rather than 'station'; thirdly 'such as we are made of', our 'embodiment', what Rosalind calls 'nature' in *As You Like It*.

What Viola says suggests that these three do not stand in any necessary relationship to each other or to 'oneself'. It is always possible, in other words, to feel that one's 'being-in-the-world' (as Martin Heidegger thinks of human being) is internally dislocated, that one's state is above one's fortunes, or that one's nature has led one where one did not really want to go. In such situations one has to rely on unreliable guides, such as appearance. As Viola well knows, these can be deceptive. The issue is not 'appearance' and 'reality' though, for Viola's parentage is really not an issue in the play: the unreliability of appearances leads to scepticism, not to any affirmation of 'reality'.

The place of 'reality' is taken by what can for convenience be called 'sincerity'. That this is no more reliable than appearance is shown by the painful scene (III.i.151–7) in which Olivia pleads for Caesario's love. After her opening aside the speech moves naturally into lyric couplets, gently singing the misery and humiliation of love with a touching directness which echoes Orlando's 'I can live no longer by thinking'. The problem here is that, while the emotion is genuine, its object is mistaken.

A similar situation occurs in Act 2:4 when Viola tells Orsino of her 'sister's' love. What is at issue here is a depth of emotion that goes beyond the kinds of self-conscious concern that characterize 'the world'. People must be seen to care for nothing else, or else it may be suspected that their attention is not altogether on the beloved, but on their own reputation and standing in the world in some way. This is not an objectively reliable criterion, but in an uncertain world it is the best that can be had. Both these cases show how unreliable it is, for in both cases deep mistakes have been made.

'Mistake', or to use Feste's word, 'misprision', is at the heart of the play.[28] It is closely related to Viola's invocation of 'time' on two occasions, one in I.ii.60, 'What else may hap, to time I will commit'; and again at II.ii.39–40:

> O time, thou must untangle this, not I,
> It is too hard a knot for me t'untie

talking of Olivia's love for her as Caesario.[29] 'Hap' and 'time' go together, for Viola is not evincing any belief in Providence, or in any kind of order whatsoever. The invocation is paradoxical, because what she is invoking is nothing but happenstance itself. What 'happens' must be 'taken': we are in situations and we must act and react. The shipwreck is a dramatic image of our being 'thrown' into situations. If we must 'take' it is possible to 'mistake', and we must make sense of this as we may.

Feste rejects reason perfunctorily, as might be expected in a play for the Christmas revels:

> To see this age! A sentence is but a chev'ril glove to a good wit – how quickly the wrong side may be turned outward! (III.i.11–13)

and later:

> words are grown so false, I am loath to prove reason with them.
> (III.i.24–5)

He describes himself to Caesario as Olivia's 'corrupter of words'. Viola reflects to herself:

> folly that he wisely shows is fit;
> But wise men, folly-fall'n, quite taint their wit.
> (III.i.68–9)

Throughout the play love is seen as folly, or even as madness. Olivia's plea to Caesario confesses:

> Nor wit nor reason can my passion hide.
> (III.i.154)

Most importantly, Malvolio, 'sick of self love', can be goaded to the edge of madness when the revellers contrive to get him to mistake his situation.

Viola avoids the perils of 'misprision' because she has no preconceptions about proper order. She exhibits an attitude which Gabriel Marcel has called 'disponibilité', a putting oneself at the disposal of things, a being open and ready to respond to the demands of a situation with good will and willingness.[30] This is nothing like being prepared for all eventualities. It is quite the opposite. That kind of preparedness depends on having thought out all eventualities, of having reduced all possibilities to a determinate and manageable number of types of possibility, so that nothing comes as a surprise, or is taken for what it is. That is a being in command of things. 'Disponibilité' means giving up that kind of command and being ready to respond to the invitations proffered by the situations in which you find yourself, whatever may turn up, or 'hap'.

Both Orsino and Olivia show a degree of 'disponibilité' in their response to Caesario. They have not so completely organized their worlds that they have no room for a sense of what may turn up. Without this the impasse would never have opened but as it is they both let Caesario in, and the complex figure can take the impasse into him(her)self, intensifying it into unendurable contradiction magically released by the appearance of Sebastian who comes on stage as a precipitation of the male in the figure (this climax forced significantly by the duel), releasing the female, Viola.

These reflections on reason invoke a shadowy counterpart, religion, which though not a part of Viola's presence is certainly part of the play, if somewhat incongruously at first sight.

\*   \*   \*

> *Marry Sir, sometimes he is a kind of puritan.*
> (II.iii.140)

When Viola asks Feste 'Dost thou live by the tabor?' he replies 'No, sir, I live by the church' (III.i.1–3). This 'misprision' establishes a paradoxical relationship between Feste and the Church which is only one of a series of allusions the most familiar of which is Maria's account of Malvolio as 'some kind of a puritan'. He is no such thing, 'or anything constantly' (II.iii.146), but the remark arouses Sir Andrew's violent response:

> O, if I thought that, I'd beat him like a dog.
> (II.iii.141)

Later, when Sir Andrew is being encouraged to win Olivia's affections 'by some laudable attempt, either of valour or of policy', he replies:

> And't be any way, it must be with valour, for policy I
> hate: I had as lief be a Brownist as a politician.
> (III.ii.29–31)

The Brownists challenged the characteristic Anglican doctrine that every member of the Commonwealth (as Richard Hooker was to formulate the view) was a member of the Church of England. The true Church, the Brownists held, consisted only of the purest. Browne himself caused alarm by preaching to the itinerant jobless who gathered to sleep at the brick-kilns at Islington. His views, separating civil society and the Church would have left the state without divine sanction. More importantly, the Church in Browne's view, is exclusive, and denied to common access.

The Church lying behind such references, is fulfilling the same function as it does in Orlando's plea to the common humanity that binds him, Adam and Duke Senior and his followers in Arden:

> If ever you have look'd on better days;
> If ever been where bells have knoll'd to church;
> If ever sat at any good man's feast;

> If ever from your eyelids wip'd a tear,
> And know what 'tis to pity and be pitied.
> *(As You Like It*: II.vii.113–18)

The Duke replies point for point, a solemn remembrance of what Orlando has earlier called 'the antique world', and which Orlando contrasts with the present by saying to Adam:

> Thou art not for the fashion of these times,
> Where none will sweat but for promotion,
> And having that, do choke their service up
> Even with the having.
> (II.iii.59–62)

The Church forms part of a traditional life, together with revelry, however odd this may seem at first sight, exactly because they have been traditional 'competitors', as it were. They are old enemies, familiar antagonists, but they also share a concern with what might be called 'ultimate realities': they are ways of thinking and feeling that consider human existence absolutely and ultimately, rather than relatively and immediately. Viola's 'disponibilité' is not hostile to such ways of thinking, but as she displays the attitude it has more to do with the relative and the immediate. That is where she is most at home. She does not deny the absolute and ultimate, but they may have to be 'committed', deferred, perhaps perpetually. Importantly she belongs to neither aspect of the traditional life, and her whole disposition, while acknowledging what has been, does not tie one's action in the present to the past.

If it is in keeping for Feste to live 'by the church', it is not surprising that, when Sir Toby bursts out against Malvolio:

> Dost thou think because thou art virtuous there
> shall be no more cakes and ale?
> (II.iii.114–5)

Feste should add:

> Yes, by Saint Anne, and ginger shall be hot i' th' mouth
> too. (II.iii.116–17)

His oath, invoking the mother of the Blessed Virgin Mary, invokes a traditional religion in support of a traditional revelry.

What the Puritans were threatening was the truce that had been established between the traditions of the Church and those other traditions that persisted in the practices of pastime to which the Puritans took exception, and which were outlawed by the Parliamentary Commonwealth. The Church's procedure had been to 'Christianize' pagan festivals such as Yule and other stations in the progress of the year, turning them into holydays, transferring their meaning. Activists such as Philip Stubbes, however, were claiming that the festivities retained an objective meaning that could not be transferred: such rituals still invoked and worshipped gods that had been supposed to have been exposed and overthrown.[31]

I think it is possible to see in Sir Toby what is perhaps still clearer in Falstaff, the condition towards which revelry 'harks back', the triumph and despair of chaos. This is not to claim that Shakespeare meant to point a moral. The fallacy of authorial intention has been well exposed by a consensus which stretches from the New Critics to the post-structuralists. The movement of the play, though, clearly shows Sir Toby being brought into the composition achieved by the marriages at the close of the play. During the play he has spoken for an increasingly reckless irresponsibility. His opening words include the pregnant sentence 'I am sure care's an enemy to life' (I.iii.2–3). 'Care' figures in *As You Like It* in the wrestler Charles's phrase, used of Duke Senior and his followers, that they 'fleet the time carelessly'. 'Careless' can mean something like 'clumsy' or 'inattentive', or, differently, 'unworried', 'untroubled by concern'. One can be 'careless' because slovenly, or because fortunate. Martin Heidegger makes 'care' in its double sense of anxiety and concern, or looking after, the core of his understanding of human being. I would like to bear that in mind as defining 'responsible' human being.

I do not mean to imply approval, only to suggest that human being can be conceived of as answering a call, or else as involved with itself. Broadly speaking, the point of view outlined by Nietzsche in his account of the Dionysian dismisses the idea of a 'call' and the point of view outlined by Gabriel Marcel, or Martin Heidegger considers human existence as 'called'. If this call is heeded, then the word 'responsible' is justified. Those who think there is a call will think both those who seem to ignore this call and those who deny its reality alike 'irresponsible'.

'Care' does not of itself imply a call. It is quite possible to see 'care' isolated in an empty universe, as for example, the Chinese poet Li Tai Po did in the poem set by Mahler as the first movement of *The Song of the Earth*. He conjures the extraordinary paradox of the Dionysian in the phrase 'the song of care shall sound laughing in your soul'. It is this extraordinary blitheness in the midst of despair that Yeats's wondering phrases at the close of 'Lapis Lazuli' both celebrate and find almost incredible:

> their eyes,
> Their ancient glittering eyes, are gay.

This is not the view of *Twelfth Night*. Sir Toby presses towards it, and we must see that he is doing this in phrases such as 'I am sure care's an enemy to life', or his reply to Sir Andrew's inquiry later in the same scene 'Shall we set about some revels?', 'What shall we do else? were we not born under Taurus?' (I.iii.133–6). Sir Andrew questions the astrological reference, getting it wrong. Sir Toby also is wrong. The Arden editors comment, 'it is characteristic of Sir Andrew to err involuntarily and of Sir Toby to do so perversely'. This is quite right.[32]

His perverseness, however, tends towards a condition of chaos he is not in the end able to enter. At the last moment Olivia intervenes, saves Malvolio, and the last act of marriages diverts and contains the Dionysian. The Apolline steps in, rather as Hymen is seen to in *As You Like It*, and recasts the world of cruelty and violence and self-destruction into the ordered form of responsible dream.

Viola's 'disponibilité' has been the key to this, waking Olivia out of 'care' into 'care', self-regarding grief into responsible concern. Viola's 'openness' without preconceptions is a feeling that the best can be made of things, that one can make shift. She is the ideal inhabitant of a world of change in which the old verities have lost their stability. The implicit alignment of the Church and revelry implies a traditional 'antique' world, which both *As You Like It* and *Twelfth Night* acknowledge has passed away. Both plays celebrate its beauty , but the sense that it has gone is much deeper and stronger in the later play.

*As You Like It* ends with the restitution of the Duke, while *Twelfth Night* ends with the establishment of the new element, Viola, in a courtly life which, it is quite clear, could not have survived without her being thrown into it. Both plays end with an unresolved element, Jacques and Malvolio: both plays end with an epilogue, spoken by Rosalind, sung by Feste. The differences are not slight. Jacques declines to join in: Malvolio swears revenge. All the 'puritanical' opposition to traditional structures in the Elizabethan world, some of it opportunistic, much of it principled, seems to become focused in him. The play makes it clear that he at least is only an opportunist:

'The devil a Puritan that he is, or anything constantly, but a time-pleaser' (II.iii.146–7), but this 'puritanical' opposition eventually formed part of the parliamentary revolution that overthrew Charles I, dismantled the Church of England, outlawed revelry and closed the theatres.[33] Malvolio is a more serious figure than Jacques, and his threat of revenge is a burst of anger quite as powerful as Sir Toby's outburst against him in the name of 'cakes and ale', and, historically speaking, much more effective.

The last word though is left to Feste. His whimsical, sad song is an invocation of the bleak silence of chaos towards which the Dionysian tends.[34] 'That's all one' is the only reflection left as the rain dissolves all difference and struggle. If Schopenhauer is right, song is the form of the tension between frustrated will and a contemplation of the ideal to which the singer is drawn in spite of himself. The nothingness of chaos appearing as an idea attracts a contemplation which temporarily and intermittently disarms the sense of baffled desire. The strange glee of Yeats's figures offers one image of the way in which we might take Feste's epilogue. Spoken by and for the players:

> But that's all one, our play is done,
> And we'll strive to please you every day.
> (V.i.406–7)

it is an affirmation of the Dionysian tendency of play itself, turning everything inside out, like a 'chev'ril glove', subverting the structures of difference the Apolline produces, straining towards the triumph of chaos, while at the same time it acknowledges the dependency of play. Play is powerless to bring chaos about: chaos is a silent circumscription, a perpetual presence (which is an absence), the knowledge of which prevents the dreamer from forgetting that it is dream. Unable to break out of the dream into nothingness or to lose himself in the dream, Feste dreams sadly, taking what comfort there is in the reflection that dream is just whimsy. It is dream that stands between the dreamer and the supreme, though final, triumph of chaos. It is dream that, however temporarily, defers the encroachment of chaos, the end of the world, as Eliot put it, 'not with a bang but a whimper'. It is a small comfort that this dream is just whimsy, a shadow-show the stage can conjure up at will.

It is worth reflecting that Nietzsche's famous affirmation 'It is a dream! I want it to go on' is not the conclusion drawn by the play. Yeats may be right about the Tragedies, but the Comedies tend in another direction altogether. In its play with social mobility and a changing world, the play leaves us with an ambiguous shrug, 'but that's all one, our play is done'. It is outside the remit of play to comment, it seems. The task of play is to 'strive to please you every day'. Perhaps the deepest implication here is that if chaos is just around the corner, not triumphantly achieved by your will but eroding and unmasking the shadow-plays of your will, then that is your own fault and your own look out: the players are only your servants, giving you what you wanted, what you will.

# 7
# Afterword: 'For the Rain it Raineth Every Day'

Whilst in Part I we have been concerned to exploit perspectives deriving from psychoanalysis and social anthropology, and in Part III we shall concentrate on semiotics of performance, I have chosen to discuss these two plays in terms of a kind of philosophical mythology. Courtly life as John Turner has presented it is the specific form of life within which tensions and anxieties and hopes that recur in other forms, our own included, must be discussed if we are to pay the right kind of attention (that is, the most fruitful) to the plays. For Graham Holderness, courtly life is a particular signifying system, creating its meanings, organizing its discourse, upon lines proper to itself, and of which the plays are particular *performances* through which we can see this signifying system with peculiar clarity. I have tried to explore particular significations, to get the poetry to unfold itself, to yield sets of meanings of which I believe our cultural tradition only became conscious some while after the conditions these meanings attempted to grasp had become established.

There is no contradiction between our perspectives, and indeed each could be applied to any of the plays we have looked at, in principle at least. We have divided our work as we have done, however, because we recognized the peculiar appropriateness of such modes of inquiry to the plays we chose individually. The Court and its life as that appears in *Love's Labour's Lost* and *Hamlet* is strongly characterized by 'competition' in the double sense upon which we have expanded, which focuses attention on the struggles of individual subjectivities to make sense of their world and headway in it; *As You Like It* and *Twelfth Night* develop a dramatic poetry rich with heady suggestions of idealized worlds of the imagination; *The Tempest* and *The Winter's Tale* foreground the dramatic process itself, *performance*, to a greater extent than the earlier plays. This, we believe, must be considered in the light of the changed status of Shakespeare's company and, more widely, in the light of the transformation of the Court and courtly life itself under James VI and I. I have tried to show that such a transformation is prefigured in *Twelfth Night* in a deep metaphor in, and of, the play, of transition.

*The Tempest* makes more of the storm and the shipwreck than *Twelfth Night* does, but the later play thrusts its survivors into the orderly world of the Mage, Prospero. In *Twelfth Night* the twins are separated and cast adrift in a world in which authority hangs suspended in the gap between the two houses in which gap a loose collection of friends, servants, and retainers gathers to while away the time. The twins are re-united, and the gap between the houses is closed (by the reunited twins): the subversive upstart is sent packing, and the unruly revellers are tamed. Yet the movement of the play is one which takes its audience from one set of understandings to another, from a world we come to see as an 'old' world into a new one. It is not a play, like *As You Like It*, which returns us to its beginnings, giving us a sense of an order restored. The whole mood of the play is one of lassitude, loss and poignancy, of surfeit and of want.

I may seem to have conducted my discussion at quite a high level of abstraction from historical particularity, but that is because I want to uncover some particularities which our time is not especially equipped to grasp. The play is at home in a world of traditional revelry, a form of life composed of the rich deposits of symbolic language and gesture, a 'restricted' rather than an 'elaborated' code, to use the terms (originating in the work of Basil Bernstein on language) as they are developed by Mary Douglas in *Natural Symbols* (1970). But that is exactly the world that is being lost under the pressures that issue in the court life of James VI and I on the one hand, and in the mounting confidence and disaffection of Parliament on the other. James's court life devotes itself to the development of the much more 'elaborated' dramatic form of the Masque, with its theatrical 'realism', while Parliament falls increasingly under the influence of the Puritan reformers who want to suppress traditional revelry altogether.

The later years of Elizabeth's court are marked by tension and watchfulness as the ageing Gloriana became more conscious of her declining powers, and as those around her became aware of this as well, with feelings of compassion, or of ambition, or of alarm. The spaciousness of Duke Senior's court, 'under the greenwood tree', reflects Orlando's 'antique world', and Spenser's *Faerie Queene* as well. The anxiety and caprice of Duke Frederick's court reflects the contemporary actuality. *Twelfth Night* is a rich, melancholy dream of idleness and self-indulgence, reflecting more the lucent syrop of Spenser's style than the virtue it depicts. It is a dream gone on too long, to overripeness. As the dream, it muffles an anxiety, a foreboding of blankness, an unknowable future: as a play it shows a lively girl who commits to Time what she cannot arrange, and who copes with it when it comes up, and who restores to life a man gone sick in his desires. It is my belief that the dream lingers beyond the play.

I have presented the end of *Twelfth Night* as an impasse. Powerless to wake out of the dream, powerless to develop its Dionysian energies towards extinction, the dreamer is depicted as being subtly enchanted by the Apolline smoothness, musing on chaos, softly conscious of the pain of desire. There is, mythologically speaking, nowhere to go: this is a boundary with nothing beyond, an end. There is no 'outside' the dream, just an incomplete incorporation into it, a sense of dissatisfaction with it, which is enough to weaken the spell to the point at which its nature as spell becomes clear. This approaches the originary moment imaged by Nietzsche as the rabble following in the train of the intoxicated God, singing their misery and their desire. Later (in the myth, which is only contingently related to actual history) the Dionysian impulse proper will break out in a frenzy of rage and cruelty, a savage hymn of disappointment. At the end of *Twelfth Night* the players shrug: they gave the audience what it wanted, an illusion, but for the players it has been what it always is, an induction into that margin of wakefulness which is the momentary realization that it is dream which precedes extinction and the silence of chaos.

This is the player's consciousness of play, offered to the consumer as an additional, luxurious, poignancy, another layer of illusion, but it has offered a glimpse of a possibility of dissent, a mode of thought which holds itself apart internally, like Kierkegaard's 'Knight of Faith', outwardly indistinguishable from any other person, but inwardly utterly unlike any other, one of a secret fellowship of isolates who are 'for other than for dancing measures', but who are sufficiently conscious of the dangers of posturing that they can smile at Malvolio's pretensions.

This is perhaps the only kind of dissent possible in the sort of court life established by James: claustrophobic, centred on the intimacy of the King's Bedchamber, concentrating courtly life in Whitehall by a kind of morbid gravity, and drawing play into its confines. *The Tempest* and *The Winter's Tale* are courtly plays in a way quite different from *Twelfth Night* or *As You Like It*. The Dionysian impulse, entranced, like the Blues singer, or the Tango dancer, knows that the only way out is self-destructive rage, and consoles itself with a sweet and bitter poetry of hopeless desiring until the time should come, if at all, when enough is enough. The question we will now be looking at is not 'what do these plays mean?' (to put it crudely), but 'how do they mean?', and not only because we have shifted our point of view, although we have, but because we have seen that we have had to, to take new conditions into account, just as these plays do.

# Part III:
# Late Romances: Magic, Majesty and Masque

*Graham Holderness*

# 8
# Introduction: Theatre and Court

### STORM IN A TEA-CUP

> I do wish I waited now in Her Majesty's Presence Chamber, with ease at my board, and rest in my bed. I am pushed from the shore of comfort, and know not where the winds and waves of a court will bear me.[1]

Robert Cecil's elegy for lost privilege, written a few weeks after the accession of James I, may be read as a characteristic contemporary lament over the vicissitudes of fortune, formulated in the conventional metaphoric terms of exile and exposure to the elements on the open sea. In the culture of an island nation it is natural to expect the perils of the sea to figure the experience of human vulnerability, from Anglo-Saxon poetry to the nineteenth-century nonconformist hymn. Cecil's formulation is however rather more specific in its metaphorical juxtaposition of the joys of court favour with the anguish of political excommunication. Again, the habit of linking the imagery of courtly participation with the symbolism of exile on the sea is a traditional mode of the English political imagination, traceable at least as far back as the Old English poems *The Wanderer* and *The Seafarer*. The emotional and psychological benefits of court society are of course bound up with conventions of social status and membership: they consist of an experience of belonging. Hence a natural punishment for the betrayal of trust and intimacy such membership entails is banishment. In Britain banishment means crossing the sea: so the ocean becomes a symbolic frontier separating membership from exile, community from isolation, the bliss of favour from the anguish of dispossession. The Anglo-Saxon poets located their radiant visions of an earlier courtly society – the warmth and comfort of the hall, the reciprocal pleasures of intimacy with the lord, the ritual exchanges of duty for favour, tribute for gift – within vivid dramatisations of the solitude and separation of exile, always embodied in the imagery of a storm at sea.[2] It is precisely this tradition that Cecil invokes, imagining himself as banished – 'pushed out from the shores of comfort'– and consigned to the implacable violence of the sea, to be driven in directionlesss wandering by the arbitrary will of wind, wave and tempest.

The sea is not being used here then simply to symbolize the generality of human suffering: in Cecil's language the symbolism of the ocean is brought into court, and the court becomes the microcosmic site of universal peril and exposure. How appropriate is this comparison, given that a court is not governed by the arbitrary and uncontrollable power of the elements, but by the rational will of the sovereign? Were the servants of the crown quite so helplessly the victims of elemental exposure, since the drifts and wrecks of court life were entirely within the control of the monarch? Any such reservation could in the seventeenth century be automatically neutralized by the systematic strategic identification of king and god: 'the state of monarchy is the supremest thing upon earth', as James himself observed: 'for kings are not only God's lieutenants upon earth and sit upon God's throne, but even by himself they are called Gods'.[3] The apparently arbitrary disturbances and vicissitudes of courtly society could be seen analogically as parallel to the elemental disruptions of the universe: meaningless only to the blindness or partial vision of suffering men; subject in a larger scheme of things to the providential dispensation and rational will of a divine sovereign. In that altered perspective both cosmic and courtly tumult become visible as intelligible and not without purpose. 'Storms' as George Herbert said of his god, 'are the triumphs of his art'.[4] Thus the suffering subject could be reconciled to the justice of his deprivation by this potent system of imaginative perception: the tumult and tempest of courtly society were no different from the storms of life itself; the subject's lot was subjection to the power of their author. For the king could pacify as well as provoke elemental disturbance: could not only banish and recall, but could control the very conditions of the subject's suffering. After the death of Buckingham in 1628, the Countess of Devonshire recorded (somewhat prematurely) that Charles I had succeeded in imposing on his court 'a great calm'.[5]

Once housed however within the discursive confines of court society, the imagery of maritime danger inevitably shifts its meaning.

Despite the enormous historical project of ideological investment aimed at naturalizing the power of the king and the authority of the court, metaphor itself, in its characteristically slippery, double-edged, riddling fashion, created the possibilities for new insight and alternative perspective. When such self-evident contradictions are fused into a metaphoric unit, they can paradoxically produce the conditions for a general calling into question of the pervasive strategies of elision and identification, whereby the court figures as a microcosmic model of the universe. Metaphor both fuses and discloses, articulates and prises apart such contradictions, likening and estranging sameness with difference. The comparison of court to ocean paradoxically opens up a fissure between court and universe, and renders possible a glimpsing of the court as an unrepresentative and even unnatural structure. As we shall see in the following pages, the kind of drama with which we are dealing – and indeed the very culture of which that drama was a constitutive part – can be seen to have operated with a similar ambivalent and double-edged power.

## 'PRESENTED AT WHITEHALL'

If Cecil's anxieties derived from a fear of losing power, they were groundless: since his retention as chief adviser to the crown was one of James' diplomatic concessions to continuity and the status quo. A matter of a few weeks subsequent to this confiding of grievance, Cecil as Keeper of the Privy Seal received a royal warrant instructing him to prepare letters patent for the acting company thitherto known as The Lord Chamberlain's Men. The formal patent licensed and authorized

> ... these our servants Lawrence Fletcher, William Shakespeare, Richard Burbage, Augustyne Phillipes, John Heninges, Henrie Condell, William Sly, Robert Armyn, Richard Cowly, and the rest of their associates, freely to use and exercise the art and faculty of playing comedies, tragedies, histories, interludes, morals, pastorals, stage plays and such others like as they have already studied or hereafter shall use or study, as well for the recreation of our loving subjects as for our solace and pleasure when we shall think good to see them during our pleasure ... [6]

The familiar phrases are those of the earliest Elizabethan patents: James' warrant was in one sense a confirmation of existing Elizabethan relationships and privileges. Under Elizabeth's arrangements acting companies had originally been assigned, nominally at least, to the protection and patronage of a great magnate such as the Earl of Leicester, or a major court official such as the Lord Chamberlain, until the formation of the Queen's Majesty's Servants in 1583. James I immediately on his accession appropriated the three leading companies – the Admiral's, Worcester's and the Lord Chamberlain's – as personal servants to his queen, to his heir apparent Prince Henry, and to himself. Thus in 1603, Shakespeare's company became the King's Men, His Majesty's Servants, and entered into the closest possible relationship an acting company could possess with the monarch and with the monarch's court. Furthermore, each member of the King's Men named in the patent was appointed to a specific court position, that of a Groom of the Chamber. Thus acknowledged as the chief national exponents of the acting profession, these nine worthies had indeed travelled a long distance, since the 1572 statute against vagrancy, the 'Acte for the Punishment of Vacabondes', had included 'Common Players' among its list of masterless and landless men. Shakespeare and his colleagues had been elevated to the position of royal servants, members of the King's household. They wore the King's livery and received the royal protection: whether they were performing in public 'within their now usual house called the Globe', or offering private entertainment for the monarch's 'solace and pleasure', all the King's subjects were instructed to see them well used, and honoured not only with the traditional respect due to their professional status – 'such former courtesies as hath been given to men of their place and quality', but with more particular marks of the royal benevolence – 'what further favour you shall show to these our servants for our sake'.

Important as this royal appropriation of the drama is, it should not lead us to exaggerate the exact status of the King's Men within the structure of James' court. The position of Groom could represent a highly responsible and politically important office; a more personal status within the sovereign's domestic polity; or a purely formal status in a large and impersonal royal entourage, depending on the specific type of court organisation favoured by the monarch of the day. In the Elizabethan court, Grooms who were personal attendants of the Privy Chamber were, like the Gentlemen of the

## Introduction: Theatre and Court 133

Chamber, personal servants of the Queen rather than figures at the centre of contemporary politics. The Elizabethan Privy Chamber was employed as a strict barrier between the monarch's private life and the public arena of politics: the task of carefully and jealously executing the rules of *entrée* or access to the Queen's person fell upon these trusted personal servants. Those with most intimate access to the sovereign's person were of course women, and Elizabeth exercised strict control over their involvement in politics. Thus the 'private' space of a monarch like Elizabeth was not strictly speaking a department of government (except in a purely personal sense) or an arena of political activity; the Queen preserved a sharp distinction between her private and her political activities, the proper location of which was the public Council Chamber. Elizabeth's chambers were staffed by a small handful of 'grooms', who were not by virtue of that office of any political importance.

James' conception of an appropriate court organisation was profoundly different from that of his predecessor. As James VI he had presided over a relatively small court, but one that was run on French rather than English lines. The most significant contrast lay in the institution of 'the Bedchamber' as a space of real political importance. Within this model the staff of the Bedchamber were not politically neutral women or disciplined personal body servants, but the key personnel of government and politics, permitted the most intimate access to the king's person. James staffed this important department initially with his Scottish entourage, subsequently with acquired 'favourites' who enacted a significant passage from household servant to great public personality:

> Cupbearers like George Villiers (later favourite and Duke of Buckingham), Carvers like Sir John Digby (later Vice-Chamberlain and Earl of Bristol) or sewers like Sir Thomas Overbury (later the favourite's favourite) went on to make spectacularly successful court careers. (Cuddy, 1987, p. 184)

This new intimacy of access and ostensibly 'participatory' monarchy conferred power only on a small elite of royal favourites, and correspondingly alienated hitherto important departments of government such as the Council. The Privy Chamber became a political arena, since those outside the charmed circle of personal retainers had to work to insert their supporters into that secondary entourage; and it became, as it had not been under Elizabeth, a notorious site of faction and intrigue.

> With the institution of the Bedchamber, even the inner councillors no longer had an automatic claim to the nearest access to the monarch; and even if the *entrée* were granted, it was enjoyed in much greater measure by the Bedchamber's staff. And they – all practised operators in Scots politics and some James's companions since his childhood – were well able to take advantage of the fact. Now . . . the Bedchamber did possess special advantages of contact with the king; Bedchamber and Council were now separate entities with, for the most part, separate membership; Council and minister now revolved in a different orbit from the king and Bedchamber. (Cuddy, 1987, p. 197)

With this shift of the centre of power at court, the Privy Chamber experienced a simultaneous expansion and formalisation, with many of its staff adopting a more ceremonial role, attending the king in his semi-public dining and entertainment. The Gentlemen of the Chamber under the Stuarts regularly complained that their position gave them no real access to the king, and therefore no effective influence in the court. The vast increases in numbers of staff indicates the dilution of their status and position: by 1625 the handful of Elizabethan Gentlemen had been augmented by fifty supernumerary 'Gentlemen Extaordinary', and by 1638 this number had risen to two hundred. The Grooms fared worse than the gentlemen: the Elizabethan incumbents were dismissed and replaced by men of markedly lower status – such as, for example, that 'Common Player' from Stratford whose career is our subject.[7]

It should be clear from the above account that the position of Groom in the court of James I had no political significance and no particularly intimate access to the king. The King's Men, if they attended at court beyond their commissions to perform at the king's request ('when we shall think good to see them during our pleasure') would have taken their relatively humble places with large numbers of purely ceremonial courtiers. No lofty political ambitions would therefore have been fulfilled by this accession to a nominal court position which actually entailed little more than inclusion in a large entourage. Nevertheless, the personal significance of such an elevation for a man like Shakespeare must have been considerable; and the significance for an acting company of this royal appropriation can hardly be exaggerated. The new relationship was not especially beneficial financially, any more than court patronage had been under Elizabeth: as Grooms of the Chamber the King's Men

## Introduction: Theatre and Court

were not feed, and their services as players were not retained by salary but paid for by the performance. Four-and-a-half yards each of red cloth for livery may have been the only gratuity they enjoyed at the King's hands. What they did enjoy was prestige, protection, and the particular opportunity of performing at court.

> In the ten years before they became the King's company, their known performances at court average about three a year; in the ten years after they attained their new service their known performances at court average about thirteen a year, more than those of all other London companies combined.[8]

One of those 'known performances' took place on 1 November 1611, and will now concern us directly: 'Hallowmas Night was presented at Whitehall before the kinges Maiestie a play called the Tempest'.[9]

# 9

# *The Tempest*: Spectacles of Disenchantment

### 'HIS MAJESTY'S SERVANTS'

We begin therefore with direct evidence that *The Tempest* was performed as a piece of court entertainment in the presence of the king himself. Eighteen months later the play was included, together with *The Winter's Tale*, in a programme of fourteen plays performed at court as part of the elaborate festivities preceding the marriage of James's daughter Elizabeth to the Elector Palatine. The presence within *The Tempest* of a formal wedding masque has led to speculation that the play may have been targeted specifically at this later occasion, and that the masque may possibly have been a later incorporation. That hypothesis is unnecessary, as a number of scholars have shown: but the theory testifies to a real awareness that this play can be located with unprecedented certainty into the cultural structures of the Jacobean court; and that within those structures it may well have experienced a dependence or contextualization on significant seasonal dates or important festival occasions that would have been quite irrelevant to its other life in the day-to-day provision of dramatic entertainment at the Globe or the Blackfriars.

By 1611 the King's Men were performing publicly at the Globe ('their usual house') during the summer months of the year; publicly during the winter season at the so-called 'private' indoor playhouse of the Blackfriars; and 'privately', by special commission, before the king and court. The same plays (though we do not know whether in the same form) appear to have been capable of transgressing these cultural divisions and entertaining the broad social spectrum of the Globe audience, the narrower social elite of the private playhouse, and the cream of the social hierarchy assembled at court. That fact in itself forms a powerful piece of evidence supporting the old theory of an inclusive Renaissance 'common culture', linking monarch, nobility, emergent bourgeoisie and urban populace, if not in actual social contact, at least in the shared experience of a common cultural repertory. Our contemporary acknowledgement of the depth of social division in Jacobean society, and our awareness of its art as deriving from a much more fragmented cultural configuration, would induce us to assume that the plays were probably adapted for performance in different contexts. But while it is obviously the case that plays existed, and have been transmitted to us, in remarkably varied textual forms, there is no hard evidence to suggest that the King's Men tailored their wares specifically for the robust appetites of the many-headed multitude, or the refined tastes of courtly society. A Quarto text of *The Tempest* lacking the Masque of Juno and Ceres would be a nice piece of evidence: but unfortunately for this theory, such confirmation does not exist.

A more persuasive argument rests on the assumption that the development of Shakespeare's dramatic works enacts a trajectory paralleling the fortunes of his own acting company, and of the acting profession in general: a historical development tracing the evolution of a highly successful and socially-recognized profession of artists from the loose combinations of theatrical entrepreneurs and common players who from the 1570s onwards were obliged by the hostility of state authorities to construct their playhouses outside the boundaries of the city. As our particular set of emphases has shown, this configuration very quickly breaks down if the courtly character and context of a very early play like *Love's Labour's Lost*, which like *The Tempest* certainly enjoyed a performance both royal and seasonal – having been played, according to its 1598 title-page, 'before her Highness this last Christmas' – is properly acknowledged. On the other hand it is certainly worth considering what kind and degree of influence the immediately contingent context of commissioned courtly performance may have exercised on the *The Tempest*, at least as we know it from its textual inclusion in the *First Folio* of 1623.

It is certainly arguable that *The Tempest* bears many significant traces of that courtly context, and for that reason can be differentiated sharply from the bulk of the Shakespearean *oeuvre*, which appears to fit more naturally into the more open, common space of the public playhouse. Though the play was categorized generically as a comedy in the *First Folio*, modern criticism has found it necessary to re-define its genre as romance: an acknowledgement that it has as much in common with the fashionable Italianate romance and tragi-comedy of Beaumont and Fletcher (who also wrote for the King's Men) as it has with other examples of Shakespearean comedy. Just as (Leonard Tennenhouse has shown[10]) the differences between Shakespeare's *Henry VIII* and his earlier cycles of history plays can be explained only intertextually in terms of a contrast between the generic composition of historical drama in, respectively, the 1590s and 1613; so Shakespeare's 'late romances' need to be seen not as the mellow autumnal flowering of a great poetic vision, but in relation to the currently dominant dramatic forms of romance, tragi-comedy, pastoral and masque. Notwithstanding the continuity of Globe performances, these generic traces link the play to a different kind of theatre, a different social composition of audience, different dramatic conventions and different criteria of artistic taste.

A number of internal features suggest that the play was written into a discursive field characterized by a predominantly educated, refined and sophisticated cultural context. To start with, the play unusually observes the classical unities of time and space. The entire action of *The Tempest* is confined to the perimeters of the desert island, and to the space of one day: and since the romance plot sprawls in a leisurely fashion across territories and times, that limitation entails a considerable amount of retrospective narrative filling, and an unusual attentiveness to the passage of time. *The Tempest* would have successfully met the stringent conditions laid down by neo-classical critics, and polemically defended, with great vigour and within the period in question, by classicists like Ben Jonson.

Furthermore, the general level of classical allusion and dependence in *The Tempest* has been regarded as unusually explicit and of unusual significance. The key sources here are Virgil's *Aeneid* and Ovid's *Metamorphoses*; and the principal argument is that these internal references to works of the classical past exemplify more than passing allusions, but rather constitute a specific engagement (in the case of the *Aeneid*, a confrontation) with the structure and meaning of the earlier works.[11]

By far the most important internal feature connecting *The Tempest* with the Jacobean court is the masque of Juno and Ceres staged by Prospero to celebrate the betrothal of Ferdinand and Miranda, and to entertain the principals of that engagement. Whatever plebeian origins the masque form may have had in popular festivities and seasonal revelry, by 1611 it was, *par excellence*, the distinctive form of court entertainment. The inclusion of parallel stylized pageant-like shows within the body of a drama can again be traced in Shakespeare's work as far back as *Love's Labour's Lost*: but there is no precise parallel to the completeness and formality of the 'masque-within-a-play' presented in Act 4:1. Although Shakespeare seems never to have written a formal court masque, his company had plenty of experience in presentations of the form. The King's Men certainly performed the professional parts in Ben Jonson's masques from 1612 onwards, and it is hard to believe that they had not undertaken the same duties prior to this documentation. *The Winter's Tale* (which was running at the Globe in May 1611) contains a dance of satyrs which parallels closely the satyric revels of Ben Jonson's *Masque of Oberon*, performed at court on New Year's Day of the same year; and the company of 'Saltiers' in Shakespeare's pastoral romance is advertised as having 'danced before the king' (IV.iv.338). Stephen Orgel has suggested that the masque of Ceres and Juno bears obvious resemblances to contemporary wedding masques by Jonson and Campion (Orgel, 1987, p. 46).

This obvious point of contact with the specifically courtly form of the masque can be broadened to a consideration of whether the play was influenced more broadly by the masque form. The scenic and pictorial effects required for a Jacobean performance – a sea, a shipwreck, a rocky coastline, a pastoral retreat or 'cell' – together with the illusionary nature of the play's many 'special effects' like vanishing banquets, may suggest that the conventions of the masque leaked out from its internalized location and coloured the character of the play as a whole. Many of the play's dialectical themes, such as the ritualized conflicts between sorcery and royal virtue, ignorance and enlightenment, fertility and virginity, can be closely paralleled by examples taken from contemporary masques proper.

We are now in a position to address our first large question of interpretation: what might *The Tempest* have meant to those courtly spectators who constituted its audience on Hallowmas night in 1611? what, can we conjecture, might James I have seen in the play? did *The Tempest*, in its court performances, function in a manner parallel or analogous to masques and other forms of specifically royal and courtly entertainment? Does this play-text, retrospectively re-read in that historical context of performance, deliver us a specifically *courtly* Shakespeare?

## 'BEFORE THE KING'S MAIESTIE'

The broad narrative framework of the play – that narrative line which we would probably find delineated in a source, if we could find one – is concerned with the standard political themes and controversies of the age: legitimacy and authority; usurpation, treachery and betrayal; loyalty and obedience; conspiracy and rebellion; the quasi-divine power of rulers, and their exercise of such power in the restoration of rights and the establishment of justice. The structure of political values problematized and resolved in the play can thus be related quite directly to the historical world in which the play had its origin.

If we pursue this narrative line through the play, it is possible to produce from its action a series of commonplace situations and exempla, all of which accord precisely with the dominant political ideology of the day. The play is concerned with usurpation, treachery, betrayal, rebellion, the deposition and restoration of a rightful ruler, the rupturing and re-establishment of a dynastic line. Tragedies of betrayal are enacted within royal families, specifically (as in *Hamlet*) between brothers. The family drama of sibling rivalry, with its contradictory exchanges of absolute trust and suspicious emulation, of unreciprocated loyalty and groundless enmity, is written large as violent political competition. The initial act of usurpation, in which Prospero is removed from his dukedom of Milan and banished by his treacherous younger brother, arises from the twin errors of absolute confidence and of ineffective authority: of trusting without limit and of ruling without power:

> *Pros.* The government I cast upon my brother,
> And to my state grew stranger, being transported
> And rapt in secret studies . . . and my trust,
> Like a good parent, did beget of him
> A falsehood in its contrary as great
> As my trust was . . .
> (I.ii.75–7,94–7)

The usurping brother Antonio enters a conspiratorial confederacy with the King of Naples, and with his military assistance engineers a coup. In return, Milan is ceded to Naples as a tributary dominion. Once stranded on the desert island however, the powerful king of

Naples becomes himself subject to precisely the same appetite for betrayal on the part of his own brother Sebastian. Antonio's usurpation is indeed the original sin of this moral pattern, since it took place within the civilized constraints, the organized reciprocities of trust and loyalty governing a sophisticated modern society, a Renaissance Italian city-state. Sebastian is lured into conspiracy by Antonio on a desert island in the empty ocean, a vacant space which simultaneously removes the restraints of civilization and enlarges the imagination to conceive of beautiful or of terrible possibilities. Where Gonzalo dreams of a Utopian commonwealth, Sebastian is possessed, like Macbeth, by the simplicity and ease of the 'one stroke' (II.i.290) which would make him King of Naples.

By this point in the action, the audience is well aware, the entire dénouement is held firmly within Prospero's grasp: his power both creates the conditions of Sebastian's attempted assassination, and aborts the conspiracy by awakening Gonzalo. In other words, Prospero is staging a re-enactment of the original conspiracy of which he was the victim – casting Alonso into an oblivious slumber akin to his own previous intellectual detachment and political torpor, and inflaming Sebastian with the temptations of opportunity that so completely seduced Antonio – but reconstructing the outcome so that no lasting harm is done, converting a potential historical tragedy into a comic resolution. That restrained and flexible manipulation of power is characteristic of Prospero's approach to what might otherwise have developed as a revenge tragedy. Although frequently possessed by fleeting fits of irrational rage, Prospero's characteristic activity is that of stage-managing events to produce an apportioning of justice, a rectification of wrongs enacted and suffered, and whatever stirrings of conscience and accessions of remorse the subjects of his moral manipulations can be persuaded to deliver. Though Prospero certainly inflicts punishment on his subject victims, their suffering is designed to be purgatorial and rehabilitative. Prospero's motives, though scarcely free from the emotion of revenge, could be defined as more firmly directed towards the objectives of punishment, reformation and restoration.

The latter ambition is probably the principal narrative resolution formulated within the play. For although the seminal and originating contestation of power that sets the scene for the play was enacted between members of a single generation, between brothers; the play focuses much more intensively on the younger generation, the generation of heirs, Ferdinand and Miranda. The ultimate effect of both conspiracies, if successful, would have been to supplant and dispossess the rightful heirs to Milan and Naples. The ultimate design of Prospero's machinations is to restore the legitimate line to each state, and furthermore to efface the contamination of treachery and usurpation colouring the previous relationship between the states, by uniting them into a single state under the joint sovereignty of the two espoused heirs.

Framed in the context of this bare narrative line, the figure of Prospero in *The Tempest* was presented to King James I and his court as a model ruler, combining the qualities of statesman, diplomat, philosopher and magician. Continually assailed by heinous acts of personal betrayal and organized conspiracy, perpetually confronted with mutiny and disobedience, treachery and rebellion, injustice and ingratitude: Prospero consistently maintains a carefully-poised diplomatic balance between righteous anger and divine forgiveness, the necessity of punishment and the desirability of reformation, the satisfaction of his personal wrongs and the safeguarding of the future interests of the commonwealth. Plays presented at court, however strongly influenced by the celebratory and panegyric form of the masque, cannot all have been read and interpreted in terms of the system of direct identification employed in the latter: presumably there was no especial inducement to encourage James to identify with the rulers portrayed in *Othello* and *The Winter's Tale*, both of which were presented in the festivities of 1613. The potentiality for some complex analogical relationship between player king and real king seems however in the case of *The Tempest* much more plausible a possibility. It seems highly unlikely, if this possibility of cross-reference (fundamental to the masque form) were available to the courtly spectators of 1611 and 1613, that the king would have been in any way displeased by this portrayal of an enlightened, educated, benevolent ruler, who is keenly attentive to the safeguarding of his own prerogative, takes a firm hand with resistance and rebellion, exercises great care over the diplomatic negotiation of royal marriages, and knows how to put on a good show to impress the guests at a state wedding.[12]

## ABSOLUTE MAGIC

A philosopher-king who together with his qualifications in the 'liberal arts' (I.ii.73) is also skilled in necromancy, and fully capable

## The Tempest: Spectacles of Disenchantment 143

of making a 'vassal' (I.ii.371-3) of a demonic pagan divinity, seems close enough to some aspects of James I to make the identification stick fairly easily. While these parallels have been abundantly acknowledged in *Tempest* criticism, it has not been sufficiently recognized that the mythological encounters between a magus-monarch and a range of supernatural powers dramatized or narrated in *The Tempest*, belong to a very widespread tradition of court entertainments enjoyed by absolutist rulers throughout Renaissance Europe. A justifiable preoccupation with the strikingly innovative formal achievements of the Jacobean masques should not induce us to ignore the general correspondences between (on the one hand) the mythographies and narrative conventions of masques and masque-like plays, and (on the other) those of the many more loosely-organized shows, pageants, ritual games, mock tournaments, *ballets de cours* which constituted the characteristic cultural activity of sixteenth- and seventeenth-century courts throughout the states of Europe. Here too the romance heritage, often mingled with classical materials, witnessed a remarkable flowering. We tend to think of romantic courtly games as largely to do with chivalry and with courtly love: or in other words with the staging of formal games and dramatized contests in which the emulative competitions of the court aristocracy could be ritually conducted; and with the construction of an elaborate decorative framework in which sexual relationships could be assimilated to the dominant values of that predominantly masculine contest. But there were also many entertainments centred more firmly around the ruler rather than the nobility, and designed principally to give shape to, and to provide compelling images for, the notion (or the reality) of divine, magical sovereignty. These tended also to employ the romance images of knights errant and imprisoned ladies and gothic castles, of necromancers and sorceresses and transformations, of imprisonment by spell and liberation by enchantment. The structural essence of their mythography is the contest of opposed and countervailing supernatural powers, usually formulated as a clash between black and white forms of magic, between a powerful sorcerer of evil propensities, and a necromantically-skilled chivalric hero. As Stuart Clark[13] has shown, many such entertainments, like the masques, involved the ruler himself in playing the role of the white enchanter, the heroic magus. The purpose of the mythic narrative was always to provide an opportunity for the exercise and demonstration of magical powers employed by the ruler for the benefit of state and people, and against the evil power of a demonic magician and his satanic creatures. Thus the evil sorcerer would be seen imprisoning or confining by enchantment innocent and vulnerable knights and ladies: often, like Circe, transforming them into beasts or monsters; often, like Sycorax in *The Tempest*, confining them in rocks or trees. The resolution of such mythic narratives would entail the defeat of the sorcerer, the breaking of enchantments and the liberation of captive subjects by the chivalric prowess and benevolent magic of the sovereign necromancer.

The myths and narrative structures of such 'court theatre' are seen by historians as coded expressions of particular forms of political power:

> Over and over again, absolute rulers were depicted as breakers of enchantments, freeing those in the grip of magical metamorphosis or illusion, defeating the magicians and witches responsible and negating their demonic powers. However fanciful this may seem, it was a natural, indeed a necessary reflection of their rulership. For absolute monarchs were divine, and the one thing that could therefore be expected of them was the working of wonders – they were thaumaturgical kings, whose gifts were authenticated in competition with the only really powerful rival thaumaturgy known in Christian political ideology – that of demonism. It was royal thaumaturgy, then, which was celebrated in this important motif of court theatre – celebrated in images of power which were themselves powerful.[14]

The magical powers exercised by Prospero in *The Tempest* – the provocation and allaying of storms, the delivering of shipwreck victims from the perils of the sea, the liberation by 'disenchantment' of a spirit imprisoned by a sorceress – would actually have seemed quite familiar to anyone acquainted with the common substance of seventeenth-century European court theatre. And such myths would have been understood, if Stuart Clark is correct, not as entertaining fantasies but as substantive contributions to a material ideology: to those real and powerful forms of belief that attributed divine status and thaumaturgical powers to political sovereignty.

*The Tempest* could thus be regarded as having more than an internalized court masque in common with the cultural forms of seventeenth-century royal absolutism: with that broad range of court entertainments designed to celebrate, endorse and affirm the authority, legitimacy and power of the monarchy. But it is of course the masque that represents the purest example of this kind of celebratory court theatre. An ancient and primitive dramatic form revolutionized by the most sophisticated cultural technology available to the theatre of the day, the hugely expensive and enormously elaborate Jacobean masque could never have existed without royal and court patronage and resource provision on a vast scale. As we have already noted, the masque was an occasional and seasonal entertainment by contrast with the repertory of the public theatres: their single and unrepeatable performances can thus be related very specifically to functions and activities of the court. The masque was technically a kind of commissioned private entertainment, directed in some ways exclusively at the patron himself, the king – at a crucial point in Jonson's *Masque of Oberon*, screens opened to disclose an inner scene parted so narrowly as to deny anyone but the king a glimpse into the heart of that more removed mystery. With its framing proscenium arch, perspective sets, movable pictorial scenery, and technological special effects the masque was a theatre of illusion; with its dancing and song, its ritualized address to the monarch, its use of noble or royal personages as masquers, its incorporation of the court spectators into the culminating revels, it was a form of 'total theatre', designed to draw an audience into an exclusive and encompassing experience – the diametrical opposite, we might say of Brecht's *Verfremdungseffekt*. The masque form was, in the most absolute and literal sense, court theatre:

> Masques were essential to the life of the Renaissance court; their allegories gave a higher meaning to the realities of politics and power, their fictions created heroic roles for the leaders of society. Critics from Puritan times onward have treated them as mere extravagances, self-indulgent ephemera. But in the culture of the Medici grand dukes, the courts of Navarre, Anjou, Valois and Bourbon, the Venetian republic, the Austrian Archdukes, Henry VIII, extravagance in rulers was not a vice but a virtue, an expression of magnanimity, and the idealizations of art had power and meaning. This was the context in which James I, and above all, Charles I, saw their own courts.[15]

## COURT AND COUNTRY

It is actually a serious oversimplification to view the masque and similar forms of courtly entertainment simply as panegyric and compliment. As recent studies such as those of Orgel have shown, the culture of the court necessarily symbolized its internal conflicts as well as its formal structure; and there was ample space for disagreement about the political function of the court masque, as the famous quarrel of Ben Jonson and Inigo Jones testifies.[16] Nonetheless, the preceding observations are sufficient to indicate the existence within *The Tempest* of an interpretative possibility consonant with its presentation before James I as a specifically courtly form of entertainment.

This is an appropriate point in the argument to remind ourselves that the theatrical company which presented *The Tempest* at court, though identified as royal servants, and personally honoured with the status of courtiers, was an independent professional company which had come into existence by a series of economic and cultural developments that were in turn relatively independent of the court and of the monarchy. Clearly the formal and constitutional identification of the Elizabethan acting company as entertainers by appointment to the nobility (Leicester's, Sussex's, Warwick's, Essex's and Oxford's Men) and later to the Queen herself (the Queen's Majesty's Servants) was of enormous importance to the status and liberty of the companies themselves. And yet the companies were fully independent commercial organizations, necessarily dependent for their economic survival and profitability on the paying public audiences of both public and (later) 'private' theatres. The construction of the first purpose-built playhouse (Burbage's 'Theatre') forms the decisive break with surviving feudal relations: it freed the companies from economic dependence either on the patronage of the aristocracy or the goodwill of an undifferentiated populace gathered in village square or inn-yard. Run entirely on commercial lines, the playhouses admitted only those prepared to pay, and established the company on its own ground, playing to the open market and not solely at any individual's behest or invitation. From the 1570s the players were no longer itinerant pedlars or household retainers to the ruling class: they represented a new kind of cultural bourgeoisie, producing and selling a commodity for cash to those prepared to pay. The 'rise of the common player' had begun:

> Under the protective shield of their lord's badge, invoking a declining, obsolescent form of service, which was in their case

sometimes little better than a legal fiction, the players established themselves as purveyors of a commodity for which the general public was prepared regularly to put down its cash.[17]

The leading theatrical companies of course managed, and continued, to straddle the gaps between public playhouse, private theatre, aristocratic household and royal court: their dramatic activities comprehended that whole social range, and their diversified cultural interventions intermeshed on the common ground of the plays they presented. We know that *The Tempest* was performed at court. Dryden identified it as a Blackfriars play.[18] There is no direct evidence to confirm that it was played at The Globe: though since that theatre remained the 'usual house' of the King's Men, it seems very unlikely that it wasn't. *The Winter's Tale* certainly was, on 15 May 1611.[19] Stephen Orgel makes the telling observation that the 'special effects' employed in the masque of Juno and Ceres – the descending and ascending of gods – were devices (conjecturally) available from the 'hut' of the public playhouse, but not in court performances before Inigo Jones installed a fly gallery into his staging in the 1630s. For the purposes of this argument it is assumed that *The Tempest* was performed, in more or less the same textual shape, at all three venues – Globe, Blackfriars and Banqueting House; and the question I wish to address is whether, on the stage of the public playhouse, *The Tempest* might have offered its audience a different theatrical discourse and a different range of meanings.

## TEMPEST-TOSSED

The emphatic gesture of the play's title draws particular attention to the seminal and constitutive device of its opening. The eponymous tempest is the literal means by which the action of the play is contrived, an expository demonstration of the sovereign's necromantic powers, and a potent dramatic *coup de théâtre* – we can conjecture a certain degree of illusionistic realism in Jacobean performance, suggested by the stage direction *Enter Mariners wet* (I.i.50). The significance of the storm of course alters as the audience is offered three abruptly contrasting perspectives: the experiential view of the mariners and courtiers caught in its violence, the sympathetic and compassionate solicitude of a helpless bystander (Miranda), and the distanced, controlling vision of the magus whose power has provoked the elements in the first place. If we wish to see the play's theatrical structure in parallel with that of the court masque, the tempest is one of a series of 'anti-masques' (the drunken revelry of Caliban and his companions is another) designed to establish patterns of inversion, disturbance, disorder, which can then be observed resolving into justice, peace, harmony, when subjected to the irenic and cohesive powers of symbolized majesty and classical form. The wedding masque would in this model be regarded as the structural opposite of the tempest: its ritual formality setting to rights the disjointed elemental frame, its classical deities and allegorical personages re-populating a heaven previously fractured by climatic violence, its symbolic function that of healing division and restoring legitimacy to the state.

But the opening scene of the play is more properly a dramatic action than a symbolic anti-masque. It is important for the purposes of analysis to retain an awareness that the contrived and artificial nature of the storm is not revealed until the opening of Act 1:2, so that the protagonists of the tempest and shipwreck, and their spectators, are presented within what appears to be a genuine representation of a real maritime drama. The courtly audience of 1611 were presented with the mirror-image of another court, but a court temporarily 'out of court', a court in exile, blown off course from the route of their voyage from Tunis to Naples, entering against their will a realm of strangeness and difference, where the privileges and powers to which they are accustomed have no force, and where normal conventions of authority and obedience are inverted. The ship holds two separate communities, one of itinerant courtiers and one of professional sailors: each with its own system of values and scale of priorities. The storm creates a situation in which sailors have some idea what to do, but courtiers are, literally, all at sea. The power of a king has no defence against the power of a tempest: on the ocean the ruler's writ does not run.

> *Boat.* Hence! What cares these roarers for the name of king? To cabin; silence! Trouble us not.
>
> (I.i.16–17)

The use of the word 'roarers', with its connotations of boisterous anti-social behaviour and yob-violence, links the mutinous resistance of the waves to other kinds of rebellious or subversive defiance,

## The Tempest: Spectacles of Disenchantment

and opens the imagination to the possibility of a social energy liberated from the strictures of monarchical rule. Gonzalo invokes those very conventions of authority the storm has toppled, appealing to the priorities of a hierarchy that has already collapsed:

> *Gon.* Good, yet remember whom thou hast aboard.

The Boatswain's riposte is an ironic interrogation of the limits of political power:

> *Boat.* None that I love more than myself. You are a councillor; if you can command these elements to silence, and work the peace of the presence,[20] we will not hand a rope more – use your authority. If you cannot, give thanks you have lived so long . . . (I.i.20–5)

The professional function of a court 'councillor' is identified as that of smoothing over discord, suppressing contradiction by the operation of a camouflaging eloquence – later in the play Gonzalo's efforts to divert and comfort the king in Act 2:1 clearly exemplify this function of consolation by concealment; and Gonzalo himself offers an apt metaphorical description when he rebukes Sebastian's brutally tactless home truths as 'rubbing the sore', rather than 'bringing the plaster' (II.i.137–8). The Boatswain satirizes the powerlessness of Gonzalo's councilling capacities when confronted with the lawless turbulence of the storm: and extends this to the truistic observation that even the symbolic majesty of the king's 'presence' would here have no effect of pacification. Such a 'peace', attainable in the normal conditions of the court, would in the Boatswain's view be in any case an artificially constructed ideological composition: something a councillor could 'work', could impose by 'command'. The elemental power of the tempest shatters that fragile composition, and can be negotiated only be the exercise of real 'work', of strenuous physical labour – 'hand[ing] a rope' is diametrically opposed to the ineffective persuasive gestures of courtly rhetoric.

The opening scene thus foregrounds questions relating directly to the problems of power as they affect the structural organization of the court. The storm not only throws men into direct conflict with the elements: it also subverts and topples the social hierarchy which under normal circumstances orders and governs those men's lives. The storm provokes a crisis of authority within the displaced court, and between its émigré community and the collective society of the ship; but not within the structure of the latter, which holds firm and purposeful in the face of overwhelming disaster. The courtiers are accustomed to giving orders, not acceding to them; and since the world of a ship in a storm is outside their jurisdiction, they have no idea how to obey the commands of a legitimate authority exercising its power wisely and well. The Boatswain is not a substantial character in the play: after the shipwreck he disappears completely, and lies under his own hatches until released by Ariel for the final scene of revelation and resolution. If the Boatswain is akin to one of the turbulent and rebellious figures of an anti-masque, yet no specific ritual of integration is required to restore him to loyalty and obedience: on his re-appearance he seems entirely reconciled to the status quo, seeing the delivery of his ship and his re-discovery of the court as interconnected benefits:

> *Boat.* The best news is that we have safely found
> Our king and company; the next, our ship . . .
> Our royal, good, and gallant ship . . .
> (V.1.221–2, 237)

Yet in that opening scene, the Boatswain speaks that language of plebeian common-sense so often uttered by marginal and incidental characters in Shakespeare's plays: the plebeians at the beginning of *Julius Caesar* and *Coriolanus*, the servants of Gloucester in *King Lear*; and in the late romances, the fishermen of *Pericles*, the shepherds of *The Winter's Tale*. A voice from outside the court, perhaps the voice of a forgotten, marginalized or dispossessed group, calls into question the fundamental assumptions by which the court exists and is governed. How that voice was heard in the luxurious performance space of the Banqueting House at Whitehall, it is difficult to judge: but there seems little doubt that its accent and its spirit of down-to-earth realism and ironic defiance originated from the bare boards of the Globe Theatre, amongst that promiscuously mingled, undifferentiated audience of craftsmen and small traders and apprentices who constituted a very definitely 'out-of-court' constituency for the public performance of all Shakespeare's plays.

## 'PERFORMED TO POINT'

Abruptly a scene-shift alters our perspective, and we learn that the tempest we have been experiencing as a natural catastrophe that could stretch human endurance to the limit and shake to the very depths this single state of man, has been an elaborate hoax: a trick; a show; a *coup d'oeil* as well as a *coup de théâtre*; a crafted, constructed representation; an illusion bearing the semblance of truth.

> *Mir.* If by your art, my dearest father, you have
> Put the wild waters in this roar, allay them.
> (I.ii.1–2)

The storm is a triumph of art. Some two hundred lines of Prospero's historical reminiscences later, Miranda insistently re-poses her initial question, in a formulation which reveals, if it does not express, a highly sophisticated understanding of the nature of the process of representation she has witnessed.

> *Mir.* And now I pray you, sir,
> For still 'tis beating in my mind, your reason
> For raising this sea-storm.
> (I.ii.175–7)

What is 'beating' in Miranda's mind is partly her initial question, or rather the anxiety and confusion the question itself expressed and sought to resolve. But it is also the storm itself, the violence of which remains with her as a palpable sensation. Her witnessing of the storm and of the suffering of the shipwrecked passengers was in itself experienced as a mental 'storm'. But at the same time, she is beginning to realize, the reality of the tempest was in another sense a purely mental composition, a series of illusory pictures capable of provoking in her violent emotional responses unrelated to any actual material event or circumstance.

> *Pros.* ... there is no soul
> No, not so much perdition as an hair
> Betid to any creature in the vessel
> Which thou heard'st cry, which thou saw'st sink.
> (I.ii.29–32)

If what Miranda's senses conveyed to her was not the truth, then she has indeed occasion to suspect that the storm may have been from the beginning 'beating', as it is now, only in her mind. What she demands from her father is the 'reason' – literally the motive or explanation – for his elaborate display of legerdemain. But the contingency of 'reason', 'mind' and 'storm' may suggest also that she is seeking to re-locate the absent 'reason' – faculty of intellectual understanding – driven from her own mind by the violent turbulence of an imposed mental aberration.[21]

The opposition of 'storm' and 'reason' draws attention to the way in which, via Renaissance philosophy's system of correspondences, such dualistic polarities could extend the basic metaphor of a storm beyond the literal dimension of social disturbance or political tumult, to encompass the signifying fields of mental disturbance and moral disorder (the whole range of interconnected symbolizing levels will be familiar from *King Lear*). The aberrations of uncontrollable insanity and the passions of ungovernable lust figure largely in the moral scheme of *The Tempest*, and will be addressed in due course. If we are dealing with a stable and coherent system of polarities, wherein each moral quality is carefully placed and defined in relation to its opposite, and where the positive value is shown to conquer, subsume or appropriate its negative counterpart, then we are very close to the neat moral antitheses of the court masque. In such a model, political subversion would be reconciled to authority, moral transgression subordinated to virtue, madness healed by reason, lust cooled by chastity. The opening scenes of *The Tempest* certainly appear to map the play's imaginative universe in terms of such moral and philosophical dualisms. The mind can hold together the sovereign rule of reason and the disturbance of tempestuous passions; so in Prospero's magic we glimpse the co-existence of an Apolline 'art' (I.ii.1) and a Dionysiac 'power' (1.ii.10) that can both create and destroy; an art that can put the elements into a roar, or allay them; provoke and control suffering and compassion, harm or heal. The contraries run through I.ii with an almost schematic pattern:

> *Mir.* What foul play had we that we came from thence
> Or blessèd was't we did?
> *Pros.* Both, both my girl.
> By foul play, as thou sayst, were we heaved thence
> But blessedly holp hither
>
> (I.ii.60–4)

Foul and blest, thence and hither, 'heaved' and 'holp' are marshalled by the verse into a neat system of correspondences; and Prospero structures some of his fundamental assertions around them:

> *Pros.* The *direful* spectacle of the *wreck*, which *touched*

> The very *virtue of compassion* in thee,
> I have with such provision in mine *art*
> So *safely ordered* . . .
>
> (I.ii.26–9; my emphases)

A 'direful' 'wreck' can be 'safely ordered' by the provisioning of Prospero's 'art'. The virtue of compassion stands as an intermediary term linking the antitheses: since the kind of pity moved in Miranda by the disturbance she has witnessed, is also claimed as the principal motive of the author of that disturbance – 'I have done nothing' says Prospero to his daughter 'but in care of thee' (I.ii.16).

Such a system of polarized values would seem to connect the play, together with the masques and other mythical narratives, firmly to the philosophical and moral universe of the court. In such a scheme, all oppositional, negative, subversive forces can be contained and formally subordinated to the dominance of a hegemonic ideology, that of the monarch. Reason, justice, virtue, legitimate sovereignty would of course hold sway in any contemporary Elizabethan or Jacobean scheme of values. But here those abstract qualities seem to be formulated in a discursive language appropriate to the celebratory ritual endorsement of James I's political, moral and thaumaturgical authority.

Nothing would seem to express this pattern more clearly than the carefully constructed shift of perspective, between Act 1:1 and 1:2, from chaos to order, from arbitrary accident to providential dispensation, from the image of an *action* which figures experience as elemental disturbance and political dissension, to the framework of a *narrative* in which a formidably rational consciousness settles and orders all wildness and disturbance into an ideological model of propriety, justice and consolation. But it is precisely the disclosure of that theatrical operation that distances *The Tempest* from the norms and conventions of ritualized 'court theatre'. For the dramatic action of this play seems less concerned with the usual technical problems of internalizing ideology within a set of theatrical devices so breathtakingly impressive and emotionally exciting in their dénouement that the polemical or propogandist material could be conveyed by a smooth and unproblematical transition to the spectator – the methods of 'total theatre'; than with a very different process of foregrounding both the mechanisms of the action, the nature of the spectator, and the means by which the former operates upon the latter. The surrogate spectator is Miranda. One of the principal functions of Prospero's long exposition in Act 1:2 is to constitute Miranda as a spectator: to inform her, literally, that she is one, since she, rapt by fiction into self-oblivion, has been under the illusion that she was present at a 'real' event.

The kind of 'spectacle' (I.ii.26) Prospero can stage is addressed and foregrounded not only in terms of its ability to persuade and convince, but also of its capacity to *move*:

> *Mir.* O, I have suffered
> With those that I saw suffer . . .
> . . . O, the cry did knock
> Against my very heart . . .
> (I.ii. 5–6, 8–9)

The theoretical character of Miranda's involvement in the 'spectacle' is precisely that of the empathic spectator, as defined by Brecht: she is lost in an illusion, unable to understand either the significance of the action or the motion of her own feelings. But the drama which contains both her and the spectacle she has witnessed works in quite a contrary direction: more perhaps in the manner of Brecht's epic theatre. The artifice of theatrical construction and the experience of the empathic spectator are both distanced and estranged, framed and exposed, held up for the inspection of curiosity and the satisfaction of reason.

Prospero's formal constitution of Miranda as the (only) spectator of his production, involves an emphatic insistence on the daughter's family relationship to her patriarchal minder:

> *Pros.* I have done nothing but in care of thee,
> Of thee, my dear one, thee, my daughter . . .
> (I.ii.16–17)

The repetitous endearments may be read as a protective and solicitous rhetoric of affection, or as a ritual affirmation of power, secured through the provocation of an anxious consciousness of indebtedness: and indeed in the discourse of the patriarchal family, the two proposed interpretations need not in any case be regarded as opposites. In addition to reminding Miranda that she is his daughter, Prospero insists on obedience, attentiveness, and an opening of the senses to whatever may be about to unfold.

## The Tempest: Spectacles of Disenchantment 155

> *Pros.* The very minute bids thee ope thine ear.
> Obey, and be attentive.
>
> (I.ii.37–8)

Prospero continually instructs Miranda to 'open' her senses in this way, to absorb through her eyes and ears the words and images he presents before her. Yet as we have seen, on this enchanted island, where the proprietor can control both the senses and what they perceive: can blind and deafen, alert or stupefy; deceive with an illusion or convince of a reality – the evidence of the senses can hardly be trusted.

The principal object of Prospero's long autobiographical narrative is the correction or consolidation of Miranda's memory; the purpose of his initial interrogation, to discover whether or not it contains anything.

> *Pros.* Canst thou remember
> A time before we came unto this cell?
>
> (I.ii.38–9)

The answer is predictable ('I do not think thou canst', I.ii.40) since Miranda was under three when they arrived on the island: her only recollection is of the waiting-women who attended on her as a baby. More to the point, Miranda seems to have existed, prior to Prospero's revelations, innocent of the constraint and discipline of time: knowing no past, conceiving of no future, she appears ignorant of temporal transition altogether. It is her father, with his obsessive preoccupation with the passage and the meaning of time, who inducts her into mortality, expels her from her realm of timeless innocence into the fallen world of time, provides her with a past, a future, and a knowledge of the passing of the present. In order to give her a future, a destiny – marriage and accession to political power, the conventional expectations of her royal birthright – Prospero must also provide her with a past; must bring her to an awareness of the treacheries and terrors that lie concealed 'in the dark backward and abyss of time' (I.ii.50).

Prospero's famous phrase describing the past sufficiently indicates his own conception of its significance. What has been is symbolized as a 'dark backward' not simply because of the impenetrable obscurity of its perpetually recursive motion, but because it contains Prospero's own sombre personal history of legitimacy inverted and hierarchy overthrown; and the past is an 'abyss', not merely on account of the difficulty of searching its precipitous depth, but because it contains the memory of a vertiginous fall. Miranda's only memory is, by contrast, an image of maternal care: but it is a curiously impersonal one. She remembers, not a mother, but 'four or five women' who looked after her. The only reference in the entire play to Miranda's mother is the curiously formal, lapidary phrase of Prospero's, 'Thy mother was a piece of virtue' (I.ii.56), which assigns Miranda to Prospero's paternity by a curious process of deductive reasoning – 'she said thou wast my daughter' (I.ii.57). This is of course a joke, and there is no reason to doubt either the mother's fidelity or the father's trust in her. Nonetheless Prospero's allusion orphans Miranda by locating the absent mother into a vague, impersonal and legendary past before the initiation of the narrative proper. In Miranda's own memory the image of the maternal 'piece of virtue' appears shattered, fragmented and dispersed across a spectral company of female servants: and even they live in her memory with all the unreliable vagueness of a dream:

> Mir.  'Tis far off,
> And rather like a dream than an assurance
> That my remembrance warrants.
>
> (I.ii.44–6)

Into the shimmering haze of that childhood memory of unfocused maternal ambience, Prospero inserts an image of singular clarity and definition:

> Pros.  Thy father was the Duke of Milan, and
> A prince of power –
>
> (I.ii.54–5)

While femininity appears as a curiously unfocused half-recollection, a waking dream, the masculine asserts itself with masterly self-definition and strong alliterative insistence ('a prince of power') as an irrefutable concrete reality of the past and the present.

The father's claim to self-evident centrality in the life-narrative of the child is further enhanced by a remarkable metaphorical claim. Their transition to the island is symbolized as both literally and metaphorically a 'labour' of love:

> Pros.  When I have decked the sea with drops full salt,
> Under my burden groaned, which raised in me

> An undergoing stomach to bear up
> Against what should ensue.
>
> (I.ii.155–8)

Here Prospero claims nothing less than that he himself gave birth to Miranda. In an extraordinary usurpation of the reproductive capacity of the female, Prospero defines the voyage to the island not only as a transit into new life, a redemption or second birth, but as a fantasy of self-sufficient patriarchal progeniture – the sole author of the daughter's birth is the father – and with that masterful gesture of sexual imperialism, his appropriation of the feminine is completed. Since he does not share either his power or his domestic polity with a woman whose status is that of wife, consort, marital partner, Prospero is not obliged to make any concessions to an alternative centre of authority in either his public or his private life: he is literally an absolute monarch and father. He describes himself as married to 'bountiful Fortune', a feminine force who may appear to represent the authority of the 'opposite' sex, but proves instead to be an aspect of Prospero's comprehensive patriarchal polity.

> *Pros.* By accident most strange, bountiful Fortune,
> Now my dear lady, hath mine enemies
> Brought to this shore; and by my prescience
> I find my zenith doth depend upon
> A most auspicious star, whose influence
> If now I court not, but omit, my fortunes
> Will ever after droop.
>
> (I.ii.178–84)

The problem of securing an effective relationship between self and world, human power and objective circumstances, is figured here as the 'courtship' of a feminine power, 'Fortuna' conceived as goddess, patroness and wife or mistress ('my dear lady'). 'Fortune' is thereby linked in philosophical association with Prospero's own 'fortunes', and the female deity identifed as the authoress of personal destiny and immediate circumstance. Both the feminine 'other' and the externality of objective circumstances could be conceived of either as opposites with which it is necessary to come to terms, or obstructions against which it is necessary to struggle: but in Prospero's imperialistic vision both appear assimilated as aspects of his own power. His 'prescience' allows him to steal a march on Fortune, and thereby to negotiate any potential contradictions between aspiration and achievement; his magical powers permit him actively to shape and determine the character of circumstances. Thus the power of 'Fortune', appropriated as a surrogate wife, is absorbed into Prospero's firm control over his own fate ('my fortunes'); and the language in which Prospero describes the latter is decidedly masculine: success is measured by his skill in maintaining erect the 'zenith' of his ascendency, and failure by the flaccid 'droop' of his masculine potency and power that would result from a failure to seize opportunity. The female is therefore in Prospero's scheme of things nothing more than a branch of his own power.

Miranda's memory is effectively an empty space, a *tabula rasa* into which Prospero can insert his reconstructions and dramatizations of the past. What he programmes into that memory is very obviously his own composition: the Milanese past is clearly occluded by the suppression of the mother, and the transition to the island symbolized by the bizarre fantasy of masculine generation. Prospero's narrative has exactly the same capacity as his earlier theatrical demonstration: to provoke pity and compassion in the auditor/spectator.

> Mir. Alack, for pity!
> I not remembering how I cried out then
> Will cry it o'er again – it is a hint
> That wrings mine eyes to't.
> (I.ii.132–5)

Miranda's feelings of compassionate solicitude are prompted by her father's story: she almost insistently foregrounds the absence in her own memory of any direct experience or confirmation, and in the odd and arresting phrase 'it is a hint/ That wrings mine eyes to't' comes close to identifying the emotional response as something stimulated and provoked by art. Coupled with this complex perception is a trace of that anxious filial guilt I noted earlier:

> Mir. O, my heart bleeds
> To think o'th'teen that I have turned you to,
> Which is from my remembrance.
> (I.ii.63–5)

Miranda may well weep as much for the loss of selfhood and identity entailed in this utter dependence on her father to supply her with memory, as she weeps over the trouble she caused him, or the pity provoked by his narrative. We are not presented here with

## The Tempest: Spectacles of Disenchantment

anything so simple as a choice between falsehood and truth, illusion and reality, art and nature. It is not that Miranda's feelings are not genuine or sincere: only that the absence of any recollected experience inevitably characterizes her feelings as 'aesthetic' emotions, produced and provoked by artifice. The proximity to this exchange of the theatrical tempest, which showed Miranda feeling exactly the same compassion over the *tableau vivant* of a simulated shipwreck, must necessarily imply that Prospero's apparently complete control over both reality and emotion, over what is seen and what is felt, can at least raise the possibility that genuine emotion may be stimulated by art of a dubious motive, and that that paradox may in turn serve to complicate any stable hierarchy of relationships between art and nature, falsehood and truth.

## OUT OF COURT

At the heart of this long and seminal second scene, stands a passage of descriptive and analytical narrative which is necessarily central to the play and to our argument, since it contains (and in this respect *The Tempest* differs significantly from *The Winter's Tale*) the only direct description we will find of a court and of a state – Milan.

> *Pros.* Through all the signories it was the first,
> And Prospero the prime duke, being so reputed
> In dignity, and for the liberal arts
> Without a parallel; those being all my study,
> The government I cast upon my brother,
> And to my state grew stranger, being transported
> And rapt in secret studies. Thy false uncle . . .
> Being once perfected how to grant suits,
> How to deny them, who t'advance, and who
> To trash for overtopping, new created
> The creatures that were mine, I say: or changed 'em,
> Or else new formed 'em; having both the key
> Of officer and office, set all hearts i'th'state
> To what tune pleased his ear, that now he was
> The ivy which had hid my princely trunk
> And sucked my verdure out on't . . .
> (I.ii.71–7, 79–87)

Here Prospero's narrative hollows out a most significant absence in the representation of his personal history and of the play's court society, since the wisely-governed state which he originally ruled, and to which at the play's close he is about to return, is nowhere depicted, but takes its place along with all the other lost ideal kingdoms of political mythography, to be elegiacally lamented and eternally regretted. Milan under Prospero's benevolent government is said to have been pre-eminent among Italian city-states, and to have commanded a respect properly due to the humanistic virtues of its prince, whose acknowledged superiority in the 'liberal arts' lent a manifest 'dignity' both to the prince's person and office, and (an inference enabled by the syntax) to the reputation of the state itself. The narrative conjures the image of a state ruled not by ancient right or dynastic privilege, but by the exercise of those intellectual faculties and powers appropriate to a Renaissance aristocracy: the 'liberal arts' were (according to the OED) 'those considered worthy of a free man; opposed to *servile or mechanical* . . . arts suitable to persons of superior social station'. Now whether this humanistic philosopher-prince, well-versed in the core-curriculum of the aristocracy, ruled his state effectively, or placed his reliance in abstract academic pursuits hopelessly unsuitable to the exercise of effective power, we have no means of knowing: we have literally nothing but Prospero's word for it, and that word could be interpreted either way. Prospero's acknowledged mastery of the liberal arts conferred dignity on his state, yet led to his abstraction from concrete affairs and popular support (we have already seen a parallel contradiction explored in *Love's Labour's Lost*):

> *Pros.* I thus neglecting worldly ends, all dedicated
> To closeness and the bettering of my mind
> With that which, but by being so retired,
> O'er-prized all popular rate . . .
>
> (I.ii.89–92)

The latter suggestion (which Orgel glosses as 'exceeded the people's understanding', p. 106) is the only indication in the whole monologue that Milan contained any subjects other than the two rival brothers and the anonymous 'creatures' who inhabited their court. If effective government could be sustained only by an open and participatory relationship with the people, and by a vigilant and rigorous surveillance and control over what was happening in the court, then Prospero's preference for 'the liberal arts' is acknowledged as weakness and distortion, offered as confession rather than exculpation, and strangely prefigures cultural and political conflicts and divisions of our own day, between traditional humanistic models of education and public responsibility, and cultural priorities appropriate to the radical entrepreneurial individualism of a free-market capitalism. Prospero certainly appears here to be endorsing such a proto-Thatcherite position, acknowledging his own guilt and responsibility for the 'neglecting' of necessary 'worldly ends', and identifying the disinterested pursuit of knowledge and wisdom as a political distortion or deviation from the true purpose. In this respect he appears as a typical Renaissance ruler, revaluing the older mediaeval prejudice in favour of the *vita contemplativa*, and recognizing, as a compatriot of Machiavelli's, that a successful prince is likely to need more than traditional claims and dynastic prerogative to support his enterprise. The 'government' which Prospero 'cast upon his brother', and the 'secret studies' he himself preferred to pursue, appear here as contraries, divided one against the other by an imprudent bifurcation of responsibilities. Where Antonio addressed himself assiduously to the acquisition of influence and control, Prospero became 'transported' and 'rapt' (literally 'seized away') in his secret studies, carried from social engagement and public responsibility, already in a metaphorical sense conveyed to a desert island which could be populated with the activities of his own imagination.

Although it may seem natural to assume that Prospero is admitting the folly of an academic or philosophical enterprise that abstracts the ruler from worldly purposes, this assumption raises a number of problems when applied to the concrete detail of his own sociological analysis of the court. It is quite apparent in this respect that the bitter invective he employs against Antonio's opportunistic manipulation of the political apparatus of the court draws on those rhetorical traditions of anti-court satire and criticism that we can find everywhere in the drama of Shakespeare, expressed at their most pungent in *King Lear*, *Hamlet* and in *Timon of Athens*. The organizational and professional structure of the court, especially the system of patronage, is viewed cynically as a mechanism that can very easily be manipulated by an unscrupulous usurper. By the studious and machiavellian exercise of generosity and control ('who t'advance, and who/ To trash for overtopping') which Prospero himself had employed, Antonio finds it possible to secure unthinking loyalty and obedience from an entourage only recently committed to another sovereign. Courtiers are 'creatures': the technical denotation of a patron–client relationship is almost submerged within this anti-courtly discourse into the connotation of mere unconscious and sub-human bestiality. With the absolute power of a musical conductor Antonio re-orchestrates the structure of the court:

> Pros. . . . having both the *key*
> Of officer and office, *set* all hearts i'th' state
> To what *tune* pleased his ear . . .
> (I.ii.83–5)

Antonio was able in this court society to secure and manipulate the loyalty of his powerful subjects as easily and comprehensively as he could require a particular piece of music from a body of paid court entertainers.

The position from which Prospero speaks this diatribe is a distinctively 'out-of-court' location: the normal systems and conventions of a Renaissance court are viewed both externally and with hostility, as they are in such discourses as pastoral and anti-court satire. Of course such modes of expression were available within courtly discourses too: the pastoral identification of a corrupt and artificial society, or the chastened and cynical observations of a poet temporarily exiled from court favour, were common enough formulations in the cultural context of the Elizabethan, Jacobean and Caroline courts themselves. But there is in *The Tempest* no positive or ideal model of a court by which such contrary perspectives could be measured and into which they might be assimilated, as they are in the courtly pastorals of Sidney and Spenser: here is only the embittered and hostile voice of an exile decrying the political system with which he was unable successfully to engage, the functioning or malfunctioning of which led to his banishment. In other words, Prospero clearly adopts his intellectual position within the detached and disinterested cultural ambience of those same 'liberal arts' he had pursued to his destruction: and his perspective on both the court and the court society are the resigned and ironic musings of pastoral exile, moralizing satire and a fastidious intellectual superiority.

Prospero's account of the temptations of power as they beset and ultimately conquer his brother is profoundly revealing and illuminating:

> *Pros.*   He being thus lorded
> Not only with what my revenue yielded,
> But what my power might else exact, like one
> Who, having into truth by telling of it,
> Made such a sinner of his memory
> To credit his own lie, he did believe
> He was indeed the duke, out o'th' substitution . . .
> (I.ii.97–103)

With this account of the self-deceiving effects of borrowed authority, Antonio is brought firmly within the compass of the play's general preoccupation with the delusive and truth-bearing capacities of fiction, fantasy, drama, the works of the imagination. Within the transparent simplicities of Prospero's 'out-of-court' pastoral discourse, the hierarchy of significances deployed here is clear and unproblematical: Antonio is (in reality) not the duke, but a temporary regent ruling by proxy of a superior and with authority on limited loan; the combined influences of wealth, status, the unlimited potentialities of power and the self-deceptive capacities of the mind unite to convince him (in fantasy) that he *is* the duke. But we have already seen and heard enough in the play's opening scenes about the power of illusion, the relativity of memory, the instability of conceptions like reality and truth, to regard any simplistic reduction of experience to categories of truth and lies as inadequate formulations, ill-equipped to encompass the reality of the play's imagined world. Prospero completes his diagnosis of Antonio's delusions by employing the most notoriously complex and unstable distinction we are likely to find in the whole of Renaissance drama, the distinction between actor and role:

> *Pros.*   To have no screen between this part he played
> And him he played it for, he needs will be
> Absolute Milan.
> (I.ii.107–9)

The metaphorical 'screen' is first a barrier between Antonio and Prospero: that which separates their discrete identities as separate products of the same parents, and distinguishes Prospero's ducal identity from the younger brother's dynastic impotence. Antonio is only playing a part for Prospero, and the ineradicable difference between role-model and role must be preserved. But 'him he played it for' refers to both Prospero (as role-model) and Antonio himself: as Antonio's convincing discharge of the role, his 'playing' of the part, becomes linked to his own interests and ambitions, and becomes a game of hazard, an operator's 'play' for power, so the distinction between his 'real' identity and his assumed role begins to break down: his biological similarity to his brother and his submergence to the personality of his role combine to recreate him as 'absolute Milan' – absolute in the sense of uninhibited power, but also 'completely Milan', any formal differentiation between brother and brother, actor and role, person and state having utterly disappeared.

Within the abstract exegesis of a purely textual criticism a distinction such as that between actor and role, or the attendant distinctions between reality and illusion or truth and falsehood on which the primary distinction depends, can appear firm and unproblematical, as it appears to in Prospero's moralizing language – Antonio simply 'credits his own lie'. But in the theatre these matters are rather more complicated: and Prospero, the director and master illusionist, is surely here offering a reductive and oversimplified explanation of a reality which his own theatrical practice continually disturbs, problematizes, and calls into question. If, as he ultimately acknowledges, he and his fellow actors are 'such stuff as dreams are made on', then the firm and authoritative positivism of his sharp distinctions between truth and falsehood, reality and illusion, actor and role will scarcely bear very much philosophical interrogation.

## 'CORRESPONDENT TO COMMAND'

The remainder of this long scene divides naturally into a series of episodic units, linked thematically rather than developmentally to one another. The transition from one episode to the next is managed quite casually, with little or no effort towards naturalistic verisimilitude or technical narrative virtuosity. Prospero puts Miranda to sleep and calls Ariel – 'come away, servant'; the 'Ariel-scene' (I.ii.187–304) ends with the spirit's dismissal – 'hence, with diligence!' Prospero then wakes Miranda and unceremoniously introduces a 'Caliban-scene' (305–73) with 'Come, we'll visit Caliban' – (why?); at the end of this sub-scene Caliban in turn is dismissed

– 'so, slave, hence' – and the stage cleared for the introduction and trial of Ferdinand, which episode completes Act 1:2. The dramatic effect of these episodic transitions is to disrupt any movement towards naturalism of narrative or dénouement, and to display the drama's thematic structure (e.g. the clear antithesis of Ariel and Caliban, or the ritual sunderings and ceremonial convergences of Miranda and Ferdinand) with an overt and emphatic foregrounding of structural pattern. I.ii thus has a four-part structure, with Prospero at the commanding centre of each unit engaging in dialogue, interrogation, command and testing of, in order of appearance, Miranda, Ariel, Caliban and Ferdinand. Beyond this 'quartet' model the whole scene could be further split into two counterpoised halves, the second concerned pre-eminently with masculinity, especially with the male in appetitive relationship with the female (Caliban has lusted after Miranda as Ferdinand falls in love with her); while Ariel, androgynous and free certainly of any male sexual impulses, is constantly being required by Prospero to dress as a female, and therefore assimilates more readily to the feminine concerns of the initial 'Miranda' sub-scene.

The 'Ariel-scene' itself can be divided neatly into two halves, exhibiting Ariel in his character as an obedient agent of Prospero's power (I.ii.189–237), and in his capacity as an independent spirit given to expressions of defiance and gestures of rebellion (240–97). As Prospero's servant Ariel has enacted precisely what his master required:

> *Pros.* Hast thou, spirit,
> Performed to point the tempest that I bade thee?
> *Ari.* To every article.
>
> (I.ii.193–5)

This literal and punctilious execution of instructions belies Ariel's nature as a spirit, which is to express and enact violent energy and elemental disruption. Ariel's language articulates an uninhibited delight in the unfettered energy of the tempest: the exercise of power, the liberty of enormous space and unrestrained motion, the emulation of great mythological potentates like Neptune and Jupiter.

> *Ari.* I boarded the King's ship; now on the beak,
> Now in the waist, the deck, in every cabin,
> I flamed amazement. Sometimes I'd divide

> And burn in many places; on the topmast,
> The yards and bowsprit would I flame distinctly,
> Then meet and join. Jove's lightning, the precursors
> O'th' dreadful thunder-claps, more momentary
> And sight-outrunning were not; the fire and cracks
> Of sulphurous roaring the most mighty Neptune
> Seem to besiege and make his bold waves tremble,
> Yea, his dread trident shake.
> (I.ii.196–206)

Ariel's ability to invoke climatic tumult is paralleled by his/her power to provoke mental aberration:

> *Pros.* Who was so firm, so constant, that this coil
> Would not infect his reason?
> *Ari.* Not a soul
> But felt a fever of the mad, and played
> Some tricks of desperation.
> (I.ii.206–10)

In the rapid and excitable gusto of Ariel's speech the passage from tempest to madness seems a natural and spontaneous enlargement of the operations of disruptive energy. But in fact, as Prospero's interjections make clear, the incitement to madness is a predetermined and calculated strategy, parallel to the provocation of pity in Miranda by the spectacle of the wreck: it is as much Prospero's purpose to have the courtiers' and mariners' minds disorientated by madness and despair, as it was to move Miranda's sympathies with pity and compassion. Throughout this sub-scene the dialogic exchanges between Prospero and Ariel re-establish that dialectic of energy and control, disturbance and order, storm and calm, which I have identified as a pervasive structural pattern. As Ariel describes Ferdinand leaping in flames into an imaginary hell, Prospero catches him in a safety-net of policy – 'was not this nigh shore?' (I.ii.216); over the unregulated energy of Ariel's 'eternal delight'[22] in disruption and inversion, Prospero throws the constraining discipline of his strategems – 'But are they, Ariel, safe?' (I.ii.217). The bathetic stylistic tumble from psychological precipitation to comic 'soft landing', from epic and tragedy to farce, parallels Gloucester's great absurdist fall in *King Lear*.

The figure of Ariel was of course particularly attractive to the nineteenth-century romantic imagination, and we should perhaps be cautious in attributing to Ariel (or to Shakespeare) those idealizations of energy and revolutionary freedom to be found at their purest in William Blake. There can be no doubt, however, that Ariel represents a spirit whose natural habitat is liberty, one impatient of confinement and resistant to command. The spiritual power Prospero finds it convenient to control and employ can also prove recalcitrant to imposed servitude. Prospero seeks to impose on Ariel the same discipline of time he earlier imposed on Miranda:

> *Pros.* What is the time o'th'day?
> *Ari.* Past the mid-season.
> *Pros.* At least two glasses. The time 'twixt six and now
> Must by us both be spent most preciously.
> *Ari.* Is there more toil? Since thou dost give me pains,
> Let me remember thee what thou hast promised,
> Which is not yet performed me.
>                                             (I.ii.239–44)

Ariel has 'performed' (executed) Prospero's bidding (I.ii.238) in 'performing' (staging) the tempest (I.ii.194) and expects Prospero to 'perform' his part of an agreement by fulfilling his contractual obligations. Ariel is not like Miranda innocent of the dimension of time: on the contrary, he counts his years in Prospero's service with punctilious exactness ('thou did promise/ To bate me a full year', I.ii.249–50). But the constraints of time are to Ariel irksome bonds on his desire for liberty. We do not know whether Prospero is insisting on the letter of their contract ('before the time be out? No more!', I.ii.246) or rescinding a previously offered remission, but either way he is a tough negotiator who shows no inclination to compromise. In his view the service he requires of Ariel is the repayment of a debt of obligation. Just as Prospero was obliged to reconstruct Miranda's memory on her behalf, so he finds it necessary to correct Ariel's:

> *Pros.*  Hast thou forgot
> The foul witch Sycorax, who with age and envy
> Was grown into a hoop? . . . I must
> Once in a month recount what thou hast been,
> Which thou forget'st.
>                                        (I.ii.257–9, 261–3)

The content of that constructed biography of a spirit, like Prospero's earlier programming of Miranda's memory, seems to tell us as much about himself as it does about his servant. Ariel owes his master service, according to this scheme of moral obligation, because it was Prospero who released Ariel from a much worse torment of confinement, imposed on him by the black magic of Prospero's predecessor:

> *Pros.* This damned witch Sycorax,
> For mischiefs manifold and sorceries terrible
> To enter human hearing, from Algiers
> Thou knowst was banished . . .
> This blue-eyed hag was hither brought with child,
> And here was left by th' sailors. Thou, my slave,
> As thou reports't thyself, was then her servant,
> And for thou wast a spirit too delicate
> To act her earthy and abhorred commands,
> Refusing her grand hests, she did confine thee
> By help of her more potent ministers
> And in her most unmitigable rage,
> Into a cloven pine, within which rift
> Imprisoned thou didst painfully remain
> A dozen years . . . It was mine art,
> When I arrived and heard thee, that made gape
> The pine and let thee out.
> (I.ii. 263–6, 269–79, 291–3)

The accumulation of correspondences between Prospero and Sycorax is quite remarkable. Like Prospero, Sycorax was a sorcerer/ess, gifted with necromantic powers; like him she was banished, consigned to the ocean and stranded on the same island; where Prospero's life was saved by his enemies' fear of the popular affection, Sycorax was spared on account of a pregnancy (a literal one to parallel Prospero's metaphorical carrying of Miranda). Prospero's magic is more powerful than that of Sycorax: he claims that her charms were unable to release Ariel, while his enchantment could accomplish the spirit's liberation. But not only can Prospero undo Sycorax's doing: he can also reverse his own liberation, and re-confine what has been released:

> *Pros.* If thou more murmur'st, I will rend an oak
> And peg thee in his knotty entrails till

Thou hast howled away twelve winters.
                               (I.ii.294-7)

Indeed Caliban, born to the freedom of legitimate possession and inherited sovereignty, claims to have been, effectively, imprisoned by Prospero in much the same way: 'confined within this rock' (I.ii.360).

In exchange for this granting of liberty, Ariel ought to feel obligation as gratitude, and render voluntary service to his liberator. When the spirit proves mutinous and recalcitrant, Prospero exacts his obedience by threatening to repeat his former confinement, imposing the same term but with harder conditions – imprisoned this time in an oak rather than a pine. Ariel's acquiescence ('I will be correspondent to command', I.ii.297) is an obedience exacted under duress rather than a loyalty spontaneously given.

Why, finally, does Prospero require Ariel to disguise himself as a sea-nymph?

> *Pros.*  Go, make thyself like a nymph o'th' sea.
> Be subject to no sight but thine and mine, invisible
> To every eyeball else.
>                               (I.ii.301-3)

What purpose could such a disguise have, if only Prospero can see it? The peculiarly inexplicable 'excess of significance' here has prompted critics to propose some internal inconsistency in the text. Orgel observes that Ariel is of course visible to the audience, and therefore appears in an appropriate garb to sing 'Come unto these yellow sands' and 'Full fathom five' to Ferdinand. Why the instruction to adopt such a guise, which would function perfectly adequately without explication, should be so laboriously clarified and discussed before the audience, is not explained. Since Ariel later presents Ceres in the masque (see IV.i.167) this propensity of Prospero's to confer on the spirit he can successfully control the distinctive attributes of female form, must surely have some connection with his tortuous and complex relationship with gender differences and sexuality.

The 'Ariel sub-scene' is thus a cameo exploration of fundamental themes – mastery and service, loyalty and obedience, authority and rebellion – which pervade and fissure the dramatic and poetic texture of the play. They are also the characteristic themes of many of the masques, and at this point Shakespeare's play is certainly operating in terms of masque-like images and conventions. A contest of authority is enacted (and a potential crisis of authority averted) between a magician-sovereign and his mythological or allegorical servant. In addition to establishing his power over Ariel by demonstrations of intellectual superiority, spiritual power and force majeur, Prospero also pits himself, though only in imagined and narrated terms, against the negative potencies of a necromantic contender, Sycorax; a conflict very much in the manner of the magical courtly shows and thaumaturgical demonstrations discussed earlier. Prospero of course never encounters Sycorax directly, but since he confronts and reverses the legacy of her power, the result is the same: the royal magus displays and legitimates his own supernatural powers by exercising them against powerful forces of resistance and subversion.

There are however important contrasts with the masque in the manner of Prospero's exhibition of power. Since these are to be found even more strongly marked in the encounter with Caliban, they will be addressed in my analysis of the next 'sub-scene'. I want at this point simply to register some of the sub-textual or 'deep-structural' implications of the narrated contest between Prospero and Sycorax. Stephen Orgel has argued that Sycorax's female gender signifies more than her mythological relationship with legendary witches like Circe and Medea.

> The drama that Prospero recounts, and that he replays with Miranda, is a family drama; but it is one with a significant absence: the wife and mother . . . But the absent presence of the wife and mother constitutes a space that is filled, for Prospero, with surrogates and a ghostly family: the witch Sycorax and her monster child Caliban, who is so often and so disturbingly like the other wicked child, the usurping younger brother Antonio; the good child-wife Miranda, the obedient Ariel, the adolescent and libidinous Ferdinand. (Orgel, 1987, p. 18)

The reality of wife and mother being all but suppressed from Prospero's memory, and entirely effaced from that of his daughter, Sycorax represents the return of repressed femininity as a monstrous parody of demonized and illegitimate power; in Orgel's words, 'that ghostly memory so intensely present in the play, the perverse, irrational, violent, malicious, vindictive principle in nature, progenitor of monsters, lover and agent of the devil on earth' (p. 21). Sycorax is woman as challenger and rival of patriarchal power, driven by unmotivated and unreasonable anger ('unmitigable rage', I.ii.276), inhibitor of masculine freedom and activity, creature of monstrous lust and unnatural fornication, witch and sexual consort of demons. Prospero's assiduous campaign to suppress or banish the 'unruly woman', to demonize the unacceptable face of femininity and to exercise strict patriarchal control over the women in his power is exhibited again in the masque, where all the speaking characters are goddesses presented (acted) by his own familiar spirits, thus giving Prospero complete control over the representation of femininity; and of course in his vigilant surveillance and paternalistic protection of Miranda's chastity.

## 'CONFINED INTO THIS ROCK'

Sycorax was the tormentor of the 'moody' and rebellious Ariel, and Prospero invokes her name as an awful warning, to him, against treachery and betrayal. She was also the mother of that powerful figure of unreconstructed resistance, Caliban: and therefore in his case a more dangerous antecedent, since by descent from Sycorax Caliban can claim to be his 'own king' (I.ii.342). Prospero of course denies any such claim by denying Sycorax and Caliban any share in that human community which arrogates all political rights – when he arrived, the island was not 'honoured with/ A human shape' (I.ii.283–4). Caliban's servitude follows as an apparently natural consequence. He is not human; he is the offspring (according to Prospero) of an unnatural union between a witch and the devil; he was on the arrival of the humans completely uneducated, being unable even to speak; he is guilty of attempted rape,and he has that within him which, in Miranda's fastidiously ambiguous phrase, 'good natures/ Could not abide to be with' (I.ii.358–9). Prospero's enslaving of Caliban could hardly, in the light of this characterization, seem more just or appropriate. Caliban himself, of course, does not accept Prospero's claim to sovereignty; and it is that force of resistance and denial that fissures the otherwise cohesive totality of the play's particular version of colonialist discourse.

For as an impressive body of 'new historicist' criticism has already demonstrated,[23] Prospero's occupation of the island, and his relationship with its original inhabitants, offers a dramatic model of, and a dramatic commentary on, the phenomenon of sixteenth-century imperialism. The play draws on documents that recorded voyages to Virginia, and the shipwreck that landed a group of colonists on the island of Bermuda; together with other sources dealing with the 'New World', such as Montaigne's essay 'Of the Cannibals'.[24] While these intertextual relationships have long been familiar to scholars, at least in the form of 'sources', the contribution of the 'new historicism' has been to demonstrate the complexity and contradictoriness of sixteenth-century colonialist discourse. While the language which justified and encouraged imperialist exploration and the subjugation of native peoples was based on assumptions of natural superiority and racial mastery, the closer it moved towards the reality which it attempted to realize, the more strikingly it began to bear the traces of a contradictory ideology. The tension between European conceptions of the 'third world' as occupied by wild, savage, monstrous and barbaric creatures, and the actual civilizations of the peoples encountered by colonists, stands at the centre of colonialist discourse; its contrary is indeed embodied in that essay of Montaigne which provided the direct source for Gonzalo's vision of a utopian commonwealth.

The theatrical tradition that has found Caliban so fascinatingly complex a role, and has provided a very wide range of 'character' interpretations, is rooted firmly in the contradictory medium of the text itself. The more Prospero and Miranda attempt to impose upon Caliban, and upon their relationships with him, an ideological structure of unquestionable simplicity, the more the play turns and twists to offer qualification, reservation, or open contradiction.

Colonialist discourse is always concerned to establish clear and stable distinctions between colonist and colonized. The qualities of each – the civilized virtues of the one, for example, and the unredeemable ignorance and treachery of the other – must be seen as immanent, knit deep into the fabric of each society. There can be no acknowledgement that the characteristic behaviour of each party might emanate directly from the manner of their confrontation rather than from inherent characteristics of each. Caliban is introduced by Prospero as a character fundamentally and irreducibly hostile, servile and evil:

> *Pros.* We'll visit Caliban, my slave, who never
> Yields us kind answer . . .
> Thou poisonous slave, got by the devil himself

Upon thy wicked dam, come forth!
(I.ii.308-9, 319-20)

Once again, in parallel with Prospero's conversations with Miranda and Ariel, there is a contestation of memories, a dispute over the meanings of the past. Prospero's recollection of his relationship with Caliban is the standard colonial myth: the European colonist arrives full of benevolent intentions, offering to the native people kindness, education and community:

> *Pros.*   I have used thee –
> Filth as thou art – with humane care, and lodged thee
> In mine own cell . . .
> (I.ii.345-7)

Miranda also speaks with the authentic accent of the colonizer, and describes herself as bearing the charitable virtue of compassion and the gift of a civilized language:

> *Mir.*   . . . I pitied thee
> Took pains to make thee speak . . .
> (I.ii.352-3)

In each case the proffered benefits have been spurned, the proffered share in a civilized community rejected. In an accusation Caliban does not deny, he is convicted of attempting to rape Miranda. Despite the sensitivities that appropriately surround this particular form of violent crime, it seems important to acknowledge that here the allegation belongs to that bigoted, one-sided colonialist discourse shared by Prospero and Miranda. If it is true, then it was clearly an act calculated to violate both patriarchal solicitude and filial kindness; an example of treacherous ingratitude (which Caliban is of course to compound in the course of the play by plotting to murder Prospero) that seems to demonstrate conclusively the impassable gulfs that separate wisdom and ignorance, civilization and barbarity, benevolence and malice. Caliban evidently does not respond to kindness, and must therefore be controlled by punishment; he is not fit to receive the benefits of human society, since he bears some unnameable taint of moral atrocity which renders his proximity intolerable, and must therefore be confined by imprisonment.

Caliban tells the same story with interesting differences of emphasis:

> *Cal.* This island's mine by Sycorax my mother,
> Which thou tak'st from me. When thou cam'st first,
> Thou strok'st me and made much of me; wouldst give me
> Water with berries in't, and teach me how
> To name the bigger light and how the less,
> That burn by day and night; and then I loved thee,
> And showed thee all the qualities o'th' isle,
> The fresh springs, brine pits, barren place and fertile –
> Cursed be I that I did so! All the charms
> Of Sycorax, toads, beetles, bats, light on you!
> For I am all the subjects that you have,
> Which first was mine own king, and here you sty me
> In this hard rock, whiles you do keep from me
> The rest o'th' island.
>
> (I.ii.331–44)

Caliban acknowledges the gift of education, and obviously regards it as a precious benefit. Moreover the process of education is seen here very much as a personal relationship between teacher and pupil. It is inseparable from the memory of exchanged endearments – 'thou strok'st me' – 'I loved thee'; and it is recollected with a temporary reversion to the childish imagination that was so eager to learn the mysteries of naming – Caliban of course now knows the words for sun and moon, but can remember when he thought of them as the big and little lights. In Caliban's autobiographical narrative, his education is remembered as a mutual process, in which Prospero's gifts of knowledge are amply reciprocated by the native's practical knowledge of the island. If Caliban's narrative is true, he emerges from its particular shaping of the past as a creature capable of love and eager for companionship, full of gratitude and affection, and active in the discharging of felt obligations. Above all, what he registers is a claim to mutuality: he does not see himself as excluded by racial or moral contamination from a relationship of mutual obligation and reciprocal indebtedness with a human being. Did he attempt to rape Miranda, or were his spontaneous gestures of physical affection only perceived as violence?

Prospero simply tells a different story: in his version all the 'humane care' (I.ii.346) is on one side, and Caliban returns it with ingratitude, treachery and attempted violation. To Prospero and Miranda Caliban is not human: he is 'filth' of a 'vile race'. By comparison with Caliban's vision of a co-operative process of mutual education based on love, Prospero's harsh authoritarianism and conviction of righteousness seem crude indeed; and Miranda's assumption that Caliban's own native language was simply a meaningless 'gabble', unintelligible even to himself – that he could not have known what he was saying until he learned English – is perhaps worthy of inclusion among all the immense stupidities of the imperialist imagination.

Is this a sentimentalization of Caliban? After all, though he speaks movingly of education here, he also regards the principal benefit bestowed by language as the capacity to curse. Though he elegizes a lost mutual affection with Prospero in a poetry of grave and eloquent beauty, he appears to regret the failure of his attempted sexual conquest of Miranda. But as we have seen, there are in play two distinct and antagonistic versions of the story; and there can be little doubt that in this play the processes of story-telling, the means by which representations of the past are constructed, are made so obtrusively explicit that the relativities of memory and interpretation become insistently foregrounded. One fundamental ideological difference separates Prospero's and Caliban's perspectives on the past: that is, how the fact of race is to be understood and addressed in moral belief and social action. Prospero and Miranda believe that Caliban belongs to a 'vile race', manifestly inferior to their own, and scarcely deserving of inclusion within the human community. Caliban believes that the island is his, deriving from Sycorax by legitimate inheritance and possession.

It is of course the paradigmatic ideological dispute that lies at the heart of imperialism; and it is natural to assume that in a post-colonial age such as ours, possibilities of interpretation may have surfaced that would have been invisible to the Elizabethans. But in fact sixteenth-century colonialist discourse was not by any means a seamless entity, unfissured by ideological difference, free of any internal disturbance or inherent anxiety. Prospero represents a fairly cynical and pragmatic acceptance of the white man's burden: acknowledging that Caliban is a 'villain' (I.ii.309), he nevertheless confides to Miranda: ' . . . as 'tis,/ We cannot miss him. He does make our fire,/ Fetch in our wood, and serves in offices,/ That profit us' (I.ii.310–13). The solipsistic arrogance of the European imperialist does not question that the appropriate lot of a born slave should be slavery; and the physical disgust of racial hatred is withdrawn in favour of the profitability of racial exploitation. Yet the very presence within the play of Gonzalo's speech about a utopian commonwealth (II.i.145–62) draws into the play that other possibility of response to the reality of newly-discovered primitive societies: a recognition that the image of a simple, communal existence could have the power to interrogate and call into question the sophisticated corruptions of a modern commercial society. As Greenblatt, Brown, Barker and Hulme have demonstrated, these contradictory responses of confident exploitation and anxious idealization were often found interpenetrating within a single individual's experience of the colonial situation; in exactly the same way they are to be found interacting and confronting one another within the ideological universe of this dramatic text.

Why, for example, did Prospero, who of all people has cause to respect legitimate sovereignty, not recognize Caliban as the ruler of the island? Why should Caliban's subversive fantasy of lust and procreation ('I had peopled else/ This isle with Calibans', I.ii.348–9) not have taken the different form of a legitimate royal marriage with Prospero's daughter, and the authorized provision of a sovereign family? Those theatrical traditions that have made Caliban into a kind of animal (where actors and directors have, perhaps unwisely, taken Trinculo's view of him as the most authentic characterization) should not be allowed to obscure the indiscriminate and arbitrary nature of the racial disgust portrayed in the play. Miranda's physical repulsion towards Caliban is paralleled in the play by the reported sexual disgust felt by Alonso's daughter, Claribel, at the prospect of her marriage to the King of Tunis. Sebastian bitterly condemns the marriage as a case of racial miscegenation, and describes Claribel as hopelessly caught between loyalty and obedience to her father, and a correspondingly powerful emotional recoil from the imminent union with a black husband. 'Sir', he says to Alonso:

> *Seb.* . . . you may thank yourself for this great loss,
> That would not bless our Europe with your daughter,
> But rather lose her to an African,
> Where she, at least, is banished from your eye,
> Who hath cause to wet the grief on't.
> . . . You were kneeled to and importuned otherwise
> By all of us, and the fair soul herself
> Weighed between loathness and obedience at
> Which end o'th' beam should bow.
> (II.i.121–5, 126–9)

Sebastian's language precisely parallels that of his compatriot

## The Tempest: Spectacles of Disenchantment 177

Brabantio, who ridicules the assumption that Desdemona could voluntarily have chosen the 'sooty bosom' of Othello over the authorized attractions of the European master-race, 'the wealthy curled darlings of our nation'; and infers that Desdemona must, like Claribel, have been torn between loyalty and loathing, in order 'To fall in love with what she feared to look on' (*Othello*, I.ii.68,70; I.iii.98). In *The Tempest* Alonso, like Desdemona, seems to display a curious innocence of the racism that afflicts everyone else; or at least to regard international alliances and the foreign policy of the commonwealth as more important than his daughter's scruples of sexual racism.

Prospero and Miranda however concur with Claribel, Sebastian and the entire population of the Milanese court in regarding miscegenation as unthinkable. Just as Prospero, for reasons that are clearly defined as racist, could never regard Caliban as an equal or even as an associate, and therefore contributes to the positioning of him as an incorrigible slave; so Miranda, for reasons that are equally clearly racist in origin, could never regard Caliban as a potential sexual partner, and therefore contributes to the positioning of him as an irredeemable rapist. Within the moral framework of Gonzalo's utopian commonwealth, Caliban's innate disposition towards community, co-operation and love would coincide with the essential spirit of that imagined anarchistic system of free and mutual exchange. From the perspective of the moral values imported from Italy by the courts of Milan and Naples, such a commonwealth could be nothing more than a disorderly gang of 'whores and knaves' (II.i.164). Prospero's view is clearly closer to the latter than to the former, closer to Hobbes than to Montaigne: on the assumption that European values are threatened with subversion and violation by the undisciplined energies of an inferior race, he introduces to the innocent space of the desert island slavery, punishment, and a hierarchically-organized structure of domination.

## IMAGES OF EMPIRE

The central image of Caliban's attempted 'rape' clearly possesses huge symbolic resonances for both parties; yet it means something quite different to the representatives of each 'race'. It is used by Prospero, in an irascible and irrational passage of argument, as the sole justification for his seizure of the island (I.ii.344–8): he has no comment to make on Caliban's claim to sovereignty other than the accusation of falsehood – 'Thou most lying slave' – and the irrelevant allegation of sexual assault – 'I have used thee –/ Filth as thou art – with humane care . . . till thou didst seek to violate/ The honour of my child' (I.ii.345–8). As Barker and Hulme observe, it has always been customary for imperialist powers to justify their own violence in the subjugation of native peoples by reference to the violence of the natives themselves – which of course appears specifically in the form of resistance to the incursions of alien power. In post-colonial situations, withdrawing imperialist powers smugly point to the common legacy of internecine conflict as a return to an original condition. For Caliban, a sexual union with Miranda would have been an opportunity to establish his own race in the territory he regards as his.

The image of an assault or rape perpetrated by native occupants of a colonized territory upon a colonizing 'woman' (wife or daughter), later developed into a paradigmatic symbol in the fiction of imperialism. It is the potent and seminal central motif in texts such as E. M. Forster's *A Passage to India*, and Paul Scott's *The Raj Quartet*. Each of these three texts involves a peculiar displacement of the agency of violation, from the colonizer to the colonized. From the point of view of the colonized, a symbolic rape is precisely what has been practised upon them by the violent incursions of an imperialist power. Howard Brenton in the play *The Romans in Britain* inverts the motif, and makes the male body the object of attempted rape, specifically in order to restore this powerful symbol of invasion to its appropriate position.[25]

But from the point of view of the colonizer – Prospero, Ronnie Heaslop, Inspector Meyrick – the action symbolizes something quite different: it indicates how the generous offer of fellowship and of the benefits of civiliation is continually violated by the uncivilized savagery of those to whom the offer is made. The symbolic 'rape of the fair country' which offers such an exact image of imperialist domination, is systematically inverted to produce the image of a brutal native assault on the purity and vulnerability of the female colonist. In fact the modern texts to which I have referred reflect critically on this stereotype, refusing to endorse its ideological content (though it still seems to 'third world' intellectuals absurd that it should be used at all). It seems to me that it is possible to identify in *The Tempest* a degree of 'open-ness', secured through the continual juxtaposition of conflicting constructions of the past, and through the confrontation of Prospero's crude authoritarianism with more democratic and utopian political views, that in turn throws the issue of Caliban's suppression and resistance into an interactive and liberating kind of play. Caliban will simply not be confined to the position allotted to him in Prospero's hierarchical vision of an ordered colonial community.

What then might that courtly audience which witnessed a royal command performance of *The Tempest* on 1 November 1611 have made of these representations of the 'New World'? Images of empire were of course familiar elements of the Stuart court masques. The discovery and colonization of remote and exotic lands provided a whole vocabulary of fantastic imagery representing strange places and unfamiliar peoples, which could be exploited by the romantic and overtly fictive methods of the masque. The reality of maritime exploration and overseas colonization could also effectively be merged with the attractive legends and fantasies of classical literature. At the same time, since the Empire was imagined as a vast personal fiefdom, a huge extension of the royal power, the exotic and distant could be brought home: the colonies were after all outposts of British society and culture, no different in kind from communities within Britain (and Ireland) itself. The New World could be conceived as essentially nothing other than the Old World re-inscribed, expanded, its frontiers merely enlarged rather than altered. In Ben Jonson's masque *The Fortunate Isles* the classical islands of the blest (which were after all imagined by the ancients as situated at the Western end of the world) are in effect identified with Britain. In Jonson's *News from the New World*, where the 'New World' is actually a society discovered in the moon, the evident cultural differences between old and new societies are complemented by evident similarities and parallels. In *The Tempest* the comic scenes present a kind of satirical interplay of far and near, exotic and familiar. 'Were I in England now', an English actor playing a Milanese character shipwrecked on a Mediterranean island which is also somehow in the Caribbean, confides to an English audience, 'as once I was . . . ' (II.ii.27). The satirical juxtaposition of new and old worlds that we find in the comic scenes brings the remote, semi-fictional worlds of America and the 'Bermoothes' firmly into Jacobean London.[26]

From this interpretative perspective *The Tempest* can be assimilated to a genre in which elements of romance and fantasy operate as thinly-disguised signifiers for contemporary domestic reality.

The genres of fantasy do not in this cultural problematic estrange and defamiliarize the present: they can be understood simply as ways of representing the immediate reality of the everyday world. When in the court masque a member of the royal family would play a fantasy character – such as Prince Henry playing Oberon in Jonson's masque of 1611 – the remote and the familiar, the supernatural and the real merged into one indivisible medium of representation.

Clearly the 'science fiction' and 'fantasy' elements of Jacobean dramatic romance did to some extent operate in this way: the court masque itself perfectly exemplifies the fusion of fantasy romance and immediate contemporary application, mingling as it did classical, legendary and supernatural materials with sharply-pointed political comment on the issues of the day. But it is perhaps a misleading conception of the relationship between the court that witnessed performances of *The Tempest* in 1611 and 1613, and the colonial experience on which the play so extensively draws. We should not assume that places like Virginia and the Bermudas simply existed in the minds of Shakespeare's spectators as fantasy landscapes. It has been acknowledged since as far back as 1808, when Malone drew attention to some documentary materials relating to the Virginia Company, and particularly to the wreck of the *Sea Revenge* on the Bermudas, that among the sources of *The Tempest* were unpublished contemporary accounts of very specific colonial experiences. One source which has definite echoes in the play is the letter of William Strachey, not printed until 1625, which describes how in the course of a voyage organized by the Virginia Company, to transport some four hundred colonists to America, the ship bearing the governor of Jamestown, Sir Thomas Gates, was blown off course by a hurricane and stranded on Bermuda. Shakespeare's familiarity with this document is not surprising, given that a number of friends and associates link the dramatist quite closely to the Virginia Company itself. The Earl of Southampton, to whom Shakespeare's poems *Venus and Adonis* and the *Rape of Lucrece* were dedicated, sponsored the voyage which led to the foundation of the Virginia Company. Men known to Shakespeare, such as Dudley Digges and Christopher Brooke, were associated with the company. The Earl of Pembroke, to whom the posthumous *First Folio* of Shakespeare's plays was dedicated, was a prominent supporter of overseas exploration and of the American colonies. Shakespeare may even have known Strachey.

We tend to think of colonial expansion in this period as owing more to the entrepreneurial zeal of the commercial middle classes, to the speculative ambitions of the smaller landowners, and to the religious aspirations of the Puritans, than to the government or state. But as Lawrence Stone has shown,[27] the group most active among the landed classes in promoting and investing in overseas exploration was the aristocracy. They were the important entrepreneurs, the major risk-takers; Stone suggests that the kind of high-risk speculative gambling involved in financing colonial ventures appealed to the aristocracy much more strongly than did capitalistic methods of seeking profit. Thus the Jacobean court itself was a major participant in the activity of colonization. When the aristocracy who formed the nucleus of the court watched a play like *The Tempest*, they were watching a particular mediated representation of their own colonial activities.

It is clear therefore that the 'New World', which is embodied in *The Tempest* in the form of a fantasy, could have been conceived and understood by one of the play's audiences in concrete economic and political terms as well as imaginative ones. There were possibilities, in other words, for those dimensions of meaning which we can detach from the play and designate as 'historical', to merge into continuity with its auditors' immediate contemporary experiences of the 'New World'. Since those experiences were genuinely unprecedented, that process must have been somewhat different from the merging of legendary and classical imagery with the immediate cultural context of the court, which happened continually in the masque form. While Prospero's representation of a benevolent thaumaturgical ruler must have seemed to the chief auditor of a court performance, the king, to be a thinly-disguised portrayal of everyday reality, the depiction of Prospero's colonial outpost must have drawn the imaginations of aristocratic spectators out towards those uncharted seas and undiscovered countries where their money and efforts were invested in risky and exciting imperialist ventures.

What *The Tempest* reveals about seventeenth-century colonialism, as understood by a well-informed and interested contemporary, runs directly parallel to the non-fictional accounts produced by men directly involved in the colonialist enterprise itself. In drawing on the other 'textualizations' of colonialism written by Strachey, Jourdain, Montaigne and others, Shakespeare did more than pick up a few useful details of historical narrative and exotic local colour.

As Stephen Greenblatt has shown,[28] the process at work in the contruction of a text like *The Tempest* can best be understood as a process of symbolic exchange, or to use Greenblatt's own phrase, a circulation of social energy. Shifting our attention away from the monumental figure of the author, that huge individualized focus of authority which in traditional criticism determines the ways in which 'historical' material is filtered and mediated towards 'artistic' embodiment, and focussing instead on the patterns formed by discursive exchanges of meaning between social and cultural institutions (such as the joint-stock firms the Virginia Company and the King's Men), Greenblatt argues that *The Tempest* actually reproduces in fictional form the same ethical and political discourse to be found non-fictionally inscribed in Strachey's letters from Virginia. For the task of negotiating and controlling crises of authority which appears to be Prospero's main preoccupation, was exactly that facing the managers of the Virginian colony of Jamestown; and even more specifically, it was the problem encountered by Sir Thomas Gates as he sought to govern that part of the colony that found itself shipwrecked on Bermuda. Gates himself was concerned above all about the possible repercussions of his absence in Jamestown; but he found within his castaway company virtually no internalization of the ideology of colonialism. Whether in Bermuda or Virginia, the people saw themselves as exiles: and once acquainted with the incredibly favourable conditions pertaining on Bermuda, which seemed to associate the islands strangely with all the aristocratic and popular legends of the *locus amoenus*, from the classical Islands of the Blest to the Land of Cockaigne, they seem to have felt very little inclination to leave. The combined forces of utopian longing and radical religious dissent produced resistance to Sir Thomas' authority, and at least one colonist, who believed that the circumstances of the shipwreck had voided the governer's magistracy, had to be executed for subversive treason. The problems of colonial discipline were intensified rather than diminished when Gates finally arrived in Jamestown, where the settlers were discovered demoralized and starving. His solution was the immediate imposition of a draconian code of emergency laws, providing extreme and brutal punishments for the slightest offence of resistance to his own and the Company's authority. Greenblatt describes the *Laws Divine, Moral and Martial* (1612) as 'the first martial law code in America' (p. 154).

Prospero's continual confrontation with examples of lower-class resistance and upper-class betrayal precisely parallels the conflicts

# The Tempest: Spectacles of Disenchantment 183

encountered by the historical pioneers whose task was not only to discover and colonize a new world, but also to ensure its subjugation to the ideology of the old.

> Such then were the narrative materials that passed from Strachey to Shakespeare, from the Virginia Company to the King's Men: a violent tempest, a providential shipwreck on a strange island, a crisis in authority provoked by both danger and excess, a fear of lower-class disorder and upper-class ambition, a triumphant affirmation of control linked to the manipulation of anxiety and to a departure from the island. (Greenblatt, p. 154)

What Sir Thomas Gates achieved with the instruments of law and punishment, Prospero achieves with magic: or as Greenblatt observes, 'Prospero's magic is the romance equivalent of martial law' (p. 154).

Far from enacting a transformation of banal historical documentation into vivid imaginative drama, *The Tempest* rather reproduces the essential structural configuration of authority and resistance that we find at the heart of the real colonial experience. An aristocratic reading of the court performances must inevitably have been pulled in the direction of endorsement and approval for the play's pattern of disruption and re-composition. That narrative and dramatic pattern doesn't merely affirm the necessity of firm magistracy and strong government, drawing optimistic conclusions from the Bermudan and Virginian adventures by re-enacting their instructive history of loss and recovery, subversion and containment, struggle and success; it also humanizes the colonial experience by converting martial law to magic, softening and withholding physical punishment in favour of social re-integration, and mollifying vindictive justice with benevolent forgiveness. On the other hand – a qualification Greenblatt does not consider – might not *The Tempest* in its popular presentations on the public stage have offered alternative readings of the colonial experience to that very different audience,composed of lesser merchants, small tradesmen, craftsmen, artisans, apprentices? Certainly in the comic scenes involving Trinculo the clown and Stephano the drunken butler, we see characters (who approximate closer in social status to that audience of common people who clustered around the stage) moving into the downstage *platea* position of direct and humorous engagement with the audience; and the perspective we receive onto the colonial experience is suddenly and dramatically altered. Trinculo comes across Caliban:

> *Trin.* A strange fish! Were I in England now, as once I was, and had but this fish painted, not a holiday-fool there but would give a piece of silver. There would this monster make a man – any strange beast there makes a man. When they will not give a doit to relieve a lame beggar, they will lay out ten to see a dead Indian.
> (II.ii.26–32)

Suddenly, and with a remarkable shift of viewpoint, we are looking at the colonial experience not from the perspective of its managers, anxiously and carefully rehearsing and negotiating their problems of authority and resistance; but from a perspective in which self-interest, mean ambition and unscrupulous exploitation figure more prominently than the envisioned plantation of a civilized and godly community. While the colonial poetry of Ariel and Caliban draws our imaginations outwards towards the remote and exotic terrain of empire, Trinculo's satirical observations land us squarely back home in the familiar domestic environment of opportunism and exploitation, where money makes a man. On the stage of the Jacobean public theatre such immediate contemporary satire would bring the play's fantastic other-world firmly down to earth.

The discursive conventions within which this self-reflexive interweaving of far and near, exotic and banal, strange and familiar, can take place are clearly quite different from those governing the main-plot scenes in which Prospero's power and Prospero's ideology command the stage. And although the intoxicated carnival ambitions of the three clowns are kept firmly in place both by Prospero's controlling surveillance and by the aesthetic structure of the drama itself, it is hard to believe that there were not members of the public theatre audience who could not have responded with some enthusiasm and approval to Caliban's song of liberty:

> *Cal.* No more dams I'll make for fish,
> Nor fetch in firing
>   At requiring,
> Nor scrape trenchering, nor wash dish:
>   'Ban, 'Ban, Ca-Caliban
> Has a new master – get a new man!

Freedom, high-day! High-day, freedom! Freedom, high-day, freedom!

(II.ii.174–81)

While the courtly audience could take pleasure in the pastoral fantasy of Ferdinand, a royal prince, being condemned to carry firewood, those closer to the necessary execution of that hard, ubiquitous and pervasive labour might have responded more positively to Caliban's fantasy of release from the same 'wooden slavery' (III.i.62).

## MASQUE AND DRAMA

The fifth act of *Cymbeline* presents an example of the deployment of masque forms and conventions, which provides an illuminating contrast with the more formal court masque presented in *The Tempest*; and indeed with other masque elements employed in the latter play, as well as the pastoral masque gesturally performed at the Bohemian sheep-shearing feast of *The Winter's Tale*. The narrative and dramatic patterns of problematization, intervention and resolution to be found in these romance plays clearly derive from the masque form. As in the Stuart court masques, a group of characters appears to question, challenge or doubt the justice of existence, the equity of a sovereign's government, or the rationale of a divine providence. In *Cymbeline* this function is performed by a company of ghosts, those of Posthumus' father, mother and two brothers. In a poetic discourse characterized by the formalized stanzaic verse of the masques, the ghosts interrogate Jupiter's justice in permitting an arbitrary and disproportionate punishment to fall on Posthumus, the innocent victim of circumstance and misjudgement. The perplexity and anxiety of the ghosts creates exactly the right dramatic atmosphere of uncertainty and disturbance to prepare for a ritualized demonstration of divine intervention. Jupiter descends, with appropriately impressive special effects, to silence the complaining spirits, to justify the ways of god to men, to explain the rationale of divine providence, and to predict the resurrection and restoration of Posthumus' fortunes. The ghosts join in a chorus of celebration, gratitude and praise; and depart in haste to discharge willingly-accepted obligations of service, to perform Jupiter's 'great behest' (*Cymbeline*, V.iv.122).

But this is not, in the play, a court masque, but a dream. The pageant is performed around the sleeping form of Posthumus; it is coterminous with his unconsciousness; and it is not witnessed by anyone else. Clearly the dramatic narrative has as much in common with the conventions of dream-fiction – such as mediaeval dream-poetry – as it does with the Stuart court masque. As in all the mediaeval dream poems, Chaucerian and other, the principal function of the dream is to act as the vehicle of a message. Here that missive, in the form of a riddling written prophecy left on Posthumus' breast, is neither clear nor immediately intelligible: nonetheless, despite the impenetrably obfuscating effects of its prophetic discourse, Posthumus immediately accepts the dream as bearing sufficient application to his own life to carry an undeniable charge of meaning. It is either a dream, or the delusion of a madman; either nonsense ('senseless speaking'), or an impenetrable mystery ('a speaking such/ As sense cannot untie'):

> *Post.* Be what it is,
> The action of my life is like it, which
> I'll keep, if but for sympathy.
> (*Cymbeline*, V.iv.148–50)

The arbitrary logic of fantasy, and the inexplicable dénouement of circumstances, seem to find common ground on the narrative territory of Posthumus' tortuous life: dream and reality become indistinguishable. The paradox is of course at the heart of the Stuart court masque, which attempted precisely to confer on its classical narratives, legendary characters and mythological actions the lineaments of substantial truth. Posthumous is not, of course, as are Ferdinand and Miranda in *The Tempest*, constituted as the spectator to a staged production: the pageant is completely internalized as an action of the dreaming consciousness. Though it partakes of the form and employs the conventions of the masque, this masque-like fiction demands to be read as a psychological event rather than as a theatrical performance. But that internalization serves to enhance rather than diminish the capacity of masque conventions to operate as signifiers of reality, as bearers of truth.

In a parallel episode in Act 3 of *The Tempest*, a comparable group of puzzled and questioning characters witnesses the apparition of a supernatural visitor, this time the fearsome harpy of Greek legend. The descent of the mythological creature is framed by two dances of spirits, which first set the banquet, and then remove from the stage the remnants of it that survive the ravaging Harpy's devouring assault. The stage directions governing the two dances irresistibly recall the procedures of the court masque: the first dance is an invitation or offering, the second a mocking and scurrilous anti-masque of ridicule and contempt:

> *Enter several strange shapes bringing in a banquet, and dance about it with gentle actions of salutations; and inviting the king, etc., to eat, they depart*

> *Then, to soft music, enter the shapes again, and dance with mocks and mows, and carrying out the table*

In *Cymbeline* there is no distance between the actor who plays Jupiter and the role he plays. In *The Tempest* the distance between performer and part is much more openly in evidence: *'enter Ariel like a Harpy'*. Ariel is in fact a versatile performer who subsequently presents the role of Ceres in the masque proper. There is no space at all in the case of the *Cymbeline* example for any serious doubt as to Jupiter's honesty or the accuracy of his predictions. Yet in *The Tempest*, the message Ariel delivers, in the persona of the Harpy, is little more than an extensive and sustained pack of lies. He claims that both storm and shipwreck were caused by 'Destiny': though we know them to have been the product of Prospero's magic. He describes the island as uninhabited; although we are aware that it is in fact occupied by a small but highly civilized community (sophisticated enough at least to have introduced slavery). He describes himself and his 'fellow-ministers' as instruments of Fate; they are of course the agents only of Prospero's strategic manipulations. He attributes the responsibility for the punishments they are experiencing to some impersonal deity or destiny, 'the powers'; in fact of course Prospero has stage-managed them all. Finally Ariel compounds the falsehood he himself initiated, by permitting Alonso to continue to believe that his son is drowned.

The moral message that this supernatural visitation is intended to convey is clear enough: punishment can only cease, the demands of implacable justice can only be deflected, by repentance and reformation – 'heart's sorrow,/ And a clear life ensuing' (III.iii.81–2). The immediate result of the apparition on Alonso and his court is not however any sudden spiritual conversion, but only an intensification of madness and despair.

Though these two examples have in common their mutual relationship with the court masque, there the resemblance ends; for one is a convincingly-dramatized dream of truth, the other an overtly simulated tissue of lies. One is experienced, the other staged. In a characteristically metadramatic gesture, Prospero by commending the theatrical success of the performance calls attention to the mechanisms of its construction:

> *Pros.* Bravely the figure of this harpy hast thou
> Performed, my Ariel; a grace it had, devouring.
> Of my instruction hast thou nothing bated
> In what thou hadst to say; so with good life
> And observation strange my meaner ministers
> Their several kinds have done. My high charms work,
> And these, mine enemies, are all knit up
> In their distractions. They now are in my power . .
> (III.iii.84–90)

In commending Ariel's portrayal of the harpy, Prospero explicitly draws attention to the apparition as theatre rather than as myth. The supporting cast are also praised for their dramatic skills: their performance of the dance was executed with 'good life' (naturalistic representation) and 'observation strange' (surprisingly convincing portrayal of character). The quality of their performances is measured in part by the accuracy and precision with which they can be observed to have fulfilled and executed Prospero's commands. The functionalist purpose of the show itself is revealed with abundant clarity – Prospero uses theatrical representation in order to secure and maintain 'power'.

The performance of the 'court masque' proper in Act 4:1 is prefaced with a very similar passage of metadramatic contextualization, in which the internalized dramatic performance is visibly put into production before it is staged. Prospero again commends the success of Ariel's previous production, and commands another:

> *Pros.* Thou and thy meaner fellows your last service
> Didst worthily perform, and I must use you
> In such another trick. Go, bring the rabble
> O'er whom I give thee pow'r here to this place.
> Incite them to quick motion, for I must
> Bestow upon the eyes of this young couple

> Some vanity of mine art: it is my promise,
> And they expect it from me.
>
> (IV.i.35–42)

Once again the term 'perform' is employed specifically for its articulation of diversified associations: as a servant Ariel and his underlings 'perform' a 'service' for Prospero; but as actors, as theatrical presenters and dramatic impersonators they 'perform' an entertainment for some sort of audience. The specific kind of cultural context depicted here is one in which the potential historical splitting of these alternate meanings – clearly within the experience of an acting company like the King's Men – is prevented from occurring, since the players are obliged to 'perform' (act) by virtue of the same relationship of service which obliges them to 'perform' any other task their master may enjoin upon them. The relationship between patron and client–performers is closer, in other words, to the context of court theatre, where actors are bound in some formal relationship of service, and where private performances are commissioned by the king or his agents; than it is to the context of the public playhouse, where the acting company functioned as an economically independent collective of producers who marketed their products to a diversified body of consumers, and where the obligation to 'serve the public' is really very different from the patron–client relationship existing between the monarch and the 'King's Men'.

Despite the applause bestowed on his actors' performance skills, Prospero makes no secret of the subservient relationship into which those performers are bound; nor of the purely utilitarian function of their art; nor of the strictly delegated nature of the power their performance may seem to wield; nor of the reductive definition by means of which a theatrical show can be designated as a mere 'trick' of fancy, arbitrary, temporary and delusive. Prospero 'uses' his actors to accomplish a 'trick', the sole function of which is to exercise some form of 'power' over his enemies; but he is careful to stipulate that such power belongs, not to the art of drama itself, but to the authority of the sovereign who commissions, produces and directs the performance; it is a borrowed power, given and reclaimed. Within this discursive field, with its very detailed and precise foregrounding of the infrastructure of power underlying court theatre, the masque of Juno and Ceres is heralded in an illuminatingly reductive phrase: 'some vanity of mine art'.

While the utilitarian function of that 'Masque of the Harpy' seems far more constitutive than its qualities as a performance, the 'Masque of the Three Goddesses' performed for Ferdinand and Miranda initially appears to be produced in a completely opposite spirit. While the one, designed to provoke remorse in Prospero's enemies, shows the making of an illusory offering which is immediately taken away, the other seems freely presented to Miranda and Ferdinand as a betrothal gift:

> *Pros.*  . . . it is my promise,
> And they expect it from me.
> (IV.i.41–2)

Although neither promise nor expectation has actually figured in the text, the offering of a performance in the spirit of a gift seems entirely in keeping with Prospero's generous and benevolent endorsement of his daughter's own voluntary choice of marriage partner, and perfectly in keeping with the customs of courtly festivity and entertainment used at the Jacobean court to celebrate royal and aristocratic marriages.[29] That ritual of tribute, which has been identified as the ancient and original form of the masque convention,[30] is also repeated in the dramatic narrative of the masque itself: Iris declares her purpose in the words 'some donation freely to estate/ On the blessed lovers' (IV.i.85–6). The masque that enacts the offering of a gift is in itself a gift, an offering. Though Prospero's casual description of it as a 'vanity' seems to link naturally to his dismissal of the earlier performance as merely a 'trick', the word 'vanity' might well seem to differentiate the betrothal masque from the apparition of the harpy. If the Masque of Juno and Ceres is vain, empty, a playful exhibition of theatrical skills, a dazzling display of necromantic inventiveness, then its very pleasurableness may be linked to its absence of willed intention, of manipulative pressure, of didactic imposition.

The masque begins with Iris' description of a pastoral landscape, the domain of the earth-goddess Ceres. That countryside of pasture and crops is not however the scene of the masque, since Ceres is commanded away from its pastoral topography to a 'grass-plot', a 'short-grassed green' on which the Queen of the Gods may be received, and on which appropriate revels may be celebrated. These internal stage-directions do not read like instructions to the designer and scene-painter; in fact the poetic description seems much more like that kind of verbal scene-painting familiar from the bare unlocalized stages of the public theatres, than a call for expensive and elaborate scenery to visualize the landscape of Ceres' kingdom. Iris's description is rather to be understood as the formal demarcation of an acting area: as Orgel comments, 'the masque takes place on a well-tended lawn, as opposed to the wild nature of the island' (Orgel, p. 175). Whether the actual performing area referred to was the green cloth carpeting the dancing area in the Banqueting House at Whitehall, or the green rushes that carpeted the stage floor in the public theatres, a specific area is being formally marked out as the proper terrain of this kind of dramatic event. The courtly audience of Prospero's little kingdom is composed only of himself and the young couple, who although constituted as the auditors of the show are also at least partly an element in it, since the characters in the masque allude directly to their presence. These devices such as the foregrounding of the process of location, and the formal placing of an audience to mediate between the internalized show and the theatre audience itself, signals clearly from the outset the self-reflexive and metadramatic qualities of this masque-within-a-play.

Iris then heralds the apparition of Juno, and celebrates the Queen's royal authority, her 'sovereign grace' (IV.i.72). The staged descent of the goddess enacts in theatrical form the miracle of divine intervention. Juno comes to confer on the betrothed couple the gift of her blessing, and the gathering of goddesses forms a quorum for the ritual celebration of human espousal: 'A contract of true love to celebrate' (IV.i.84). The straightforward ritual unfolding of celebration and tribute is however at this point strangely diverted. Ceres and Iris begin to speak of another goddess who is not present, indeed not welcome at this celebration: Venus, the goddess of love. Her absence from a betrothal rite seems to call for explanation, and necessitates the construction of another internal narrative, describing an abortive attempt by Venus to sabotage the ceremony of betrothal by provoking a premature sexual union (IV.i.91–101). Precisely why Venus and Cupid turn away from their mission of disruption is not explained: but the additional layer of narrative incorporates into the tributary celebration a dimension of ethical instruction and moral warning, against the ever-present dangers of unchastity. The 'wanton charm' is deflected, and that authorized exchange of flesh here designated as the 'bed-right' deferred until after the accomplishment of all appropriate ceremony and ritual:

> *Iris*  Here thought they to have done
> Some wanton charm upon this man and maid,
> Whose vows are that no bed-right shall be paid
> Till Hymen's torch be lighted; but in vain.
>
> (IV.i.94–7)

That diversion of the masque narrative from celebrations of fertility (Ceres and Iris), marriage and motherhood (Juno), to a focus on the dangers of sexual licence, is engineered by the goddess of fecundity herself, Ceres. It happens that in turning the masque towards such considerations, its symbolic narrative becomes more closely aligned with the anxieties and preoccupations of its producer Prospero. His own offer of a gift to Ferdinand, in the person of Miranda herself, is made with stringent conditions concerning the recipient's use of the tendered object. The father's absolute stipulation expresses his absolute determination to retain control over his daughter's sexuality:

> *Pros.*  Then as my gift, and thine own acquisition
> Worthily purchased, take my daughter. But
> If thou dost break her virgin-knot before
> All sanctimonious ceremonies may
> With full and holy rite be ministered,
> No sweet aspersion shall the heavens let fall
> To make this contract grow; but barren hate,
> Sour-eyed disdain, and discord shall bestrew
> The union of your bed with weeds so loathly
> That you shall hate it both. Therefore take heed,
> As Hymen's lamps shall light you.
>
> (IV.i.13–23)

'As Hymen's lamps shall light you' – not 'since Hymen's lamps will illuminate your passage', but 'insofar as Hymen's lamps will authorize the propriety of your union'.

By delivering this admonition against any breach of the marriage laws, by insisting that until the god of marriage at the appropriate time signals his permission for sexual congress to commence, sex between Ferdinand and Miranda must remain strictly prohibited, Iris and Ceres are speaking not from the mythological perspectives of their legendary characters, nor from the aesthetic coherence of the masque itself; they are speaking directly on behalf of Prospero, communicating his views and even employing his language. Prompted by the play's own insistent self-revelations, we reflect on this fact with small surprise: the masque is after all performed by Prospero's spirits, who are there to do his bidding. One of the masque's principal characters, we learn a little later, is actually played by Ariel: 'When I presented Ceres . . . ' (IV.i.167). The masque is revealed to be not a vanity of art, or a generously disinterested gift, but a further demonstration of Prospero's magical, artistic and ideological power. Both the contents and the conditions of its performance bespeak Prospero's will and Prospero's intentions. The masque is disclosed and foregrounded as a form of political power, by means of which Prospero coerces the imaginations of his subjects into a willing obedience. The vision is sustained by the power of his own imagination: when his vigilant surveillance of the island temporarily lapses, and is caught momentarily off guard, the entire show collapses into chaos:

> *Enter certain reapers, properly habited. They join with the nymphs in a graceful dance, towards the end whereof Prospero starts suddenly and speaks, after which, to a strange hollow and confused noise, they heavily vanish*

Here the grotesque counterpoint of the anti-masque occurs not within the aesthetic structure of the performance itself, but in a space between the performance and its producer; a movement that simply could not be imagined taking place within the court masque proper. The elaborate idealizing structure of the masque is demolished in the very course of its enactment; and its supporting infrastructure, the very conditions of its possibility, are revealed for what they are – an elaborate machinery of ideological coercion. This extraordinary image of the total breakdown of court theatre prompts Prospero to his famous meditation on the nature of dramatic illusion:

> *Pros.* Our revels now are ended. These our actors,
> As I foretold you, were all spirits, and
> Are melted into air, into thin air,
> And, like the baseless fabric of this vision,
> The cloud-capped towers, the gorgeous palaces,
> The solemn temples, the great globe itself,
> Yea, all which it inherit, shall dissolve,
> And, like this insubstantial pageant faded,
> Leave not a rack behind. We are such stuff

> As dreams are made on, and our little life
> Is rounded with a sleep.
>
> (IV.i.148–58)

Prospero's grave and meditative eloquence confers on these observations a portentous quality of enormous generality, as his imagination moves from the specific example of the 'revels' just brought to an abrupt close, to the world of theatrical illusion that can realize and embody images of the great world ('towers', 'palaces', 'temples'), to the world of reality which that medium of dramatic representation seeks to simulate. What begins as a passage of dramatic criticism seems to end as a sermon of philosophical meditation on the transience and fragility of life itself. But Prospero's observations are not prompted by reflections on drama in general, but by the contemplation of a very particular kind of drama, the court masque. The play (*The Tempest*) that contains the masque, Prospero himself, and the metaphysical disquisition that forms between them, is radically unlike that kind of drama. This clear demarcation of the distance between court masque and popular drama is one of the clearest indicators we will find of the true historical distance between the theatre of the court and the theatre of the public and 'private' playhouses.

# 10
# *The Winter's Tale*: Country into Court

The two-part structure of *The Winter's Tale*, with its shift from courtly Sicilia to pastoral Bohemia, isolates and defines its image of court society with an unmistakable clarity.

> *The Winter's Tale* has hatred in the first part and love, where there was hatred, in the last . . . Not only does the middle part stir the mind and heart of itself, but by the contrast of its beauty, love, youth, confidence, happiness, country life, and venial roguery, it intensifies the dramatic effect of the ugliness, the oppressive adult madness, hatred and murderous crime at court in the first part.[31]

Within the starkly-distinguished antitheses of pastoral convention, the Sicilian court is represented as the scene of suspicion, mistrust, surveillance, conspiracy, injustice, and tyranny; while the Arcadian simplicity of rural Bohemia reveals a society of freedom, openness, community and love. The two antagonistic stage-worlds of the play revolve around the polar axis of the famous sixteen-year gap, with its fill-in Chorus from a personified Time, and throw off a series of ancillary and subordinate oppositions: art versus nature; class-division against communal solidarity; tragedy confronted by comedy. As always in pastoral discourse the *locus amoenus* of the bucolic paradise provides a constant point of reference by which the constraints, inhibitions, corruptions and injustices of the court society may be measured.

Yet the ambivalence of pastoral convention is also very much in evidence throughout *The Winter's Tale*. In itself pastoral is originally a sophisticated courtly form, a *convention* which represents the works of nature through the constructions of artifice. Shepherds and shepherdesses appear in the Bohemian scenes, but the focus of the play's action is on a prince and princess of pastoral romance:

the former disguised as a 'swain', the latter concealing by her simple nurture the nature of a royal lineage. Life in Arcadia is never more than a temporary sojourn for these aristocratic figures, whose ultimate home is always a regenerated and reconstructed court. Nor are the courts depicted anything like the systematically corrupted courts of Jacobean tragedy. In the Sicilian court Leontes is actually an isolated figure, the object of continual resistance and remonstration. The well-meaning Polixenes, victim of Leontes' suspicious jealousy, becomes in his turn a tyrannical suppressor of natural affection, his court of Bohemia condemned by the passionate naivety of pastoral romance. But Polixenes' indispensable chief counsellor is Camillo, who begins, as soon as the king has tragically intervened into the blossoming relationship of Florizel and Perdita, to re-plot the dénouement of the play as a comedy of resolution and reconciliation. It is the chastened Sicilian court of the last act, which in a scene of reciprocal recognition and mutual discovery produces the living statue of Hermione, that provides the opportunity for (and thereby declares its own claim to considered as) the most convincing synthesis of art and nature.

## 'MANNERLY DISTINGUISHMENT'

*The Winter's Tale* opens with a brief 'establishing' scene, conducted in the form of an exchange of courtly compliments between Camillo and the Bohemian courtier Archidamus. Smooth and innocuous on the surface, this conversation nonetheless begins to open up some of the contradictions which will in the course of the play tear apart the fabric of the Sicilian court. Archidamus' speech seems to represent some of the exaggerated affectations of courtly elegance, and is perhaps being reproved by Camillo's terse statement of down-to-earth opinion: 'You pay a great deal too dear for what's given freely' (I.i.17–18). A bluff common-sense which will later form the characteristically tough and resilient texture of Paulina's remonstrances against Leontes' tyranny, is here opposed to the elaborate linguistic codes of courtly discourse. Archidamus' suggestion that there could ensue a competition between Bohemia and Sicilia, each vying to bestow on the other the maximum of pleasure and 'entertainment', may also point to a fault-line in the cultural geology of this particular court, one which it shares with the court of *Love's Labour's Lost*. Camillo's description of the relationship between the two kings raises as many ambiguities as the questions it answers:

> *Cam.* Sicilia cannot show himself over-kind to Bohemia. They were trained together in their childhoods, and there rooted betwixt them then such an affection which cannot choose but branch now. Since their more mature dignities and royal necessities made separation of their society, their encounters, though not personal, have been royally attorneyed with interchange of gifts, letters, loving embassies, that they have seemed to be together, though absent; shook hands, as over a vast; and embraced, as it were, from the ends of opposed winds. The heavens continue their loves! (I.i.20–32)

The love between the two men, beginning in childhood companionship, is figured here as an elaborate process of courtship: conducted at a distance, by the formal exchanging of communications and protestations of affection. The contradictory suggestions of intense intimacy and enormous distance construct a peculiarly incongruous relationship of identity and difference. In the space between private affinity and public friendship lies the seed of Leontes' tragedy. The love the two men carried through from childhood is described as 'rooted between them': rooted in the body of each, joining them indissolubly into a single destiny – later Polixenes describes their childhood selves as 'twinn'd lambs'. Yet they are not the same person, and the organic twinning of childhood could scarcely survive into adult lives in which 'mature dignities' and 'royal necessities', the public identity and responsibility of an aristocratic existence, would demarcate a necessary 'separation of their societies'. What is 'rooted between them' is described as 'affection', here carrying all the positive charge of that word as a sign of natural and reciprocal love. But 'affection' as often alluded to disorganizing and lustful passion, as in Leontes' subsequent astounded exclamation: 'Affection! thy intention stabs the centre . . . '(I.ii.138). 'Rooted' may in this context suggest a phallic resurgence, a grasping tenacity of desire that could well lead to a rather different kind of branching from the fulfilment of friendship anticipated by Camillo.

The latter association, but faintly shadowed here, becomes slightly more explicit when Polixenes speaks to Hermione of the same childhood relationship:

> *Pol.* We were as twinn'd lambs that did frisk i' th' sun,

> And bleat the one at th' other: what we chang'd
> Was innocence for innocence: we knew not
> The doctrine of ill-doing, nor dream'd
> That any did. Had we pursu'd that life,
> And our weak spirits ne'er been higher rear'd
> With stronger blood, we should have answer'd heaven
> Boldly 'not guilty', the imposition clear'd
> Hereditary ours.
>
>                                    (I.ii.67–74)

The imagery of phallic erection marks the birth of conscious sexuality as the end of innocence. What children are said to '[ex]change' in relationship is not only pure and prelapsarian, it is also purely reciprocal: 'innocence for innocence', like for like. Sexual maturity restores the growing man to the common destiny of original sin, and makes the mutual exchanging of innocence a nostalgic memory. Of course puberty comes to each man alike, but what then grows between them, as a common experience, is precisely what cannot any longer be shared or exchanged; those 'passions' of 'stronger blood' that must perforce be turned outwards towards a new and different object. Polixenes's apparently innocuous speech actually re-enacts the old masculine myth of the fall of *man*, in which Hermione, although addressed as a 'sacred lady', implicitly plays the role of temptress and seducer, as well as that of a vessel of purity. As in the idealizations of courtly romance, or indeed in *Hamlet*'s penetrating explorations of them, woman appears as both virgin and whore:

> *Pol.*      O my most sacred lady,
> Temptations have since then been born to's: for
> In those unfledg'd days was my wife a girl;
> Your precious self had not then cross'd the eyes
> Of my young play-fellow.
>
>                                    (I.ii.76–80)

The induction into hereditary sin follows the development of sexual maturity; and the initiation into that maturity is caused by the temptations of women. Sexual guilt is not only the end of innocence: it marks also the loss of a paradisal male companionship and a perfect mutual self-sufficiency.

I am not gesturing towards that kind of Bradleian psychological interpretation in which Leontes' jealousy could be related more to Polixenes than to Hermione; though I think such inferences are not merely 'fanciful',[32] and are likely to be encountered as possibilities in performance. If a play explores patriarchal ideologies in any way at all, whether as subversive interrogation or restorative recuperation, it will need to address (as we have seen in discussion of other plays) the nature of male friendship as well as the conditions of feminine subordination.[33] The condition of childhood is defined in these exchanges as an existence without distinctive identity: two children are as alike as 'twinn'd lambs' (I.ii.67), and Leontes sees in Mamillius a restoration of his own childhood self (I.ii.151–60); as he later recognizes in Florizel and Perdita identical resurrected replicants of the two children he had lost ('I lost a couple, that 'twixt heaven and earth/ Might thus have stood' V.i.131–2), and in the son of Polixenes a duplicate of the father, of that youth from whom Leontes himself was once indistinguishable (see V.i.123–9). Within the undifferentiated community of childhood there is existence without identity: children are identical 'kernels' (I.ii.159) that only subsequently harden into individuated, exclusive and defensive shells.

It is in the context of this vision of innocence as life without identity, separation and possession that we should read Leontes' horror at the prospect of an open society in which possession is common and freedom of movement universally permitted. The king's jealous fantasy constructs a whole symbolic vocabulary of closure and access: of unlocked gates, pierced barriers, broken distinctions. A woman is as false as a criminal gambler, as 'one that fixes/ No bourn 'twixt his and mine' (I.ii.133–4); a man's fish-pond may be poached by his neighbour; 'other men have gates, and those gates open'd,/ As mine, against their will' (I.ii.197–8); there is no sure defence of the female womb against the incursions of a hostile invader – 'no barricado for a belly. Know't,/ It will let in and out the enemy,/ With bag and baggage' (I.ii.204–6); and Polixenes' escape prompts Leontes to a paranoid nightmare vision of free communications: 'How came the posterns/ So easily open?'. The answer to that particular question comes from an anonymous lord, who simply reminds Leontes that his own power has traditionally been delegated to others: 'by his great authority,/ Which often hath no less prevailed than so/ On your command'. Camillo has held the keys to the city gates: power and possessions are by the conditions of this society never in practice personally held, but shared and distributed among members of the aristocratic elite.

This discourse of perimeters fractured and spaces invaded is rooted of course in Leontes' attitude towards the body of his wife.

> *Leo.* Three crabbed months had sour'd themselves to death,
> Ere I could make thee open thy white hand . . .
> (I.ii.102–3)

The fact that that same hand appears, in Leontes' infected vision, to have opened so much more readily to Polixenes, seems a particularly tormenting possibility. It is the very *similarity* between what Hermione is imagined to be doing with Polixenes, and what she legitimately does with Leontes, between the permitted and the transgressive, the authorized and the forbidden, that disrupts Leontes' sense of necessary discriminations and stable distinctions.

> *Leo.* How she holds up the neb, the bill to him!
> And arms her with the boldness of a wife
> To her allowing husband!
> (I.ii.182–4)

That sense of mutual identity that formed the intimate bond of childhood friendship, becomes in the conditions of adult relationship a dangerous and poisonous subversion of 'mannerly distinguishment':

> *Leo.*    You have mistook, my lady,
> Polixenes for Leontes. O thou thing –
> Which I'll not call a creature of thy place,
> Lest barbarism, making me the precedent,
> Should a like language use to all degrees,
> And mannerly distinguishment leave out
> Betwixt the prince and beggar.
> (II.i.81–7)

Leontes' need for a firm maintaining of distinctions in delineating possession of the female body, is here linked to the wider issue of 'distinguishment' between social classes. The woman who recognizes no difference between husband and friend is not only breaching moral codes and conventions, she is also releasing into the body politic a subversive contamination, by means of which appropriate customary social distinctions would disappear, and society collapse into an undifferentiated barbarism.

The adulterous queen is a traitor in the political as well as in the ethical sphere.

> Leo. There is a plot against my life, my crown;
> All's true that is mistrusted . . .
> (II.i.47-8)

### 'GO PLAY, BOY, PLAY'

Leontes' ambiguous and self-revelatory exhortation to Mamillius to 'play' appears as a focal point of a speech (I.ii.180-207) already extensively quoted, in which the diseased imagination of the jealous husband riots through a whole vocabulary of political fear and sexual disgust. In linking together some of that rich and complex word's range of meanings – the innocent and unconscious 'play' of the child, the libidinous 'play' of the supposedly unfaithful wife (compare our modern 'playing around'), and the play-acting dissimulation of the cunning husband acting the honest dupe only the better to entrap those suspected of betraying him – the 'play' (*The Winter's Tale*) forces an important juxtaposition of childhood innocence with adult knowledge and corruption.[34] Yet just as the discourse of pastoral created its 'out-of-court' images from a space firmly within courtly culture, so there is continuity and connection (where Leontes can only see grotesque incongruity) between these different types of play. What exactly are children doing when they play? What are adults doing when they emulate such childish games in their own cultural behaviour?

*The Winter's Tale* foregrounds these questions from the very beginning by including scenes involving the child Mamillius. We first see Leontes engaged in what purports to be a playful conversation with his son; and subsequently we see the son playing games with his mother and her waiting-women. In the latter scene (Act 2:1), the substance of the 'play' actually involves a very adult consciousness of sexual and courtly behaviour. Mamillius himself insists that he is no baby, and professes 'love' to a female courtier, documenting the profession with some exercises in fashionable satire against cosmetics. The women invite him with sublimated licentiousness into the sexual games of courtly love:

> 2nd Lady  Hark ye,
> The queen your mother rounds apace: we shall

Present our services to a fine new prince
One of these days, and then you'd wanton with us,
If we would have you.
(II.i.15–19)

The free operation of childhood fantasy can deliver nothing more than coded representations of the adult world: Mamillius' 'tale' of 'sprites and goblins' (II.i.25–6), which he does not live to complete, ironically adumbrates the demons of suspicion and mistrust that animate the adult society, the imaginary 'spider' in Leontes' cup (II.i.40), the 'bug' (*bwg*) of threatened punishment which Hermione scornfully rejects as a childish trick of attempted intimidation (III.ii.92). It is after all the doomed child who gives the play its title: 'a sad tale's best for winter'.

The earlier exchange between Leontes and Mamillius displays even more clearly the 'fallen' quality of this family's 'play'. Leontes talks to the boy as he observes Polixenes and Hermione together in the garden:

> *Leo.*           Mamillius,
> Art thou my boy?
> *Mam.*                      Ay, my good lord.
> *Leo.*                                   I'fecks:
> Why that's my bawcock. What, hast smutch'd thy nose?
> They say it is a copy out of mine. Come, captain,
> We must be neat; not neat, but cleanly, captain:
> And yet the steer, the heifer and the calf
> Are all called neat. – Still virginalling
> Upon his palm! – How now, you wanton calf!
> Art thou my calf?
> *Mam.*                      Yes, if you will, my lord.
> (I.ii.119–27)

That patient humouring of the adult ('whatever you say') gives some indication of the extent to which Leontes' meanings are unintelligible to the child – the extent to which this verbal play between father and son is irreversibly contaminated with adult knowledge and adult anxiety. The observation of a resemblance between parent and child, the wiping of a little boy's snotty nose, allusions to familiar farmyard animals – these should be constitutive elements of a 'natural' family relationship. Yet each detail is poisoned with the double meanings supplied by Leontes'

# The Winter's Tale: Country into Court 203

imagination, the double vision implicit in his attention to the two objects of his observation, false mother and true son, innocence and experience. The question of resemblance asks for the reassurance of authentic paternity, since Hermione's unborn daughter is about to be declared Polixenes' bastard. The boy's nose, a 'copy' of his father's, is 'smutch'd' like Leontes' tainted reputation. Gestures towards the rural landscape of the play's second half – 'the steer, the heifer and the calf' – occur only in the form of symbolic associations between cattle and cuckolds. A word that denotes innocence and purity is distorted, through its application to a musical instrument, to indicate a sly and cultured sensuality – 'still virginalling/ Upon his palm!'

There is no innocent play at Leontes' court, not even for children. Yet the adult occupants of the court spend their time at play, since that is their appropriate courtly occupation. The nature of their play is largely verbal, but its elaborate linguistic games are constructed around relationships of friendship and affection which naturally attract a language of desire and fulfilment, of courtship and sexual conquest. The instrument of this style of courtly play is, as it is in *Hamlet* and in *Love's Labour's Lost*, the tongue; and the tongue can also become an instrument of sexual pleasure.

> *Pol.* There is no tongue that moves, none, none i'th'world,
> So soon as yours, could win me . . .
> *Leo.* Tongue-tied, our queen? speak you.
> . . . Is whispering nothing? . . .
> Kissing with inside lip?
> 
> (I.ii.20–1, 27, 284–6)

That competition of endearment between Leontes and Hermione with which the play begins, ends with a result confirming that Hermione's tongue, moving in the discourse of courtly persuasion, can in practice 'move' Polixenes more strongly than could Leontes' eloquence. Leontes explicitly commands a releasing of Hermione's powers of persuasion, the unlocking of her 'tongue' to articulate speech. Is it possible that the tongue that has moved so successfully in the art of exhortation has engaged more directly with the object of its persuasions; has moved from open courtly compliment, to clandestine 'whispering', and thence to the intimacy of a sexual kiss?

In urging her husband's friend, at her husband's command, to stay, Hermione deploys the language of courtly love.

> *Her.*    Will you go yet?

> Force me to keep you as a prisoner,
> Not like a guest; so you shall pay your fees
> When you depart, and save your thanks? How say you?
> My prisoner? or my guest?
>
> (I.ii.51–5)

The language-game is that of courtly romance, with its imagery of imprisonment and indebtedness; and it is a language to which Polixenes can courteously respond:

> *Pol.* Your guest then, madam:
> To be your prisoner should import offending . .
>
> (I.ii.56–7)

Now such language is not only appropriate to the rank and situation of the speakers; it has been specifically commanded by the king. In urging Hermione to persuade Polixenes, Leontes is commissioning a particular form of courtly 'entertainment', in exactly the same way as Prospero commissions entertainments for his daughter and her fiancé. Hermione is required to act out a dramatization of ritual courtship, wooing Polixenes to accede to her will. The point of fracture, the fault-line within this courtly discourse, manifests itself when the conscious and carefully-preserved distance between performer and role appears to collapse, and Hermione seems to become, though only in the eye of the entranced spectator, what Leontes has asked her to play. As Hermione brings the elaborate conceits that belong to the verbal exuberance of this courtly game to a teasing conclusion, Leontes evidently overhears:

> *Her.* Th'offences we have made you do, we'll answer,
> If you first sinned with us, and that with us
> You did continue fault, and that you slipp'd not
> With any but with us.
> *Leo.*           Is he won yet?
>
> (I.ii.83–6)

Hermione is jesting here about herself and Polixenes' wife in relation to their respective husbands: but reading the plural pronoun as singular, she could appear to be discussing an adulterous affair. That is clearly Leontes' immediate impression, since his question 'is he won yet?' shares with the conversation to which he is listening the same technique of merging meanings from sexual and diplomatic behaviour. Certainly the word 'slipp'd', which confers salacious overtones on the concept of transgression, provides Leontes with some choice descriptions of the imagined infidelity – 'sluic'd' (I.ii.194), 'slippery' (I.ii.273).

In the immediate source of *The Winter's Tale*, Greene's *Pandosto: the Triumph of Time* (1588), this type of courtly behaviour is regarded as profoundly ambivalent. Pandosto welcomes his friend Egistus with loving embraces, and encourages his wife Bellaria to join him,[35]

> ... wishing his wife to welcome his old friend and acquaintance: who, to shew how she liked him whom her husband loved, entertained him with such familiar courtesy as Egistus perceived himself to be very well welcome.

That 'very well welcome' indicates a tone of ironical observation potentially present in Greene's narrative, as if the narrator himself views such 'entertainment' and 'familiar courtesy' as inherently open to suspicion.

> Bellaria, who in her time was the flower of courtesy, willing to show how unfeignedly she loved her husband by his friend's entertainment, used him likewise so familiarly that her countenance bewrayed how her mind was affected towards him, oftentimes coming herself into his bedchamber to see that nothing should be amiss to mislike him. This honest familiarity increased daily more and more betwixt them; for Bellaria, noting in Egistus a princely and bountiful mind, adorned with sundry and excellent qualities, and Egistus, finding in her a virtuous and courteous disposition, there grew such a secret uniting of their affections, that the one could not well be without the company of the other: in so much, that when Pandosto was busied with such urgent affairs that he could not be present with his friend Egistus, Bellaria would walk with him into the garden where they two with private and pleasant devices would pass away the time to both their contents. (pp. 185–6)

Greene does not imply that there is ever more to this relationship than 'honest familiarity', but he draws attention to a potential continuity between the public show of intimacy and its private consumption. As an appropriate enterprise to be undertaken by the 'flower of courtesy', Bellaria's courtship of Egistus represents the perfection of society manners, and the expression of a 'virtuous and courteous disposition'. But the ostentatious 'familiarity' of this type of 'entertainment' seems to imply the existence of a deeper intimacy. Greene is interested in the inner states such outward behaviour may reflect and reveal. Bellaria's 'countenance bewrayed how her mind was affected towards him': the description compliments Bellaria on the accuracy with which she mimes attachment, but at the same time implies that what can be read in the countenance may be a simple reflection of genuine feeling. Thus the relationship between 'entertainment' and 'affection' is as problematical in Greene as it is in Shakespeare, who engages in the same kind of play with the same words. Greene leaves it open to his readers (perhaps to those 'Gentlemen Readers' of his dedication, some of whom may have shared the author's detached suspicions about courtly manners) to define for themselves the quality of that 'secret uniting of their affections' which involves Bellaria visiting Egistus' bedchamber, and in Pandosto's absence passing their time in 'private and pleasant devices'.

Without ever suggesting the possibility of Bellaria/Hermione's guilt, Greene nonetheless expresses a distinct mistrust of courtly manners, in which the encouragement of elaborate public displays of intimacy, and the availability of privacy, create for married people potentially dangerous situations of sexual freedom, and leave the protagonists acutely dependent on the moral self-discipline of their own 'virtue'. The problem is located specifically in the true relationship between 'entertainment' and 'affection', between the overt displaying of familiarity and the emotional bonding such display would normally be expected to express. If courtly 'entertainment' is in reality the outward sign of affection, then where is the line of demarcation between different qualities of 'affection' to be placed? And if 'entertainment' is rather a matter of theatrical display, the enactment of publicly-prescribed rituals of courtesy, does it not become (as represented by Osric in *Hamlet*) inauthentic, the hypocritical dissimulation of the sycophantic diplomatist? Furthermore, since (as John Turner has demonstrated in preceding discussions) in a court society sexual relationships are in any case regulated by the authority of the monarch, who maintains a watchful surveillance over a potentially dangerous field of activity, even 'private' relations between respectable married people may require careful monitoring, and may become subject to the kind of reconfiguration that happens when a spectator's perceptions intervene into the process he is observing.

The difficulty and uncertainty of distinguishing between behaviour and feeling is the theme of Leontes' first utterance of jealous passion, a speech which makes much play with Greene's vocabulary of ambivalence:

> Leo. To mingle friendship far, is mingling bloods.
> I have *tremor cordis* on me: my heart dances,
> But not for joy – not joy. This entertainment
> May a free face put on, derive a liberty
> From heartiness, from bounty, fertile bosom,
> And well become the agent: 't may, I grant:
> But to be paddling palms, and pinching fingers,
> As now they are, and making practis'd smiles
> As in a looking-glass; and then to sigh, as 'twere
> The mort o'th' deer – O, that is entertainment
> My bosom likes not, nor my brows.
> (I.ii.109–19)

The excitement of jealous passion derives from a contemplation of boundaries crossed, distinctions broken down. 'Friendship' of this public and ceremonial kind demands a 'mingling' of emotional intimacies; but here 'friendship' appears to be mingling with its opposite, betrayal. Just as Leontes' emotional disturbance resembles sexual delight (the 'dancing' of his heart has to be explained as deriving from another cause) so the apparent treachery of Hermione and Polixenes is rooted in ceremonies of affection inseparable from courtly entertainment, in 'liberty', 'heartiness' and 'bounty'. These terms are problematized by Leontes' suspicions – 'bounty' for example is ironically acknowledged as a 'fertile bosom' capable of engendering a variety of creations, from the generosity of friendship to the obscenity of lust – but they are in themselves in any case problematical by their very nature. The conviction that the strict division between appearance and reality has broken down pushes Leontes towards a revulsion from the inauthenticity of theatrical display, from the actor's 'practis'd smiles', studied in a looking-glass, or from the exaggerated sigh of a performed courtly affection. Yet the performance is one commissioned by the agency of his own power.

Once, in Leontes' imagination, the boundaries between courtesy and intimacy, entertainment and affection, friendship and betrayal are crossed, that imagination becomes itself an instrument for demolishing all limits, abolishing all distinction between fantasy and the real, eliding disparities of space and divisions of time. Prospero's imagination was, we remember, crossed and interrupted in its functioning by the thought of betrayal, its power over the masque collapsing as the memory resurfaces of Caliban's plot. Leontes' imagination derives its inspiration from the conviction of betrayal, and he himself becomes the victim of his own fantasy. Assured that his wife has ruptured the distinction between entertainment and affection, mistaken Leontes for Polixenes, Leontes himself becomes unable to distinguish between what his imagination half-creates and what it perceives:

> Leo. Affection! thy intention stabs the centre:
> Thou dost make possible things not so held,
> Communicat'st with dreams:- how can this be? -
> With what's unreal thou coactive art,
> And fellows't nothing: then 'tis very credent
> Thou mays't co-join with something; and thou dost,
> (And that beyond commission) and I find it,
> (And that to the infection of my brains
> And hardening of my brows).
> (I.ii.138–46)

'Affection' here must carry a double charge of meaning, since it seems to refer both to the positive and negative connotations of the word: to the carnal 'affection' supposed breeding between Hermione and Polixenes, but also to the positive 'affection' Leontes has cherished towards both parties. The results of that emotional growth are described in both the public and the psychological domains: a sensation of his own 'affection' pierces to the heart, 'stabs the centre' of Leontes' being; while contemplation of an illegitimate 'affection' between wife and friend convinces him that the very soul of the world is under lacerating attack, stabbed to its centre and in danger of annihilation. 'Affection' (emotional attachment/ sexual excitation) has a natural link with fantasy, 'communicat'st with dreams', and is capable of creating something out of nothing – 'what's unreal'. Yet, as Leontes' tortuous (and quite illogical) philosophical interrogation insists, this combination of affection and imagination clearly brings something into being, constructs images of the 'possible'. Those concrete imaginative embodiments of possibility acquire an undeniable vitality and substance: they become indistinguishable from the real. It then becomes feasible to infer the nature of reality from the visions of imagination: it seems 'credent' to Leontes that imagination must 'co-join with something' – must have at its roots some solid ground, some participation with the concrete,

## The Winter's Tale: Country into Court

some sharing in the construction of reality. The individual subject's own sensations can thus be regarded as infallible tests of experience, measures of reality. Since Leontes' 'affection' for wife and friend has been poisoned by a knowledge of the 'affection' they appear to share, and since that contamination is sensibly experienced in the 'infection' of his knowledge and the 'hardening' of his brows (the growth of a cuckold's horns, and the ossification of his countenance into an expression of vindictive anger), then his dreams of adultery and betrayal can be taken as proven.

Our senses tell us what is real; but our senses can be possessed by fantasy or compelled by a performed dramatization. Leontes appeals to the evidence of the senses with an absolute assurance of their infallibility: 'Ha' not you seen, Camillo? . . . or heard . . . or thought . . . my wife is slippery?' (I.ii.267–74). Camillo has seen, heard and thought nothing: but for Leontes that 'nothing', that vacant absence, is filled with voyeuristic fantasies of secret intimacy: 'Is whispering nothing? is meeting noses?/ Kissing with inside lip?' (I.ii.284–6). The very potency of imagination then becomes it own attestation, the vividness of its imagery its own undeniable proof. Seeking to persuade Camillo of the truth of his suspicions, Leontes' final appeal is to his own state of mind: could such a psychological condition exist unless its imputed cause were authentic?

> *Leo.* Dost think I am so muddy, so unsettled,
> To appoint myself in this vexation . . .
> Without ripe moving to't? Would I do this?
> Could man so blench?
>
> (I.ii.325–6, 332–3)

Clearly these speeches have profound implications for the play's reflections on its own medium, as well as for the psychological crisis dramatized in Leontes: and as I will be demonstrating presently, there are significant implications here for the relationship between *The Winter's Tale* and Jacobean 'court theatre'. As Miranda discovers in the second scene of *The Tempest*, what the imagination seizes as reality need not necessarily be truth. If a work of art does not contain within itself that internal distantiation which enables the reader or spectator to deconstruct its compelling construction of the real, then it can only operate, like Leontes' jealous fantasy, to naturalize the products of imagination and to confuse them systematically with reality. The temptation to do this can be irresistibly powerful, since there is no denying the problematical nature of 'reality', or the reality of the products of the imagination. But a play is neither pure imagination nor a self-evidently fictitious delusion: it is rather imagination caught in the act of judging itself, creating images of the real and simultaneously questioning both its own reality and the reality to which it alludes. Leontes is a man who loses all sense of distance, of detachment, of distinction. He cannot tell the difference between dream and reality, between role and actor, between art and nature. In comedy he would be the man who jumps on to the stage to intervene in the action of a play; in tragedy, the man who kills his wife on the evidence of a handkerchief. In romance he would be the man who falls in love with the statue of a woman.

## 'PLAY'D TO TAKE SPECTATORS'

Leontes' bursting in (a motif familiar from our discussion of *Hamlet*) on the family gathering of his wife and child in II.i marks the irruption of 'infection' into the territory of legitimate 'affection'. He accuses his wife of adultery, conspiracy and of carrying Polixenes' 'bastard'. Hermione's response is at first uncomprehending, suspecting some practical joke; then sharply definitive –

> *Her.* How will this grieve you,
> When you shall come to clearer knowledge, that
> You thus have publish'd me!
> (II.i.96–8)

– then formally measured and formidably dignified:

> *Her.* Good my lords,
> I am not prone to weeping, as our sex
> Commonly are; the want of which vain dew
> Perchance shall dry your pities: but I have
> That honourable grief lodg'd here which burns
> Worse than tears drown: beseech you all, my lords,
> With thoughts so qualified as your charities
> Shall best instruct you, measure me . . .
> . . . Do not weep, good fools,
> There is no cause: when you shall know your mistress
> Has deserv'd prison, then abound in tears
> As I come out: this action I now go on
> Is for my better grace. Adieu, my lord:

I never wish'd to see you sorry; now
I trust I shall.

(II.i.107–14, 118–24)

That initial distinction between 'clearer knowledge' and the kind of murky knowledge that has been 'publish'd', is precisely the distinction that is absent from Leontes' diseased imagination. He has 'publish'd', rendered manifest and self-evident, what his senses have convinced him of: he simply cannot conceive of any distance or distinction between conviction and understanding. Hermione does not spend long on protestations of her innocence. She gives utterance to a powerful sense of righteous resentment and fierce indignation ('honourable grief'), described as a concealed, inner state ('lodg'd here'). The contradictory images of water and fire sharply differentiate her condition from the stereotypically 'feminine' response of 'weeping' and 'tears'; what she feels is rather a hard moral anger which 'burns', preserving an injured dignity and provoking thoughts of revenge and restitution – 'I never wish'd to see you sorry; now/ I trust I shall'. We can already see in this statement of intent, coupled with Paulina's 'mankind' (man-like) determination, the basis of that fierce sorority which will devise and execute Leontes' sixteen-year purgatory. In glossing the phrase 'this action I now go on/ Is for my better grace', commentators are usually drawn more strongly towards 'grace' than towards 'action'. 'Action' probably combines legal and military associations: a legal process which is also a just cause, and a battle to clear a wounded reputation. The word also belonged to the vocabulary of theatrical practice, though more in the limited sense of 'physical gesture' (as in Hamlet's 'suit the word to the action') than in the conceptual sense of a dramatic 'action', a meaning which separated out at a later stage. Nonetheless it is contingently clear that Hermione intends not to profess her sinlessness in direct exculpation or special pleading, but to perform her innocence by means of a considered and constructed theatrical representation.

The arraignment of Hermione is for Leontes a 'show trial', designed rather as a public confirmation of manifest guilt than as a process of inquiry convened to establish guilt or innocence. It is the king's defence against the charge of tyranny: though since as he announces the inception he also anticipates the outcome, the trial becomes an instrument of autocracy rather than a demonstration of justice.

> Leo.     Let us be clear'd
> Of being tyrannous, since we so openly
> Proceed in justice, which shall have due course,
> Even to the guilt or the purgation.
>                                                   (III.ii.4–8)

Hermione seems well aware of these conditions. Leontes is both her accuser and her judge. Her purity has already been interpreted as sinfulness, her chastity read as depravity; further protestations of innocence can only be received as endorsements of treacherous and conspiratorial guilt.

> Her.            ... mine integrity
> Being counted falsehood, shall, as I express it,
> Be so receiv'd.
>                                                   (III.ii.26–8)

The ordinary means of human communication have been so profoundly confused and contaminated by Leontes' jealous and tyrannical obsession, that no direct confessional protestation of innocence can have any persuasive force. Hermione anticipates that the issue can be clarified only by the intervention of some external agency: and she anticipates such a disclosure in the form of an open, performative revelation of the truth.

> Her.            ... if powers divine
> Behold our human actions (as they do),
> I doubt not then but innocence shall make
> False accusation blush, and tyranny
> Tremble at patience.
>                                                   (III.ii.28–32)

Those divine powers who are spectators (*ab extra*) of human actions may commission some representation which will inevitably affect the spectators at Hermione's trial, especially Leontes, with shame and terror at their own proven injustice. Leontes himself has every reason, on the basis of his former relationship with his wife, to know the accusation to be false; and that intimate personal knowledge cannot be published or performed. Since that reassurance of trust is broken, and there is no appeal to personal faith, innocence can only be enacted:

> Her.        You, my lord, best know
> (Who least will seem to do so) my past life

Hath been as continent, as chaste, as true,
As I am now unhappy; which is more
Than history can pattern, though devis'd
And played to take spectators.

(III.ii.32–7)

There is no substitute for real interpersonal knowledge in relationship; but if that cannot be relied on, then a dramatic narrative ('history') must be 'devis'd' and 'played to take' (to move, capture, persuade) an audience of 'spectators'.

    *Her.*       For behold me . . . here standing
To prate and talk for life and honour 'fore
Who please to come and hear.

(III.ii.37, 41–2)

At the very moment when Hermione could be expected to unfold the inner truth of her being, and to attempt the most direct emotional communication with her accuser, her metadramatic language suddenly throws the very nature of theatrical representation into sharp and heightened relief. The action being performed here is of course a symbolic representation of the truth: Hermione's innocence. But the manner of its performance structures into the medium of its representation a self-reflexive internal distantiation, capable of disclosing the performative medium itself as an object of attention, and of laying bare the probability – the necessity, perhaps – of distance between word and deed, feeling and expression, knowledge and representation, role and actor. These lines should simultaneously address, as they would have addressed within the self-reflexive medium of the Jacobean public theatre, both the on-stage audience of the trial, and the actual theatre audience of paying spectators who have 'come to hear'. Hermione is doubly on trial, as a character in a drama and as an actress (originally actor) on stage: she appeals to the one audience for justice and to the other for approval.

Within the common environment of a single complex theatrical medium, Leontes and Hermione 'act' their parts, and constitute their spectators, quite differently. Leontes is the Stanislavskian character, utterly abandoned to the inner necessity of his role, to the closed interiority of his experience; the broken, convoluted language of his discourse is Shakespeare's method of rendering probable and natural a condition of psychological extremity. Locked within a character, Leontes is also imprisoned within a language: he can neither understand what other people say, nor be understood by them. Hermione, by contrast, appears as a Brechtian role, in which the representation of character is acknowledged to be a representation, at the same time as it conveys the palpable substance of character. The experience of tragic suffering, which folds Leontes in onto a tormenting subjectivity, draws Hermione out towards performative communication, to a direct engagement with those spectators whose attention both interprets and constructs the significance of her character.

The contrast between their respective modes of theatrical existence is made quite explicit, as Hermione points out the absorbing power of Leontes' delusion, and her own independence of it:

> *Her.* You speak a language that I understand not.
> My life stands in the level of your dreams . . .
> *Leo.* Your actions are my dreams.
> (III.ii.80–1, 82)

Hermione's independent existence has been incorporated into her husband's fantasy, and there reinterpreted in terms of suspicion, jealousy and fear. Leontes' reply is designedly ironic – 'You had a bastard by Polixenes,/ And I but dream'd it!' (III.ii.83–4) – but unwittingly defines with remarkable clarity the true nature of the situation: Hermione's 'actions' are rehearsed and performed in the theatre of Leontes' mind. For him, 'action' and 'dream' are indistinguishable. For her, the necessity of clarifying the difference and distance between them has become a life-or-death imperative.

That clarity of dramatic and psychological understanding enables Hermione to reflect convincingly back onto the conventions of courtly behaviour from which this terrible misinterpretation originally arose.

> *Her.* For Polixenes,
> With whom I am accus'd, I do confess
> I lov'd him as in honour he requir'd,
> With such a kind of love as might become
> A lady like me; with a love, even such,
> So, and no other, as yourself commanded:
> Which, not to have done, I think had been in me
> Both disobedience and ingratitude
> To you, and toward your friend, whose love had spoke,

Ever since it could speak, from an infant, freely,
That it was yours.

(III.ii.61–71)

The faint echo of Cordelia's appeals to her father in the first act of *King Lear* emanates as much from a similarity of context as from verbal parallels. Just as Cordelia's low-key description of a grave filial piety contrasts sharply with the unlimited excesses of love professed by her sisters,[36] so the 'love' Hermione describes is very unlike the chaotic unbridled lust of Leontes' imagination, since it is inextricably involved with notions of duty, propriety, moral obligation. To love someone 'as in honour he required' is to describe a relationship at some distance from romantic conceptions of intensely subjective passion and intimate interpersonal bonding. 'Love' is not here opposed, as it almost always is in post-romantic models of sexual relationship, to 'duty', but is rather an aspect of it. 'Honour', always a key term in the value-systems of such an aristocratic society, has to do with personal qualities, but much more to do with their formal public recognition, and with the kinds of respect conventionally paid to a person of particular rank and relationship. To love Polixenes was both an obligation and an appropriate (a 'proper') response to his presence in Leontes' court: to fail either in the correct, approved emotion or in the proprieties of its public manifestation, would represent a serious combination of personal and civil misdemeanours – disobedience to her husband, and ingratitude towards his friend. Hermione is partly of course pointing out that she was only doing as she was told, so that no blame even for the misunderstanding should be imputed to her. But she is also offering an important account of the nature of courtly relationships between men and women of rank, and deploying a language in which the possibilities for confusion of the kind Leontes has experienced would be significantly reduced. Courtly 'love' of this kind is obviously quite different from the *amour courtois* of the romances, but it is comparable in its capacity as a public performance of private relationship. Public and private realms are also in this courtly discourse kept apart, an appropriate distance between them maintained: actor is not confused with role, personal intimacy with diplomatic affection, or subjective emotion with public duty. In the case of all these linked oppositions, the condition of their interrelationship within this conception of courtly love is the capacity of its discursive conventions to keep them apart.

A similar emphasis on the necessary distance between actor and performance colours the important role of Paulina. Since she represents in the play the voice of honest resentment at injustice, of what D. H. Lawrence called 'true, righteous, indignant anger', Paulina would seem to have little of the 'actress' about her. But a closer look at the complexity of her generic roots will supply us with a much more distinctly 'metadramatic' context for the interpretation of this particular manifestation of the 'unruly woman'. In the passage of Greene's *Pandosto* which narrates the finding of Fawnia [Perdita], we find the prototype for Shakespeare's Paulina. The generic quality of this section of narrative displays a particularly strong drawing towards naturalism. This can take the form of very precise descriptive details elaborated round the presentation of the child:

> The babe, who writhed with the head to seek for the pap, began again to cry afresh . . . (p. 200)

– or of a punctiliously naturalistic explication of even the most romantic fantasy events:

> Taking therefore the child in his arms, as he folded the mantle together the better to defend it from cold there fell down at his foot a very rare and rich purse . . . (p. 200)

These gestures towards a naturalistic style and genre, which seem to foreshadow later literary attempts at a vividly detailed poetry of common life (Wordsworth) or a realist synthesis of naturalism and myth (George Eliot), develop into a scene of *fabliau* humour between the shepherd and his wife, in which the language of common life is employed to construct a boisterous and energetic piece of popular comedy reminiscent of Chaucer:

> . . . his wife, thinking it was some bastard, began to crow against her goodman, and taking up a cudgel (for the most master went breechless) swore solemnly that she would make clubs trumps if he brought any bastard brat within her doors. The goodman, seeing his wife in majesty with the mace in her hand, thought it was time to bow for fear of blows . . . (p. 200)

The termagant wife's moral outrage is of course subdued by her husband's revelation of the wealth the baby brings with her, and the total package is immediately re-interpreted as a gift of divine providence. He urges her not to 'blab' the story when she meets with her 'gossips', but the wife has her own store of cynical peasant wisdom on which to draw: 'profit is a good hatch before the door' (p. 201). Greene's prose is rooted here in traditions of folk narrative, popular humour and common language: in its colloquial dialect ('crow', 'make clubs trumps', 'bastard brat'), its class irony ('his wife in majesty with the mace in her hand'), and its sexual chauvinism ('for the most master went breechless'), it speaks in an authentically popular accent. All these elements re-appear in *The Winter's Tale*, but interestingly deconstructed and re-arranged.

The 'wife in majesty' becomes in Shakespeare's play Paulina, courageous defender of the queen's reputation, stigmatized by Leontes as unnaturally unfeminine: 'A mankind witch!' (II.iii.67). Where in Greene the spectacle of a woman abrogating masculine power is mocked by the ironic contradictoriness of a peasant 'majesty', wielding a rolling-pin in place of the royal 'mace', in Shakespeare the woman makes a necessary and just claim on a power abused by a specifically masculine brand of tyranny. The sarcastic sexism of Greene's narrative is put into the mouth of Leontes. 'What?' he demands of Antigonus, 'canst not rule her? . . . He dreads his wife!' (II.iii.46, 79).

> Leo.   And, lozel, thou art worthy to be hang'd,
> That wilt not stay her tongue!
> (II.iii.108-9)

The rueful reply of Antigonus draws directly on the popular traditions reflected in Greene: 'Hang all the husbands/ That cannot do that feat, you'll leave yourself/ Hardly one subject' (II.iii.109–11). Leontes himself adopts the very tone and language of Greene's peasants:

> Leo.      Take up the bastard,
> Take't up, I say; give't to thy crone . . .
>     A callat
> Of boundless tongue, who late hath beat her husband,
> And now baits me!
> (II.iii.75–6, 90–2)

The incorporation of this popular discourse even extends to some rustic Chaucerian allusions:

> Leo.   . . . thou art woman-tir'd, unroosted

> By thy dame Partlet here.
>
> (II.iii.74–5)

Although at this point the action of the play is potentially tragic, this throwing into play of stylistic contradiction creates a generally comic effect. But the comedy is not that traditional popular comedy of hen-pecked husbands and shrewish wives that we find in Greene: it is rather a comedy of estrangement arising from the contradictory stylistic conjunctures and theatrical incongruities permitted to jostle one another across this very open and non-exclusive stage. Leontes' own 'jealousy' is exposed, articulated thus in a vulgar folk idiom, as a crude and common sexual chauvinism. On the basis of this popular language, Paulina is able to mount a spirited critique of courtly sycophancy, that climate of deference that has assisted the growth of Leontes' madness and permitted the development of an autocratic 'tyranny'. ''Tis such as you', she says to the retainers of Leontes' entourage:

> *Paul.*   That creep like shadows by him, and do sigh
> At each his needless heavings; such as you
> Nourish the cause of his awaking . . .
> You, that are thus so tender o'er his follies,
> Will never do him good, not one of you.
>
> (II.iii.33–6, 126–7)

And although to some degree the incongruous juxtaposition of a popular naturalism with a courtly tragedy proves in itself an illuminating revelation, the stylistic conjunctures allow for more complex theatrical effects than that of giving voice to the accent of popular wisdom. Once Paulina has delivered her great passionate condemnation of Leontes' tyranny on the queen's (apparent) death (III.ii.175–214), something odd and complex begins to happen in her dramatic language. Leontes himself pleads for more punishment – 'Thou cans't not speak too much; I have deserved/ All tongues to talk their bitterest' (III.ii.215–16). One of the anonymous 'lords' that creep like shadows around the court intercedes between the repentant king and his formidable accuser: although Leontes has apparently succeeded for no very good reason in killing his entire family, it is still inappropriate that the system of deference should be breached, that 'mannerly distinguishment' should fail to be preserved:

> *A Lord*   Say no more:

Howe'er the business goes, you have made fault
I' th' boldness of your speech.
                                    (III.ii.216–8)

The courtier mediates between the power of the king and the subversive energies of the unruly woman, attempting to reassert a discredited authority, to patch up a fractured hierarchy. Paulina initially appears to comply with this imposed regulation, and voluntarily to accept subordination:

> *Paul.*   Alas! I have showed too much
> The rashness of a woman: he is touch'd
> To th' noble heart. What's gone and what's past help
> Should be past grief. Do not receive affliction
> At my petition; I beseech you, rather
> Let me be punish'd, that have minded you
> Of what you should forget. Now, good my liege,
> Sir, royal sir, forgive a foolish woman:
> The love I bore your queen – lo, fool again!
> I'll speak of her no more, nor of your children:
> I'll not remember you of my own lord
> (Who is lost too): take your patience to you,
> And I'll say nothing.
>                                    (III.ii.220–32)

Here the anti-court satire and popular resistance from which Paulina has been drawing reach an accommodation with the requirements of a deference society: but they do so not by submission but by negotiation, not by honesty but by irony, not by sincerity but by the elaborate doubleness of performance. The savage indignation and righteous anger against Leontes' tyranny are of course there in Paulina, but the occasion of their expression is impersonated, since the queen is not dead. The dramatic medium chosen for the application of punishment is not an anguished emotional sincerity but a biting sarcasm, punctiliously deliberate and emphatic in its phrasing, carefully preserving the distance between ostensible deference and actual condemnation. Femininity itself becomes the object of an apparent self-critique, conducted with mock humility ('The rashness of a woman', 'a foolish woman'), which operates in fact to discredit masculine authority and to assert female pride and power. Certainly Paulina is already preparing the ground for an ultimate reconciliation between guilty king and injured queen. But she does so by constituting the king as a penitent, appointing herself the voice of his conscience, and thereby arrogating the power of moral authority to herself and the absent Hermione. Guilt and innocence, repentance and restitution, are firmly located onto a public stage, to be formally enacted before witnesses, 'Play'd to take spectators'.

### 'IF THAT WHICH IS LOST BE NOT FOUND'

When Leontes instructs Antigonus to expose to the elements Hermione's new-born daughter, he anticipates the play's turn towards romance and towards a more open theatrical medium than the one he himself has dominated:

> Leo.　　　　As by strange fortune
> It came to us, I do in justice charge thee,
> On thy soul's peril and thy body's torture,
> That thou commend it strangely to some place
> Where chance may nurse or end it.
> 　　　　　　　　　　　　(II.iii.178–82)

The notion that the baby has emerged 'strangely' into the world is of course entirely imaginary: there is in reality nothing odd or illegitimate about the circumstances of its birth. The 'strangeness' of its genesis derives directly from the visionary fantasies that Leontes has constructed and substituted for what in the privileged view of the audience appears to be an unproblematical reality: the daughter we know to be his seems to him undeniably to be Polixenes' 'bastard'.

The scene in which Antigonus abandons the baby on the sea-coast of Bohemia could be said to mark by stylistic and theatrical means that strangely artificial break between acts 3 and 4 which introduces the 'strange' improbabilities of the play's second half, and indeed 'estranges' the play's entire theatrical structure (though the preceding discussion of Paulina will perhaps suggest that the firmness and finality of this 'break' can be exaggerated). It could be argued that too much of Leontes' perspective is being taken on trust here,

## The Winter's Tale: Country into Court 221

since nothing could be 'stranger', in naturalistic psychological and dramatic terms, than his sudden and vaguely-motivated collapse into paranoid jealousy. But while in the course of the first half of the play the strangeness of Leontes' madness attains a certain degree of visibility, the naturalistic manner of its psychological dramatization still dominates the theatrical texture. Although that mental aberrance is clearly diagnosed, disapproved, resisted and finally cured, by the intervention of a range of characters and circumstances (Camillo, Hermione herself, Paulina, Antigonus, various anonymous Lords, and of course most significantly the Delphic Oracle) they are all obliged to negotiate their interventions within the cramped and constrained confines of Leontes' own court. Particularly significant is the omission of any attempt to stage the delivery of the Oracle, which is merely reported to the Sicilian court, and described only in the brief 'on-the-road' scene which begins Act III. This choice of narrative structure involved declining a theatrical opportunity irresistibly suggestive of the performance techniques of the masque: a scene of religious ritual, of sacrifice and divine intervention, derived from the familiar pagan mythologies of Greece, and offering obvious opportunities for a deployment of the potent special effects, spectacular and auditory, of a 'total theatre'. But there is no 'Masque of Apollo': the ceremony is reported in some few seconds of stage time, and it is delivered by written message into the entirely secular and psychological domain of Hermione's trial. Leontes' immediate response – 'There is no truth at all i' th' Oracle' (III.ii.140) – seems far less astonishing (must, indeed, as a classical reference, have seemed out of its dramatic context like plain common-sense to a Jacobean audience) uttered from within the secular naturalism of the Sicilian court, than it would have done if Shakespeare had chosen to stage the oracular pronunciation, in parallel with *Cymbeline* and with *The Tempest*, as a masque-within-a-play, where the thematic and religious 'truth' of the Oracle could have been embodied within the compelling performance conventions of a ritualistic court-theatre.

The folk-lore and romance motif of the abandoned princess could thus be said to open up the play's theatrical possibilities, to facilitate the incorporation of 'strangeness'. The first sign of that transition is a sudden accession of theatrical plurality, with a wide and diversified range of characters and techniques suddenly simultaneously possible on stage. Liberated from the closed worlds of court, palace and prison that form the locations of the play's first half (punctuated only by the briefly functional 'road to Delphos' scene), we find the stage representing an open space, a literal and metaphorical margin suitably placed on a possibly non-existent coast-line. The elements of the scene could be broken into the following sequence: a naturalistic conversation between Antigonus and a 'Mariner', establishing the concrete details of sea-coast, storm and danger (III.iii.1–15); a description of a dream in which the supposedly dead Hermione appears to Antigonus, in a speech which terminates with the intervention of the famous bear (16–58); and a sub-scene of comic romance in which shepherd and 'clown' find the baby and describe both the shipwreck and the killing of Antigonus. The dramatic moment could be loosely compared with the opening of *The Tempest*, though the contradictions between event and tone, or between representation and reception, are actually much more extreme, since this is a 'real' shipwreck in which people are drowned, and a man is 'really' eaten by a bear. Theatrically the potentially tragic tone and perspective of the play's first half are brought to an abrupt termination while poor Antigonus is still running from the bear. The rapid switch from the solemn and melancholy apparition of Hermione to the romance discovery of the child, or the sharp transition from Antigonus' psychological dilemma to the comic account of his being eaten alive, mark more than a change of scene, location, theme and direction: they signal a clearly-defined passage from one genre, and from one theatrical medium, to another – from tragic myth to romantic comedy:

> *Ant.* To me comes a creature
> Sometimes her head on one side, some another;
> I never saw a vessel of like sorrow . . .
> (III.iii.19–21)

> *Shep.* Here's a sight for thee; look thee, a bearing-cloth for a squire's child! look thee here; take up, take up, boy; open't. So, let's see: it was told me that I should be rich by the fairies. This is some changeling . . . (III.iii.112–17)

> *Ant.* Weep I cannot,
> But my heart bleeds; and most accurs'd am I
> To be by oath enjoin'd to this.
> (III.iii.51–3)

## The Winter's Tale: Country into Court

> Clown ... the men are not yet cold under water, nor the bear half-dined on the gentleman: he's at it now.
>
> (III.iii.104–5)

The extensive and spirited debate around the question of how exactly that 'bear' was represented on the Elizabethan stage is more illuminating as a disclosure of theatrical contradiction than as an authentication of historical fact. Was the bear a real animal, taken from the neighbouring bear-pit in Southwark? If so, was it a tame animal, familiar to the audience as a performer of tricks, likely to elicit a response of amusement and of gratified applause at a successful *coup de théâtre*? Or might it have been a much more intimidating beast, fierce with unreclaimed savagery, productive of genuinely non-theatrical fear? Was it an exotic creature drawn from semi-fantastic travellers' tales of the Arctic polar-bear? Or was it a well-known local character, familiar from a neighbouring context of semi-theatrical entertainment? Was it, for that matter, a real animal at all: or possibly a pantomime figure constructed by a bear-skinned actor? Ben Jonson's *Masque of Oberon* contains a chariot drawn by two white bears: whether those creatures were real or simulated, there could have been nothing stylistically pantomimic about them, since the performance text is calling there for an effect of exotic magnificence, for a demonstration of power in action. Shakespeare's bear is the axis of a transition from tragedy to farce, and could conceivably therefore have been the instrument of that transition, with Antigonus and a performing bear, or a bear-skinned pantomime actor, executing a familiar 'tumbling' routine (certainly seen at court on 3 February 1610 in *Mucedorus*, which contained a scene in which the Clown falls over a white bear). The theatricality of the bear's intervention probably depended on the very contradictions the scholars have struggled to explain, and must have been in performance capable of tying and releasing a complex configuration of opposites: the wild and the tame, the savage and the domesticated, nature and art, reality and illusion, naturalistic representation and self-reflexive performance. Above all, there appears to be evidence[37] that the apparition of the bear signified a seasonal transition from Winter to Spring, and even more specifically an inverse mirror-image of the passage from the festivities of Carnival to the stringencies of Lent. The theatrical effects of the bear's intervention, however it may have been staged, should be thought of as an irruption of the unexpected, a sudden subversion of authoritative codes and conventions, an opening out of the dramatic world into unpredictable disturbance. Such an effect could be achieved either through the shock of apprehension caused by a real bear, or the comic disorientation of a simulated, pantomimic animal.

## COURT AND COUNTRY

The rustic Bohemian scenes, and the sheep-shearing feast that stands at the heart of the play's second half, are introduced by a conversation between Polixenes and Camillo which establishes very clear distinctions and parameters for the juxtaposition of courtly and pastoral discourses:

> *Cam.* Sir, it is three days since I saw the prince. What his happier affairs may be, are to me unknown: but I have (missingly) noted, he is of late much retired from court, and is less frequent to his princely exercises than formerly he hath appeared.
> *Poli.* I have considered so much, Camillo, and with some care; so far that I have eyes under my service which look upon his removedness; from whom I have this intelligence, that he is seldom from the house of a most homely shepherd; a man, they say, that from very nothing, and beyond the imagination of his neighbours, is grown into an unspeakable estate.
> *Cam.* I have heard, sir, of such a man, who hath a daughter of most rare note: the report of her is extended more than can be thought to begin from such a cottage.
> *Poli.* That's likewise part of my intelligence: but, I fear the angle that plucks our son thither. Thou shalt accompany us to the place, where we will (not appearing what we are) have some question with the shepherd . . .
> (IV.ii.30–50)

Florizel's sojourns in the country are from this point of view represented as dishonourable 'retirements' from court, and as truancy from the appropriate activities of a prince. The court of Bohemia has become exactly what the court of Sicilia (like the court of Elsinore) was: a location of intrigue, suspicion, surveillance, mistrust. The king has his son watched, and recieves information on his movements from an 'intelligence' service of spies. Not only does Polixenes now adopt the characteristic actions previously performed by Leontes – observing, dissimulating, plotting – he even adapts the characteristic tricks of his brother king's language – the 'angle' that plucks Florizel to Perdita recalls both the violated fish-ponds of Leontes' imagination (II.ii.195), and his violent imagery of seduction and apprehension - 'she I can hook to me' (II.iii.7); and Polixenes' decision to play a part, to disguise himself, links back to Leontes' 'play' speech, which also contains the identical image from fishing: 'I am angling now,/ Though you perceive me not how I give line' (I.ii.180–1). The country they announce their intention of entering is by contrast a terrain of miracle and marvel, where a shepherd can grow from nothing to a condition 'beyond the imagination of his neighbours', and where a shepherd's daughter may be a universally-admired beauty. It is of course the country of romance, and seems from this initial contradiction to offer a challenging simplicity and naive spontaneity with which to measure the brooding and suspicious self-consciousness of the court.

The pastoral scene of the 'sheep-shearing feast' (Act 4:4) displays the character of, and contains all the elements of, a court masque: yet those elements appear de-contextualized, estranged, distanced and re-valued. The occasion of the scene is a fertility ritual celebrating a seasonal festival. At its centre is a young royal couple hoping in the course of this ritual celebration to become, like Ferdinand and Miranda, betrothed. Both are costumed in an unfamiliar disguise, their royalty hidden beneath the rustic uniforms of their assumed personae. The feast involves a formal ritual welcome and offering, followed by song, music, dancing and an anti-masque of satyrs. The characters' language is full of classical allusions to myth and to the imagery of gods descending: though no god or goddess ever actually appears. The elements of the scene have so much in common with the court masque that its failure to resolve into one, its continual denial of expectations inevitably provoked by its theatrical allusions, raises the possibility of a calculated strategy of negative association, of calculated self-differentiation, between theatre and masque.

The expectations aroused by Polixenes' words of a clear and mutually exclusive antithesis between court and country are very soon disappointed. The first 'rustic' character the audience encounters is the ex-courtier Autolycus, a thief and confidence trickster, 'one that fixes/ No bourn 'twixt his and mine' (I.ii.133–4). That suggestion of continuity between court and country is strengthened by the 'sheep-shearing' scene itself, which opens with a series of exchanges between Florizel and Perdita that both evoke and subvert the conventions of courtly drama. The very first line of the scene draws attention to the transformation and transgression enacted by costume: a change of clothes can turn a shepherdess into a queen, a woman into a goddess:

> *Flo.* These your unusual weeds, to each part of you
> Do give a life: no shepherdess, but Flora
> Peering in April's front. This your sheepshearing
> Is as a meeting of the petty gods,
> And you the queen on't.
> *Per.*           . . . Your high self,
> The gracious mark o'th' land, you have obscur'd
> With a swain's wearing, and me, poor lowly maid,
> Most goddess-like prank'd up . . .
>                               (IV.iv.1–5, 7–10)

The royal personage does not appear, as in the conventions of the court masque, naturally associated with the presented role. What is being focused on here is not the potentiality of theatre to enact transformation, but the mechanisms by which such apparent transformations may be enacted. Florizel's language foregrounds the 'unusual weeds' which by a simple device of disguise convert the peasant girl to a goddess or queen. In actual fact of course, as the romance plot prescribes, Perdita's dress is merely bringing her public appearance into line with the true royalty of her nature: she is actually an aristocrat in a pastoral play rather than a peasant playing the queen of the May. The distance between literal assumption and romance 'reality' is intensified by that fundamental misapprehension: but in any case the emphasis on the process of costuming, and its capacity to construct highly plausible identities which seem to carry some undeniable substance of the 'real', locates the focus firmly on theatricality itself, rather than on the representations and personifications that theatricality might succeed in performing.

Florizel counters Perdita's fears about the impropriety of their relationship by citing a series of precedents from classical mythology, all examples of gods descending to earth to intervene in human affairs:

> *Flo.*           Apprehend

## The Winter's Tale: Country into Court    227

Nothing but jollity. The gods themselves,
Humbling their deities to love, have taken
The shapes of beasts upon them: Jupiter
Became a bull, and bellow'd; the green Neptune
A ram, and bleated; and the fire-rob'd god,
Golden Apollo, a poor humble swain,
As I seem now. Their transformations
Were never for a piece of beauty rarer . . .
(IV.iv.25–32)

The passage from court to country evidently inverts the trajectory of Perdita's elevation to deity, the distance between prince and swain being equivalent to that between gods and men.

*Perd.* It is my father's will I should take on me
The hostess-ship o' th' day.
(IV.iv.71-2)

Methinks I play as I have seen them do
In Whitsun pastorals: sure this robe of mine
Does change my disposition.
(IV.iv.133–5)

Perdita's view of her own 'transformation' is based on that common-sense, slightly puritanical mistrust of the false appearance and misleading impression constructed by theatrical representation: she sees herself as 'prank'd up' (IV.iv.10) in 'borrowed flaunts' (IV.iv.23), artificially displaying a pretended, undeserved rank and dignity. That the wearing of a simple costume, or the utterance of a certain specialized discourse, could appear, if only temporarily and within a strictly circumscribed cultural environment, to break down fundamental social distinctions and moral categories, was, as we have seen, a cause of indignant objection from the critics of both theatre and court. Here that popular critical puritanism is voiced paradoxically by a character who is already involuntarily engaged in a contrary act of dissimulation. The kind of transformation Perdita believes to be dangerous seems to Florizel an innocuous and convenient kind of play: secure in the stable possession of rank and power, the courtier can mimic the appearance of a lower status without any comparable risk. In fact of course Florizel is deluding himself here: since to the courtly values of his father such a transformation of prince to swain, adopted and enacted outside the secure perimeters of the court's own conventions of play, is as risky, as dangerous, as deserving of punishment as the emulation by a shepherdess of courtly eminence and privilege. The discursive tensions operating within this scene derive in part from the prince's attempt to stage a performance of court theatre in an 'out-of-court' location, to direct and produce his own betrothal masque:

> *Flo.* Your guests are coming:
> Lift up your countenance, as it were the day
> Of celebration of that nuptial which
> We two have sworn shall come.
> (IV.iv.48–51)

'As it were' – neither the occasion nor the performance is exactly what Florizel wants, and the element of simulation is acknowledged even in his own speech. However effective may be the transformational possibilities of costume and ritual, gesture and speech, this remains very much an amateur court masque, the totality of its performative medium continually ruptured and breached by both internal and external pressures and contradictions. The imitation of courtly entertainment takes place in the context of a dramatization of country carnival, with a ballad-mongering pedlar (who is really an ex-courtier and thief) engaging in popular and bawdy humour with common people; and the anti-masque of satyrs which links the play so closely with a specific masque performance, that of Ben Jonson's *Oberon*, is danced by performers who are given a plurality of positions within and outside the world of the drama. Their satyric dance ('a gallimaufry of gambols', IV.iv.329) is an appropriate contribution to the rustic carnival: they are thus designated as performers within the play's imagined world. But their actual social identities within that imagined world are also designated, so they appear as kin to the amateur players of *A Midsummer Night's Dream*:

> *Servant* Master, there is three carters, three shepherds, three neat-herds, three swine-herds, that have made themselves all men of hair, they call themselves Saltiers . . .
> (IV.iv.325–8)

Yet prior to their representation of common men representing a festive performance, they are also actors, whose professional careers link the courts of fictional Bohemia and historical London, through their participation in an enacted popular festival played both at court and on a contemporary public stage:

> *Servant* One three of them, by their own report, sir, hath danced before the king . . .
>
> (IV.iv.337–8)

The scene's well-known discussion of 'art and nature' clearly has its place within this complex discursive and performative medium. At first glance the debate between Polixenes and Perdita seems to pose an antithesis between art and nature that parallels exactly the antagonisms constructed by the play's bipartite structure: country and court, Carnival and Lent, innocence and experience. Polixenes advocates the incorporation into Perdita's ritual floral tribute of flowers that she regards as illegitimate and artificial, hybrids which unworthily emulate natural creativity by violating nature's own laws of 'mannerly distinguishment'. Perdita's resistance is countered by a sophisticated argument that easily disposes of the simple distinction upon which her pastoral ideology rests:

> *Poli.* Yet nature is made better by no mean
> But nature makes that mean: so, over that art,
> Which you say adds to nature, is an art
> That nature makes.
>
> (IV.iv.89–92)

The plausibility of Polixenes' argument is however subverted by his inferred endorsement of miscegenation as a principle of nature: his horticultural parallels would actually endorse that marriage between a prince and a shepherdess which his courtly ideology vehemently opposes. The problem thus seems brought to rest on the pastoral ground of a romance community in which love is more important than class. The simple dignity of Perdita's *mots d'escalier* seem irresistibly eloquent of this egalitarian pastoral sentiment:

> *Perd.* I was not much afeard; for once or twice
> I was about to speak, and tell him plainly,
> The selfsame sun that shines upon his court
> Hides not his visage from our cottage, but
> Looks on alike . . .
>
> (IV.iv.443–47)

Yet of course this simple country wisdom is actually the product of a sophisticated courtly pastoral: though she does not know it, Perdita is actually acting the role of a shepherdess, and her true nobility shines clearly through her bucolic disguise:

> *Poli.* . . . nothing she does or seems
> But smacks of something greater than herself,
> Too noble for this place.
>
> (IV.iv.157–9)

This does not however reduce the entire dramatic fiction to a courtly fantasy; for in this scene court meets country in a theatrical environment which both mingles and distinguishes its diverse elements of court masque, popular festival, romantic fantasy, popular naturalism, rarefied pastoral and clownish folk-humour. The formal elements that constitute the dramatic totality are not simply merged on the ground of a unified common culture: on the contrary, they are juxtaposed in such a way as to render visible both their form and their ideological content.

### 'THERE'S MAGIC IN THY MAJESTY'

The concluding scenes of both *The Tempest* and *The Winter's Tale* include the 'discovery', to an assembled on-stage audience, of a *tableau vivant* featuring characters believed by some of the spectators to be dead. In Act 5:1 of *The Tempest* Prospero deliberately adds to Alonso's established belief in the demise of his own son the additional conviction that Miranda too is dead (V.i.141–53), before revealing the betrothed lovers engaged in a game of chess:

> *Here Prospero discovers Ferdinand and Miranda playing at chess*
>
> *Mir.* Sweet lord, you play me false.
> *Ferd.* No, my dearest love,
> I would not for the world.
> *Mir.* Yes, for a score of kingdoms you should wrangle,
> And I would call it fair play.
>
> (V.i.171–5)

The image thus disclosed is designed both as a further revelation of Prospero's necromantic power, extended even to an apparent mastery over life and death, and a consolidation of his political and dynastic ambitions, since the young couple destined to unite Milan and Naples are a key component in his strategy of restitution. The rarity of references to chess in Shakespeare's plays persuades Bryan Loughrey and Neil Taylor that the choice of this game for the royal couple's leisure occupation is calculated and deliberate.

## The Winter's Tale: Country into Court       231

The associations of chess with play, love, war and political strategy are all appropriate allusions: but above all chess is employed here because it was, *par excellence*, an aristocratic game:

> ... chess was the natural choice of recreation owing to its traditional associations with the nobility and the conventions of courtly love. There can be no doubt that the game possessed aristocratic connotations: it was almost invariably referred to as a princely or royal game, and 'mentioned again and again in literature as one of the typical recreations of the feudal nobility'.[38]

Prospero is here therefore elaborating on his achievement in the masque-scene, extending his demonstrated capacity to create on the desert island the convincing simulation of a court. The representation of courtly entertainment is here of course notably attenuated, since Prospero has dispensed with the services of his actors and focused the activity of courtly play onto the microcosmic terrain of a chess-board. What he hopes to demonstrate by his theatrical 'discovery' is the successful exercise of his mastery of circumstances and his control over the lovers' sexuality, which can be validated only within the authorized union of a dynastic marriage. It is the more surprising therefore that the lovers appear to be enacting on the level of courtly play a dangerous game of sexual suggestion. 'Sweet lord, you play me false', says Miranda, and subsequently admits that she would wholeheartedly embrace that betrayal of trust. Ferdinand is cheating at chess: and as Loughrey and Taylor have shown, the traditional associations of the game would seem to point to a strategic assault on the virgin's chastity (when Perdita in *The Winter's Tale* rebukes Florizel in similar words, she is certainly accusing him of libidinous aspirations: 'I might fear, my Doricles,/ You woo'd me the false way', IV.iv.150–1). At the very least this emergence of unrepressed sexuality operates to destabilize Prospero's imagined mastery over his own dramatic representations; and if we were to press the associational possibilities of the chess-game further, it might well prove to have an unsettling effect on the achieved composure of this play of betrayal and political ambition.

The equivalent moment in the final scene of *The Winter's Tale* is the revelation of Hermione's 'statue', which is then apparently brought to life by the exercise of magic. For the space of time during which Leontes and the other courtiers are under the impression that the form of the living woman displayed before them is actually a statue, 'magic' is merely a metaphor for the incredible capacity of art to imitate life: 'prepare' Paulina tells them, 'to see the life as lively mock'd as ever/ Still sleep mock'd death' (V.iii.18–20). 'The life' rather than 'life' seems to relate the observation to painting rather than necromancy – the statue depicts *likeness* ('to the life') rather than embodying *life*; and implicit in Paulina's speech is a self-conscious awareness that the 'still sleep' of Hermione's mysterious absence has indeed been a mockery of death. Leontes sees in the statue a quasi-magical power of naturalistic representation; but he also receives it as an aesthetic object conveying a stern moral admonition:

> *Leo.*         O, thus she stood,
> Even with such life of majesty, warm life,
> As now it coldly stands, when first I woo'd her!
> I am ashamed: does not the stone rebuke me
> For being more stone than it? O royal piece!
> There's magic in thy majesty, which has
> My evils conjur'd to remembrance . . .
>                     (V.iii.34–40)

For all his talk of 'magic' and 'conjuring' Leontes is still at this point convinced that he is looking at a work of art, and that it is the craftsmanship of the 'stone' that rebukes him with remembrance of Hermione's unnecessary death. But of course that kind of restoration of a lost original by artistic imitation would reproduce Hermione as she was, in the image possessed and retained by her observers. Both Leontes and Polixenes comment on the obvious signs of ageing that mar the statue's verisimilitude:

> *Leo.*         But yet, Paulina,
> Hermione was not so much wrinkled, nothing
> So aged as this seems.
>     *Poli.*         O, not by much.
>                     (V.iii.27–9)

Whatever kinds of art and 'magic' are at work here – Paulina's stagecraft, Julio Romano's sculpture, concealments and revelations that charm imagination and baffle understanding – they are not seen as deriving, as they do in *The Tempest*, from the sovereign power of the patriarchal ruler. The powerful men of *The Winter's Tale*, two kings, are here firmly constituted as spectators of the enacted performance, as open-mouthed dupes of a female conjurer's legerdemain.

## The Winter's Tale: Country into Court          233

In order to demonstrate how completely in this play masculine power is subordinated to the art, magic and power of the female, it is useful to make a comparison with *Much Ado About Nothing*, which uses the same narrative of a woman unjustly accused, concealing herself in simulated death in order to reappear for a scene of reconciliation and re-composure. In the comedy the two gender groups, of military-aristocratic men and subjected but resistant women, are arraigned in mutual antagonism: a solution to the deadlock is propounded by an apparently independent witness, the Friar who was to have married Claudio and Hero. In fact Friar Francis' solution is simply a strategy for restoring the status quo. Somehow Claudio's faith in Hero must be restored, so the interrupted wedding may continue. His suggested method of achieving that end is extremely revealing:

> *Friar* When he [Claudio] shall hear she died upon his words,
> Th'idea of her life shall sweetly creep
> Into his study of imagination,
> And every lovely organ of her life
> Shall come appareled in more precious habit,
> More moving, delicate and full of life,
> Into the eye and prospect of his soul
> Than when she lived indeed.
> (IV.i.222–9)

What the Friar proposes here is nothing less than to acknowledge that Hero's apparent and symbolic death should be regarded, for the purposes of the moment, as real. The fact that the woman herself has been unjustly slandered and maliciously 'framed' is recognized; but the affirmation of her innocence and the denunciation of her wrongers seems less of a priority than the symbolic destruction of this irrevocably contaminated female body. In fact it has been contaminated with nothing but masculine suspicion, jealousy, mistrust and fear: nonetheless only its total ritual destruction can achieve the clearing of Hero's name. She will be restored, not to life, but to her pristine innocence. The image of her corrupted flesh will be replaced in Claudio's imagination by a restoration of that idealized image of courtly adoration which initially attracted him, and which proved so inadequate as a basis for a real sexual relationship.

Although the play's dramatic and moral crisis calls into question the whole system of patriarchal authority, Friar Francis has no wish to challenge or subvert it. He wants it restored, with all its contradictions effaced and suppressed. His success in this endeavour is so complete that it involves the voluntary participation of the wronged woman herself in the fabrication of this curious myth:

> Hero  And when I lived I was your other wife;
> And when you loved you were my other husband.
> Clau.  Another Hero!
> 
> (V.iv.60–2)

This conspiracy to construct an illusion of Hero's death and rebirth leaves the male ideology that created the entire crisis in the first place virtually intact. Claudio and Don Pedro have had to admit that they made a mistake; but Claudio does not have to suffer the indignity of contact with a contaminated woman, Don Pedro does not have to witness his friend dishonoured, and neither is in any way obliged to inspect or interrogate the ludicrous premises of their own ideology; neither is required to consider that the contamination arose from masculine anxiety rather than feminine betrayal.

In *The Winter's Tale*, by contrast, the same crisis is negotiated entirely by the courage and resourcefulness of a woman. And where in *The Tempest* all theatrical performances are under the control of the sovereign magus, here a masque-like show is arranged by a powerful ('mankind') female presenter:

> Paul.      Music, awake her: strike!
> 'Tis time; descend; be stone no more; approach;
> Strike all that look upon with marvel.
> 
> (V.iii.98–100)

Inga-Stina Ewbank shows that these words are 'in tone and phrasing very like a presenters's call for the chief figure of the masque to appear'.[39] The speaking statue was not, according to Ewbank, an established masque device, but *The Winter's Tale* seems to have given it currency, since it subsequently appears in masques by Campion and Beaumont. Its deployment in *The Winter's Tale* is certainly designed to operate with the miraculous power of masques and other forms of court theatre. But just as the masque in *The Tempest* is clearly revealed to be 'power on display', so Paulina's 'Masque of the Statue' is a 'magic' trick with perfectly rational and naturalistic causes. It is at the same time no mere display, and its meanings are deep and powerful. But it is by no means an ideological consolidation of existing power. When Hermione does speak, she speaks only to her daughter: her silence towards Leontes is remarkable, and she defines the purpose of her preservation as a desire to see 'the issue' of her daughter's loss and recovery. The text continually turns back on its own romance materials, criticizing their implausible dénouements as the creaking machinery of 'an old tale' (V.iii.117); and Leontes' arbitrary assigning of Paulina to Camillo in marriage is machinery of an almost grotesque improbability. If there is here 'magic' in 'majesty', it is certainly not that found in the total theatre of the court masque.

Once again, as in *The Tempest*, the conventions of court theatre are incorporated, interpolated into the dramatic medium of this product of the popular theatre; but they are included only to be estranged, framed into critical visibility and self-reflexive interrogation. Although it is prepared to employ the machinery of court theatre, *The Winter's Tale* operates across an entirely different, though not entirely separate, aesthetic and ideological terrain, and continually declares the necessity of a theatrical language other than that of the court itself. It reflects critically on the self-deluding powers of an absolutist fantasy that habitually constructs and then credits its own simulations of the real; it explores the kind of absorption into a dramatized action or a theatrical role that loses all sense of distance and distinction; it subverts the priorities of a patriarchal polity by problematizing masculine authority and endorsing feminine power; and even at that point, in the Bohemian scenes, where it approximates most intimately to the conventions of courtly drama, it releases into play a diversified plurality of theatrical energies that surround, contextualize, frame and subvert the rarefied languages of pastoral, romance and masque. The spectacle of an amateur court masque roughly improvised in the midst of a boisterous popular festival, presents us with a compelling and historically significant image of the court as it could appear not to itself, but to those artists, intellectuals and spectators who, even though they might occasionally be invited to the court's festivities, were also able to inspect its values and its pretensions from the outside.

# Endgames

## Graham Holderness

The institution of the English Renaissance court – specifically the courts of the Tudor and Stuart monarchs – has long exercised some complex and peculiar compulsion over the imaginations of subsequent generations. Such interest has been largely historical (latterly sociological) and cultural (latterly anthropological), and it is precisely at the interface of what we normally call history and what we traditionally designate as culture, that both our studies of Shakespeare, *The Play of History* and *Out of Court*, have been joined. In this book our attention has engaged with the court as a profoundly important historical institution, and simultaneously as the source of a particular symbolic language, which seems to have been powerful enough to enter and pervade the general culture at almost every level. The plays of Shakespeare, which were often performed in the Elizabethan and Jacobean courts, and which frequently construct their dramatic worlds out of particular images of court society, evidently participated in both the 'historical' and the 'symbolic' realities of the court, and can be discussed in relation to either. But as we have shown in our detailed analyses of particular plays, the Shakespearean drama does not mediate between the historical court and its own symbolic language in any direct or simple relationship: and in many ways that new secular drama of the Elizabethan public playhouses was, and remained, sufficiently independent of the court to be capable of projecting and estranging both the historical and the cultural experience of the court into a remarkable degree of visibility.

We have thus been working across three separable but interconnected analytical spaces, which can be conveniently symbolized by appropriately theatrical metaphors. The Tudor and Stuart courts were central theatres of public life, social intercourse and political power. In a cultural environment largely given over to lavish and ostentatious display, not only of material wealth and dynastic power, but of the terms and procedures, the methods and conventions of government, the personnel of the court, monarch and aristocracy, openly enacted on a symbolically raised public platform the continuous narrative of their civic duty. The personality of the monarch was of course central to all such institutions, but the court was the necessary clothing of the monarch's power: whether a king happened to be ruling in an autocratic or a participatory way, the machinery of the court was never dispensed with. Thus in earlier historical studies the court was primarily conceived of in biographical and in constitutional terms: it was the domestic environment of the monarch whose individual personality dominated the political life of the nation; or it was the working machinery of law, finance and administration, the material apparatus of government which actually ran the country.

A large proportion of those historical studies that have shaped our own historical tradition has been the work of intellectuals organic to a class which inherited the power of the feudal aristocracy, and which could not avoid looking back at Tudor and (especially) Stuart power, and at the cultural discourses of its execution, from a hostile perspective. British 'Whig' history, founded on the basis of a constitutional monarchy and a parliamentary system, inevitably saw the court primarily in terms of its function in the operation of a potentially autocratic 'personal' rule. Although within that same historical framework Elizabeth was usually magnified as the great Gloriana, it was primarily for her populist and participatory style of ruling; and the story of the Stuart court was constructed as an admonitory narrative illustrating the perils of a court separated from and antagonistic to its 'country'. When 'Whig' history became proletarianized by liberal and socialist historians who demanded that historical attention should be focussed on the social and economic lives of the people rather than on the tiny and isolated fragment of a ruling class, the distancing of the court into the framework of a remote, external and hostile perspective became a matter of political duty as well as one of historiographical emphasis. As we shall see, this particular historical perspective exerts considerable ideological pressure on the discursive possibilities framing the analysis of court society, culture and drama.

Such historical resistances have been overcome sufficiently to make way for a new branch of historical studies, with its own area of specialization: 'court history'. Sociological studies such as those of Norbert Elias, identifying and describing the aristocratic 'court societies' of European absolutism, have interacted with work on the English aristocracy by British social historians like Lawrence

Stone, to give a new impetus to historical interest in the court as a sociological and cultural institution. British historians have begun to graft these new currents of thought onto the existing empiricist methodologies of earlier historiography (such as that of G. R. Elton) describing the machinery of government, and now study Renaissance courts in much more detail as the specific locations of a society's configurations of power.[1] Drawing on this type of historical work, we have been able to build on the argument of our earlier book *The Play of History*, which demonstrates how firmly rooted are Shakespeare's plays in a sophisticated historical, sociological, geographical and imaginative grasp of the nature of other societies. Since, in terms of its conditions of production, this imaginative historiographical drama was linked to only one of the available contemporary models of court society, that of England (consisting in this case of the courts of one Tudor and one Stuart monarch), we have concentrated our explicitly historical focus on that contextual relationship. But when we examine specific dramatizations of court society within the plays, we encounter a range of reference that is European in scope: so we have been able to deal with imagined or reconstructed representations of historical courts located in Navarre and Denmark, semi-fictional princely and monarchical courts attributed to Milan and Naples, Sicily and Bohemia, and imaginary ducal courts, set in Illyria, or displaced to the Forest of Arden.

More recently a new kind of attention has been directed at the Renaissance court, a focus which takes as its starting-point the obvious fact that such institutions were as much cultural as political arenas, and that the 'business' of a Tudor or Stuart court might have been understood more as transactions in the symbolic language of authority than as negotiations in the material details of implementing power. A court was the scene of pageantry, display, ritual, a continuous process of self-dramatization. On this open stage of public life, the figures of history did not simply appear as themselves: they played parts, enacted roles, performed in a continuous drama which simultaneously 'acted' the story of the national life and 'enacted' it, made it happen. Although from one perspective, that of the dispossessed and disenchanted spectator, this dramatic quality laid the court open to the charge of radical inauthenticity, with its 'potentates', in Raleigh's words, 'acting but others' actions',[2] a recognition of the centrality of this courtly self-dramatization authorizes and legitimates a deeper interest in, and a more particular attention to, the precise forms in which the court conducted and composed its drama. It can also bring into play that theoretical acknowledgement of an unbroken continuity between culture and history, between the ritual dramatization of politics and political power, which currently dominates cultural analysis in Renaissance studies. If 'politics' can take time off to engage in 'performance', then it is possible that such performance might have been conceived as an extension of politics rather than as a separate activity. Analysis of the contents of what was performed might disclose, not an autonomous aesthetic domain of court activity, but sublimated and crystallized forms of political power. *Power on Display; The Illusion of Power;*[3] the very titles of the important contemporary essays in Renaissance cultural analysis declare their theoretical conviction that the self-dramatization of a court is a dramatization of power. Frequently this conviction joins with the hostile externality of Whig history, to insist on a thorough stripping of the delusive camouflaging sham that is culture, and a complete exposure of the reality it existed to conceal; underlying the 'illusions' of cultural 'display' we can be guaranteed an encounter with the hard, solid bedrock of historical reality: 'ultimately' Leonard Tennenhouse observes at one point in his study of 'the politics of Shakespeare's genres', drama can be interpreted as the mask of reality, 'all for show' (p. 179).

If terms like 'illusion' and 'display' are used to define culture as a series of 'insubstantial pageants' whose purpose is to conceal and mystify something ('power') that is thought of as patently more 'real', then the chief motive for studying the plays of Shakespeare (or of any other dramatist) is to expose the mechanisms of that process of mystification, and to dissolve the plays back into the material reality from which they were originally constituted. Yet a complete understanding of such cultural artefacts is possible only if they are acknowledged to have both materiality and a more complex relationship with the 'functions' of a society's ideology. To secure such acknowledgement we need to draw on those 'expressivist' theories of culture which were defined in our introduction as diametrically opposed to the 'functionalist' theories which in practice dominate the critical methods of new historicism and of cultural materialism. The debate is in one sense a re-enactment of an earlier intellectual battle fought out within the theoretical problematic of marxism. When cultural analysis tried to work with a reductive interpretation of Marx's 'base/ superstructure' model, the result was always inevitably a de-materialization of culture, which became largely understood as a smoke-screen concealing economic and political realities. Using the same model, attempts were made to insist that 'culture' always had a 'relative autonomy' of the economic base. In practice that proposed 'relativity' was always likely, in the analysis of particular examples, to collapse back into determinism, or the 'autonomy' to become so relative as to constitute something like complete cultural and artistic independence. When the perspectives of social anthropology began to penetrate cultural studies, particularly through the work of Clifford Geertz and René Girard, their attractiveness to historicist, post-structuralist and neo-marxist aesthetics lay in their capacity to grasp the totality of a society, simultaneously in both its political and economic structure, and its cultural superstructure – neither of which, in practice, could truly be separated from the other. If the purpose of culture is to 'express' the nature of a society, to embody in myth and ritual its deepest social experience, then detailed readings of such myth and ritual become valid methods of understanding a society.

Anthropology offers us two useful methods of inquiry in our approach to Renaissance drama. Firstly, it provides us with an opportunity to take seriously beliefs and cultural practices that a harder-headed materialism can only scorn as the antiquated relics of a vanished culture. Historians addressing the practices of festivity in Renaissance courts are now much more capable of recognizing that 'magic' could have possessed a much stronger meaning and reality than any that we could attribute to it. Tracing the cohesive influence within Renaissance culture of neo-platonist beliefs, which had the effect of consolidating and reviving much older myths and rituals, historians are able to acknowledge that cultural practices traditionally thought of as overtly and self-consciously symbolic or allegorical – preserving, in semiotic parlance, a respectful distance between sign and signifier – are much more likely to have been experienced and understood as possessing a genuinely 'magical' efficacy. In the course of the festivities arranged to welcome Katherine of Aragon to England in 1501, there was staged at the court of Henry VII a 'disguising' which involved the romance trope of knights assaulting a castle that contained eight ladies, four dressed in English costume, four in Spanish. Having successfully completed their assault, the knights drew the ladies into a dance. Commenting on this scenario Thomas M. Greene observes that the siege and assault enacted a sexual myth, appropriate to the projected royal wedding, of feminine resistance overcome by male fortitude, the violent sexual encounter then modulating into a dance of conjugal harmony. The performance was not, in Greene's view, simply an imitation of a 'real' event that would subsequently happen; it was rather a ritual enactment designed to *make* it happen:[4]

> The dance does not lack a faint magical dimension. It is not merely a symbol of that harmonious marriage and that harmonious conjunction of two nations which the future is expected to witness. I think we can discern within the dance, and within others on analogous occasions, vestigial, half-conscious beliefs that representations are efficacious. Men and women dance, or used to dance, at weddings in order to *accomplish* concord. The performers in Westminster Hall that night were dancing harmony between England and Spain, prince and infanta. They danced a charged presage, a charmed augury of concert. Although for many of the spectators, doubtless, it was the splendour of the show that counted most . . . a certain 'serious' teleology emerges from that solemnity.

In order fully to understand such festive occasions, it is therefore necessary to appreciate the possibility of a teleology, and an aesthetic, in which the sign and the thing signified are indivisible, in which there is no distance and thus no potential 'slippage' between representation and reality. We can add to Greene's analysis a conviction that the people of the Renaissance not only experienced but *understood* their culture in this way. As late as the 1630s William Hudson offered to the king an explanation for the nomenclature of the Court of the Star Chamber.

> And so I doubt not but *Camera Stellata* . . . is most aptly named; not because the Star Chamber where the Court is kept is so adorned with stars gilded, as some would have it, for surely the chamber is so adorned because it is the seal of that court . . . and it was so fitly called because the stars have no light but what is cast upon them from the sun by reflection, being his representative body, and as his Majesty himself was pleased to say when he sat there in his royal person, representation must needs cease when the person is present. So in the presence of his great majesty, the which is the sun of honour and glory, the shining of those stars is put out . . . [5]

There is a clear distinction here between the kind of symbolic display or artistic design that functions *representationally*, patently imitative of something other than itself, expressive through its own concrete imagery of an absent plenitude; and the kind of physical presence, such as that of the king's person, which unites within itself the symbol and its referent, literally housing that heavenly majesty that was merely mimicked by the chamber's gilded stars. The Renaissance intellectual can therefore be seen to have been prematurely capable of understanding both the post-structuralist dissociation of sign and signified, and the anthropological intuition of the essential unity of reality and myth.

Secondly, anthropology offers the illuminating possibility of 'reading' the products of a remote culture without the suspicion and hostility of an external perspective; of approaching Renaissance court festivity and theatre imaginatively, from the point of view of the participant. Traditionally that distinction between an 'objective' and an 'imaginative' approach has been considered a key difference between 'historical' and 'literary' approaches to the past. However, if the original relationship, consolidated in the 1970s, between 'history' and 'literature', consisted largely in the historicization of literary criticism, it is certainly the case that historians have now come to terms with what (for want of a more precise theoretical term) we call the 'imaginative' dimension, and even now include (though not without controversy) 'empathy' among their methods of inquiry.[6]

We have tried in the foregoing pages to employ these 'imaginative', 'empathic' methods of inquiry in our readings of Renaissance cultural production. We have been interested in the viewpoint of the participant in that culture, as well as in that of the detached retrospective observer. But Renaissance culture, and in particular the exclusive and competitive courtly culture we have used as our framing context, contained its spectators as well as its participants. In our introduction John Turner warned against the assumption that Geertz's concept of the 'theatre state' can be universally applied: nineteenth-century Bali was not Elizabethan and Jacobean England. Thomas M. Greene's distinction between the participant and the spectator in Henry VII's celebration for the Infanta further illustrates this profoundly important qualification. In Geertz's examples theatre is ritual, and there are no spectators (apart from anthropologists), only participants. Where theatre is genuinely ritual, the incorporation of the 'actor' is a total experience, an empathic and imaginative absorption into a created reality. The celebrants of Greek Dionysiac ritual were participants, completely involved in a communal celebration of belief; when those rituals developed into theatre, the spectators of tragedy were no longer participants, but observers – a development identified by Augusto Boal as the original death of community drama.[7] The split between participant and observer, revealingly played with in Sir John Davies' *Orchestra*, immediately ruptures the totalizing experience of ritual drama, and constructs the possibility – central to all our readings of court experience – of that division between the member and the outcast, the favoured and the dispossessed, the dancers who enact a ritual of magical efficacy, and the dance that may be available to the spectator only as a brilliant display, all for show. Yeats' passionate longing for the unified image that would indissolubly join artist and medium, performer and performance, dancer and dance,[8] can be glimpsed as an achievement among the rituals of Tudor and Stuart court theatre; but it was at best an unstable unity, already at the moment of its completion dissolving into the kind of spectacle that made itself available to the envious or unsympathetic onlooker for a detached and critical judgement.

This brings us to our second theoretical space and our second theatrical metaphor: for within the theatre of public life constituted by the court, and to some degree continuous with its everyday self-dramatization, the court constructed its own dramatic space on which to stage its own representations of itself. As we have shown in our discussion of the various types of 'court theatre', this self-dramatization could take a number of different forms, many of which functioned, in the manner identified by Orgel and Tennenhouse, to mystify and legitimate dynastic and political authority. The purest form of this self-validating cultural enterprise was the Stuart court masque. But on that same court stage were enacted, amidst a wide-ranging and diversified repertory, the plays of Shakespeare. Those plays must therefore be included among the productions of the court's activity of self-dramatization: they must be considered as having been, in some complex and mediated sense, specimens of court theatre.

Shakespeare's career as a dramatist discloses a consistently clear and demonstrable relationship between theatre and court. That connection, as we have shown, may take any one of a range of different forms; and our discussions of particular plays have been able to employ different theoretical frameworks. Tracing historical and cultural links between theatre and court may involve processes such as re-locating the plays into their original court performances; offering descriptive analyses of the plays' own dramatizations of different courts, or pursuing their enactment of conflicts that arise from the social structures and value-systems of an isolable 'court society'; or meditating on those larger, more universal questions that perpetually arise in the course of the drama's symbolic play with 'court experience'. Each of us has felt, while working within a common context of historical and artistic problems and methodologies, relatively free to pursue more particular, individual interests, so that specific individual contributions are marked by differing emphases and preoccupations: the theatrical, the psychoanalytical, the philosophic. Often these separate theoretical dimensions are to be found indissolubly unified within the dramatic textures of the plays themselves: thus for example Prospero's famous speech 'Our revels now are ended', (*The Tempest*, IV.i.148–58), which follows on the collapse of his impromptu court masque, is simultaneously a critique of court theatre, a symptomatic explanation of his own sudden and inexplicable excess of anxiety, and a grave and earnest meditation on the transience of performance and the fragility of human existence. Theatre, whether regarded descriptively from within the perspective of its own framework of allusion, or analytically in terms of its conditions of production, continually and insistently poses these large-scale questions, and can thereby seem to participate in the very transcendental signification it continually constructs and deconstructs. Yet Prospero's court masque is very clearly located in the constructive activity of a particular mind, 'grows' in Blake's words 'in the human brain'.

Court and theatre were of course quite separate as well as linked cultural spaces; and at this point we can nominate our third analytical space, that of the public theatre. Our third theatrical metaphor becomes no longer a metaphor but a literal, purpose-built physical space constructed specifically to contain the new secular drama – the Elizabethan public playhouse. For the plays which we acknowledge as specimens of court theatre also had another existence, distinct if not wholly separable, on the cultural margins where popular entertainment flourished. This binary existence, whereby plays performed to a fee-paying popular audience were transferred for occasional or seasonal performances at court, has always been acknowledged as a constitutive feature of the Shakespearean drama. Discussions of this relationship have usually taken one of three forms, which we can loosely designate as the 'aristocratic', the 'populist' and the 'communal'. The drama can be seen as very much the product of aristocratic protection and royal patronage, a ruling-class form of entertainment sportingly prepared to slum it among the apprentices and criminals of Southwark. Such aristocratic appropriations (currently being mimicked at the level of farce in debates over Shakespeare's true identity) are continually challenged by interpretations that stress the bourgeois character of the drama, its relative independence of royal and aristocratic culture, and its roots among the London populace and in plebeian traditions of entertainment. In this perspective any royal affiliation tends to be seen as an embarrassing historical accident, forced on the players by the undeveloped conditions of emergent bourgeois hegemony. Thirdly, there is the argument for an inclusive common culture, linking court and theatre, aristocracy and populace in an integrated 'organic community'. In this model the drama itself, which clearly mediated between Whitehall and Southwark, is frequently used as illustrative evidence to demonstrate the kind of undivided sensibility enjoyed by the inhabitants of that cohesive Elizabethan culture. In this study we have proposed a different conception of the relations between theatre and court as we find them evidenced and debated in Shakespeare's plays. For as John Turner observes in our introduction, if in the Renaissance the monarch and nobility could summon the theatre into court, the players could also bring the court into the theatre. Under the very different conditions of representation pertaining in the public theatres, the image of the court could be refracted and dispersed, 'framed' and particularized, analysed and evaluated, in ways that were not possible for the court's own species of theatre. Those potentialities could not have disappeared from the drama when it transferred from the Globe to the court. The court itself was therefore prepared to include in its programmes of entertainment, side by side with its masques and magical shows, a type of drama within which its own image could be subjected to a process of dispersal and reconstruction.

A key cultural *rapprochement* here, and a common focus of our joint attention, is the interaction between the Shakespearean drama and the court masque. There is a clear cultural contradiction between the developing secularism of the popular drama, and the increasing investment by the court in a quasi-magical cultural form. The masque was a much more primitive dramatic form, its stylized conventions, emblematic gestures, mythological figures, allegorical themes and associations with song and dance linking it back to ancient forms of folk-drama; and its recurrent motifs of gods descending, oblation, sacrifice, suggesting continuities with pagan ritual. If we were to compare the extremely secularized view of history (and indeed of monarchy) provided by Shakespeare's historical plays, with the elaborate ritualized neo-platonism of a Caroline masque, we would inevitably feel some sense of the historical contradiction between a 'people' growing gradually more confident that history was on their side, and a court relying more and more heavily on primitive ritual and magic to sustain its power.

On the other hand, as we have seen, Shakespeare's dramatic career testifies to a continual and active relationship with the forms of the masque. Masques are incorporated into the plays from the very beginning (*Love's Labour's Lost*) to the very end (*Henry VIII*). *As You Like It* ends with a Hymeneal masque celebrating marriage and reconciliation: Hymen appears (probably as a *deus ex machina*, since the stage directions do not indicate that a character presents the god) and presides over dancing and song. The gulf between court and country is closed by this uniquely appropriate dramatic form: pastoral style and aristocratic culture meet in a sophisticated courtly disguising that celebrates a primitive fertility ritual: 'Hymen peoples every town'. Yet, as Nick Potter points out in his discussion of *As You Like It*, the play's final emphasis on the conditional mood, and on the deceptiveness of appearances, throws the compelling synaesthetic poetry of the masque form into relief, opening up a fissure through which we can glimpse a 'counter-cursive movement in the play, working to destabilize and to unravel exactly the settled harmony towards which the play is tending'. 'If', as Hymen states, 'truth holds true contents' (*As You Like It*, IV.v.129), then the possibility of organic unity symbolized by the masque is a real one. But as Nick observes, 'Hymen's words are most ambiguous', and it is surely no accident that the god's riddling conditional provided the title for one of the important post-structuralist essays on the perpetual slippage between sign and signified in Shakespeare's plays.[9] This is the kind of subversive relationship between drama and masque that we find throughout Shakespeare's work, from the interrupted pageant of the nine worthies in *Love's Labour's Lost*, which indicates, in John Turner's words, 'disjunctions in real life between the playful and the real that eclipse the harmonious power of art', to the fragmentation of Prospero's masque in *The Tempest* under the twin pressures of external betrayal and internal anxiety.

Throughout these joint productions of theatre and court we find a similar self-definition of the drama as distinguishable from, though engaged with and even participating in, the court's own symbolic language. And it is that very capacity to frame and estrange the image of the court, to reflect its experience in a mirror that was not its own, that we find continuously held, with self-conscious deliberation, in place within the plays. This is not to argue that either the mirror or the reality it reflected can be regarded as simple, stable, 'objective' entities; or to venture any foolhardy conclusions about the 'author' who constructed, held or polished the mirror. It is however an attempt to suggest that these plays are full of a cultural consciousness of their own originating position, 'out of court'; not entirely separate from or opposed to the court, but tangentially and contradictorily linked, in a phrase which inscribes both the court and its margins in a single contradictory totality. To be 'out of court' is not to be in court, but it is to be in, and to be acutely conscious of, a relationship with the court: to be outside, but always looking, with however sceptical and critical an eye, into the heart of that compelling, unignorable centre of political, cultural and artistic power.

To employ such imagery of 'reflection' may appear to be running counter to the modern post-structuralist insistence that 'reflective' models of art should be discarded in favour of theories of art as 'ideological production'. It is quite clear that we cannot speak of drama as 'reflecting' a society, since the art is in no way separable from the society, and the society, far from being pre-existent in some 'objective' form conveniently available for representation, is already present in art that is already expressive of its own ideological consciousness. But we have risked, in attempting to speak of this drama, the employment of 'reflective' imagery, since we have been at pains to stress the capacity of drama to offer a relatively independent witness to the processes of human history, in the face of theories and methodologies that regard art as little more than the secretarial assistant to an executive ideology. We have not sought to deny that certain ideological 'functions' can be attributed to the drama; but in our analysis of relations between theatre and court, we have discovered and demonstrated that such functions, whatever they may be, can hardly be contained within what we know of the ideological apparatus of the court as a central state institution.

One seriously misleading method of 'reflective' analysis is that of using drama as descriptive evidence about the nature of a society.

In terms of their contents, these plays continue to assume the focussed centrality of the court as an unquestionable given. Yet the testimony of history provides quite a different image of the court's place and function in Elizabethan and Jacobean societies. Much of the work so far done by cultural historians preserves this image of the court as an isolated and unified centre.[10] But another recent historical account starts from a different premise, and begins by denying that the English Renaissance court really can be considered as an isolated and undifferentiated unit.[11] It was rather a multi-centered, politically-heterogenous entity dispersed across the social environment of the metropolis: 'no firm social or geographical boundaries ever separated the court from other fashionable milieus in the capital' (p. 55). Furthermore the court is not perceived in this analysis as in any way expressive of the insular exclusivity of aristocratic ideology: it was rather the centre for a much more widely-based social competition, 'open to infiltration by peers and gentry with no formal connection to the king's household or government' (p. 55). This relatively dispersed centre of patronage and power was characterized by a kind of 'cultural differentiation', a relatively open-ended cultural environment appropriate to a mobile and developing society.

If such historical arguments were accepted, would that condemn these dramas as false to the historical experience of the court? In fact, as we have seen, the plays clearly adumbrate and acknowledge in their formal properties and in their conditions of production, such an open, competitive society. At the same time they testify to another historical reality, this time ideological rather than political or economic: which is that the dominant classes of Renaissance England held firmly and insistently to the unified undifferentiated model of court society, as expressive of the collective and constitutional authority of the monarch, and as an apparatus for confirming and maintaining the hegemonic exclusivity of the aristocratic 'community of blood'. The provisional unity of the popular drama, internally fissured by a self-reflexive play of contradictions, externally ramifying into the complex, multiple, undifferentiated social life of the Renaissance metropolis, provided the perfect vehicle for this ambivalent disclosure of unity-in-diversity: simultaneously in, and out of, court.

# Notes

## INTRODUCTION

1. Sir John Davies, *Orchestra, or a Poem on Dancing*; all quotations from sts. 122–30, in *The Complete Poems of Sir John Davies*, ed. Alexander B. Grosart (London, 1876) vol. 1, pp. 207–10.
2. S. T. Coleridge, *On the Constitution of Church and State According to the Idea of Each* (Everyman's University Library edn., 1972) p. 51.
3. Stephen Greenblatt notes of this poem that 'the landscape is more psychological than literal'. See his *Sir Walter Ralegh: The Renaissance Man and his Roles* (Yale University Press, 1973) p. 69. *The Tempest*, and maybe *Twelfth Night*, similarly picks up this commonplace image of the castaway to explore the predicament of the person cut off from access to court.
4. Quoted in Greenblatt, ibid., p. 20.
5. This Latin tag is the epigraph of Marston's first satire. See *The Poems of John Marston*, ed. Arnold Davenport (Liverpool University Press, 1961) vol. 1, p. 67.
6. For Marston's Castilio, see ibid., p. 68; for Sir Annual Tilter, see Jonson's epigram 'To Sir Annual Tilter', which ridicules the knight for pretending to the witty device written for him by another. Shakespeare too, of course, was involved in this lucrative business, writing an impresa for the Earl of Rutland in 1613 for the fee of forty-four shillings in gold: see *Tudor and Jacobean Tournaments* by Alan Young (London: George Philip, 1987) p. 72.
7. La Bruyère, *Les Caractères ou Les Moeurs de ce siècle*, ed. Robert Garapon (Editions Garnier, Paris, 1962), De la cour, 99, p. 252. 'In a hundred years' time the world will still exist, just as it is, the stage and the sets will be the same, but not the actors. All those who now rejoice over a favour received, or grieve and lament over one denied, will have vanished from the boards. Other men are already stepping on to the stage, who will act the same parts in the same play; they will vanish in their turn; and those who do not yet exist will some day be no more; new actors will be there in their stead. What reliance can one place on a character out of a play?' Tr. Jean Stewart (Penguin, 1970) p. 149.
8. The phrase *to dance attendance* is not surprisingly a sixteenth-century coinage, dating according to the *OED* from 1522, when it appeared in Skelton's *Why Come Ye Not to Court?*
9. Norbert Elias, *The Court Society*, tr. Edmund Jephcott (Basil Blackwell, 1983) p. 88.
10. John Danby, *Shakespeare's Doctrine of Nature: A Study of 'King Lear'* (Faber and Faber, 1949) p. 18.

11. Quoted, as an illustration of conventional wisdom in 1586, by David Loades in *The Tudor Court* (B.T. Batsford Ltd., London, 1986) p. 126.
12. Perry Anderson, *Lineages of the Absolutist State* (New Left Books, 1974) p. 18.
13. For a reading of the Essex story in this light, see Mervyn James, 'At a crossroads of the political culture: the Essex revolt, 1601', in *Society, Politics and Culture: Studies in early modern England* (Cambridge University Press, 1986) pp. 416–65.
14. W. B. Yeats, *Essays and Introductions* (Macmillan, 1969) p. 107.
15. See Louis Montrose, 'Of Gentlemen and Shepherds: The Politics of Elizabethan Pastoral Form', in *ELH* vol. 50, no. 3 (Fall, 1983) pp. 415–59, and especially its conclusion where Montrose shows how 'Elizabethan practice confirms that pastoral has an affinity for paradox'.
16. Michael A. R. Graves, *The Tudor Parliaments: Crown, Lords and Commons, 1485–1603* (Longman, 1985) p. 149.
17. Ibid., p. 154.
18. See our readings of these plays in *Shakespeare: The Play of History* (Macmillan, 1988), especially pp. 85–8.
19. David Loades, op. cit., p. 2.
20. David Starkey, in David Starkey *et al.*, *The English Court: from the Wars of the Roses to the Civil War* (Longman, 1987) p. 18.
21. Michael D. Bristol, *Carnival and Theater: Plebeian Culture and the Structure of Authority in Renaissance England* (Methuen, 1985) p. 123.
22. C. L. Barber, *Shakespeare's Festive Comedy: A Study of Dramatic Form and its Relation to Social Custom* (Princeton University Press, 1959) p. 15.
23. Sir Philip Sidney, *A Defence of Poetry*, ed. Jan van Dorsten (Oxford University Press, 1966) p. 66.
24. Bristol, op. cit., p. 138. I am much indebted in this paragraph to Chapter 9 of his book.
25. Philip Stubbes, *The anatomy of abuses*, 1583 (Johnson Reprint Corporation, New York, 1973). All these quotations come from the section entitled 'Of Stage-playes and Enterluds, with their wickednes'.
26. John Davies, Epigram 159, 'To our English Terence Mr. Will: Shakespeare', from 'The Scourge of Folly', in *The Complete Works of John Davies of Hereford*, ed. Alexander B. Grosart (AMS Press, Inc., New York, 1967) vol. 2, k, p. 26.
27. Clifford Geertz, *Negara: The Theatre State in Nineteenth-Century Bali* (Princeton University Press, 1980) p. 123.
28. I am thinking here in particular of Stuart Clark's essay, 'French Historians and Early Modern Popular Culture', in *Past and Present* no. 100 (August, 1983) pp. 62–99. Geertz himself suggests this extension of his work in his conclusion to *Negara*.
29. Clifford Geertz, 'Deep Play: Notes on the Balinese Cockfight', in *The Interpretation of Cultures* (Basic Books, New York, 1973) p. 453.
30. William Wordsworth, 'Preface to *Lyrical Ballads*', in *The Prose Works of William Wordsworth*, ed. W. J. B. Owen and Jane

Notes to pp. 15–29

Worthington Smyser (Oxford University Press, 1974) vol. 1, p. 148.

## PART I: THE COURT AND THE NEW LEARNING

1. Francis Bacon, *Essays* (World's Classics edn., Oxford University Press, 1902), Essay L: 'Of Studies', p. 139.
2. Bacon, *The Advancement of Learning* (Everyman's Library edn., 1915) p. 82.
3. Bacon, *Essays*, Essay XV: 'Of Seditions and Troubles', p. 40.
4. See for an account of this latter term Jonathan Dollimore, *Radical Tragedy: Religion, Ideology and Power in the Drama of Shakespeare and his Contemporaries* (The Harvester Press, 1984), esp. pp. 153–81. His discussion of Bacon on pp. 75–8 has been helpful to me.
5. Bacon, *The Advancement of Learning*, p. 83 ('unto' for 'into' here).
6. See the discussion in our *Shakespeare: The Play of History* (Macmillan, 1988) pp. 126–7.
7. David Starkey, in David Starkey et al., *The English Court: from the Wars of the Roses to the Civil War* (Longman, 1987) p. 7.
8. Richard David, Introduction to the Arden edition of *Love's Labour's Lost* (Methuen, 1951) p. xxxi.
9. C. L. Barber, *Shakespeare's Festive Comedy: A Study of Dramatic Form and its Relation to Social Custom* (Princeton University Press, 1959) p. 87.
10. Ibid., p. 89.
11. David Loades, *The Tudor Court* (B. T. Batsford Ltd., London, 1986) p. 89.
12. Starkey, op. cit., p. 3.
13. See Frances A. Yates, *The French Academies of the Sixteenth Century* (The Warburg Institute, University of London, 1947) p. 123.
14. Louis A. Montrose, '"Sport by sport o'erthrown": Love's Labour's Lost and the Politics of Play', in *Texas Studies in Language and Literature*, vol. 18 (1976–7) p. 547.
15. Lawrence Stone, *The Crisis of the Aristocracy 1558–1641* (Oxford University Press, 1965) p. 481.
16. Peter de la Primaudaye, *The French Academie*, tr. T.B. [C?] (First Edition, 1586) p. 44.
17. Michael D. Bristol, *Carnival and Theater: Plebeian Culture and the Structure of Authority in Renaissance England* (Methuen, 1985) p. 86.
18. Francis Bacon, op cit., Essay LVIII: 'Of Vicissitude of Things', p. 160. David Starkey quotes this same phrase, op. cit., p. 21.
19. Montaigne, *Essays*, tr. John Florio (Everyman's Library edn., 1910) vol. 3, p. 23.
20. Loades, op. cit., p. 97.
21. David E. Cooper, *Metaphor* (Blackwell, 1986) p. 42.
22. Mervyn James, 'English Politics and the Concept of Honour 1485–1642', *Past and Present* Supplement 3 (The Past and Present Society, 1978) pp. 28–32.

23. Quoted by Mervyn James, op. cit., p. 29.
24. Barber, op. cit., p. 92.
25. Ibid., p. 109.
26. Stone, op. cit., p. 492.
27. Montrose, op. cit., p. 546, p. 545, p. 544.
28. Ibid., p. 546.
29. Loades, op. cit., p. 98.
30. Louis Adrian Montrose, 'Of Gentlemen and Shepherds: The Politics of Elizabethan Pastoral Form', in *ELH* vol. 50, no.3 (Fall, 1983) p. 426 and p. 448. The argument summarized here is made on p. 432.
31. Sir Philip Sidney, *A Defence of Poetry*, ed. Jan van Dorsten (Oxford University Press, 1966) p. 67.
32. Bristol, op. cit., p. 138.
33. Barber, op. cit., p. 193.
34. Ibid., p. 8, p. 15, p. 15.
35. Ibid., p. 61. This phrase summarizes an argument made throughout the book.
36. *The Political Works of James I*, ed. C.H. McIlwain (New York, Russell and Russell, 1965) p. 38.
37. Wordsworth, *The Borderers* (1842 version), ll. 1529–30.
38. D. W. Winnicott, *Playing and Reality* (Penguin, 1974) p. 61. See pp. 60–1 for an account of the breakdown of play that is useful here.
39. Barber, op. cit., p. 118 and p. 113.
40. Jeremy Hooker, *Poetry of Place: Essays and Reviews 1970–1981* (Carcanet Press, 1982) p. 24.
41. Montrose, '"Sport by sport o'erthrown": *Love's Labour's Lost* and the Politics of Play', p. 548.
42. La Bruyère, *Les Caractères ou les Moeurs de ce siècle*, ed. Robert Garapon (Editions Garnier, Paris, 1962) 'De la cour' 64, p. 242. 'Life at Court is a serious, melancholy game, requiring concentration: you have to arrange your pieces and lay your schemes, you must have a plan, follow it through, thwart your opponent's, you must be daring on occasion, and play according to the inspiration of the moment; and after all your forethought and calculation, you may meet with check, sometimes with checkmate; often, if you manage your pawns well, you may get as far as Queen, and win the game; the cleverest play prevails, or the luckiest'. Tr. Jean Stewart (Penguin, 1970) p. 149.
43. See Peter Mercer, *'Hamlet' and the Acting of Revenge* (Macmillan, 1987) chap. 4, esp. p. 68ff.
44. See John Fielding, '"To be or not to be": Hamlet, Culture and Winnicott', in *Winnicott Studies: The Journal of the Squiggle Foundation*, no. 1 (Spring, 1985) pp. 58–67, for a psychoanalytic discussion of the play that begins from the same place that my own thinking began, in the pages of D. W. Winnicott's *Playing and Reality* (see below, n. 73) but that develops its insights in an ahistorical manner characteristic of the British psychoanalytic tradition.
45. See Sigmund Freud, *Totem and Taboo*, in the Pelican Freud Library,

vol. 13 (Penguin, 1985) p. 71.
46. For a fuller discussion of this, see our *Shakespeare: The Play of History*, pp. 150–9.
47. René Girard, *Violence and the Sacred*, tr. Patrick Gregory (Johns Hopkins University Press, 1977) p. 37.
48. *The Political Works of James I*, ed. C. H. McIlwain (New York, Russell and Russell, 1965) p. 38.
49. Girard, op. cit., p. 37.
50. W. B. Yeats, *Autobiographies* (Macmillan, 1955) pp. 295–6.
51. Perry Anderson, *Lineages of the Absolutist State* (New Left Books, 1974) p. 148.
52. Montaigne, op cit., vol. 3, pp. 22–3.
53. William Golding, *Free Fall* (Penguin, 1963) p. 171.
54. M. Masud R. Khan, *The Privacy of the Self: Papers on Psychoanalytic Theory and Technique* (Hogarth Press, 1981) p. 103.
55. Bacon, op cit., Essay IV: 'Of Revenge', p. 11.
56. Montaigne, for instance, numbered this text amongst the fifty-seven he had painted on the beams of his library. See Peter Burke, *Montaigne* (Oxford University Press, 1981) p. 9.
57. Eleanor Prosser, *Hamlet and Revenge* (Stanford University Press, 2nd edn., 1971) p. 143.
58. Although a world-view is imaginable in which each of these two words might make full sense, it seems to me just such a world-view that *Hamlet* seeks to problematize – which is what makes an account of the play like that given by H. D. F. Kitto, in his *Form and Meaning in Drama* (Methuen, 1956) pp. 246–337, so hard to take.
59. A comical anthropological caution against all those who want to universalize the play, however, may be found in Laura Bohannan's piece, 'Shakespeare in the Bush', in *Natural History* vol. 75 (1966) pp. 28–33.
60. T. S. Eliot, 'Little Gidding' II. Eliot had *Hamlet* in mind here.
61. R.A. Foakes, 'The Art of Cruelty: Hamlet and Vindice', in *Shakespeare Survey* 26 (1973) p. 22.
62. See Rosalie L. Colie, *Paradoxia Epidemica: The Renaissance Tradition of Paradox* (Princeton University Press, 1966) for a full exploration of these points.
63. Mervyn James, 'At a crossroads of the political culture: the Essex revolt, 1601', in *Society, Politics and Culture: Studies in early modern England* (Cambridge University Press, 1986) p. 460, n. 154.
64. Quoted in *Ghosts and Other Plays* (Penguin, 1964) p. 294, n. 24.
65. Graham Holderness, *Hamlet* (Open University Press, 1987) p. 44. See also pp. 44–6. That book, like the present chapter, forms part of a long dialogue between us.
66. D. H. Lawrence, *Twilight in Italy* (Penguin, 1960) p. 78.
67. Rosalie Colie, 'Reason and Need: *King Lear* and the "Crisis of the Aristocracy"', in Rosalie L. Colie and F. T. Flahiff (eds), *Some Facets of 'King Lear': Essays in Prismatic Criticism* (University of Toronto Press, 1974) p. 186.
68. Ibid., p. 187.

69. S. P. Zitner, 'Hamlet, Duellist', in *University of Toronto Quarterly* vol. 39, no.1 (October, 1969) p. 6.
70. See Sir Israel Gollancz's reprinting of Belleforest's history in *The Sources of 'Hamlet'* (Oxford University Press, 1926) p. 196, p. 258 and p. 174.
71. From a letter written by Conrad on the eve of his marriage. Quoted by Jocelyn Baines, in *Joseph Conrad: A Critical Biography* (Penguin, 1971) p. 210.
72. Castiglione, *The Book of the Courtier*, tr. George Bull (Penguin, 1976) p. 299.
73. D. W. Winnicott, *Playing and Reality* (Penguin, 1974) p. 98. A discussion of the range of critical treatment of Ophelia may be found in Elaine Showalter's essay, 'Representing Ophelia: women, madness, and the responsibilities of feminist criticism', in Patricia Parker and Geoffrey Hartman (eds), *Shakespeare and the Question of Theory* (Methuen, 1985) pp. 77–94.
74. R. A. Foakes, '*Hamlet* and the Court of Elsinore', in *Shakespeare Survey* 9 (1956) p. 38.
75. Machiavelli, *The Prince*, tr. George Bull (Penguin, 1961) pp. 90–1.
76. Ibid., p. 88.
77. Sir Philip Sidney, *The Countess of Pembroke's Arcadia* (Penguin, 1977) p. 154.
78. Michael Long, *The Unnatural Scene: A Study in Shakespearean Tragedy* (Methuen, 1976) p. 132.
79. Bacon, op. cit., p. 10.
80. Quoted in Eleanor Prosser, op. cit., p. 7.
81. René Girard, op. cit., p. 47.
82. Ralph Berry, '"To Say One": an essay on *Hamlet*', in *Shakespeare Survey* 28 (1975) p. 114.
83. Maynard Mack, 'The World of *Hamlet*' (1952), reprinted in *Shakespeare: 'Hamlet'*, Casebook Series, ed. John Jump (Macmillan, 1968) p. 104.
84. Ibid., p. 96.
85. Inga-Stina Ewbank, '*Hamlet* and the Power of Words', in *Shakespeare Survey* 30 (1977) p. 94.
86. Peter Mercer, op. cit., p. 52.
87. Karen Horney, 'The Value of Vindictiveness', in *New Perspectives in Psychoanalysis: Contributions to Karen Horney's Holistic Approach*, ed. Harold Kelman (W. W. Norton & Co., New York, 1965) p. 47.
88. Bacon, op. cit., Essay XXIII: 'Of Wisdom for a Man's Self', p. 65.
89. John Danby, *Shakespeare's Doctrine of Nature: A Study of 'King Lear'* (Faber and Faber, 1949) p. 209.

## PART II: IDEALIZED COURTS AND DREAMS OF FREEDOM

1. The Arden editor's conclusion is for 'a date of composition probably early in 1599, and a first performance in the autumn of that year' (*The Arden Shakespeare, As You Like It*, 1975), while the Oxford

editors (*William Shakespeare, the Complete Works*, ed. Stanley Wells and Gary Taylor, 1986) suggest that the play was composed and performed 'not long before' the date of its entry in the Stationer's Register, 4 August 1600. If the connection with Essex's fortunes is acknowledged, it would seem that the later date is perhaps more convincing, because Essex had been imprisoned in his own home from shortly after Christmas 1599 until September 1600, following a period of imprisonment in York House under the care of the Lord Keeper lasting from 29 September 1599 (the day after his having burst into the Royal Bedchamber before Elizabeth had risen) until just after Christmas that year.

If the play was composed much before autumn 1599, his despatch to Ireland could look like exile, but not to the greenwood. If Arden is taken to resemble Lear's images of confinement, then it could easily stand for Essex's being confined to his own home until September 1600, especially as the extraordinary behaviour which precipitated it would have faded from memory by then. Duke Senior's making the best of exile might then seem an entirely appropriate noble cheerfulness.

2. I agree completely with Brecht's view, well described by Margot Heinemann in her contribution to Dollimore and Sinfield (eds) *Political Shakespeare* (1985), that Shakespeare dramatises the conflict between a declining feudal world, which he represents as tragic, and a nascent bourgeois world, in which he sees new opportunities.
3. C. L. Barber's influential *Shakespeare's Festive Comedy* (Princeton, N.J., 1959), discusses the roots of festivity well at first, but when he comes to look at the plays he seems to forget his awareness of disparity and presents too insistently the view that the plays resolve conflict and promote harmony.
4. *Power on Display: the Politics of Shakespeare's Genres* (1986).
5. See *The Arden Shakespeare, As You Like It*, p. xxvi.
6. *The Living Monument* (1976), p. 5.
7. Conrad Russell, *The Crisis of Parliaments: English History, 1509–1660* (1971), p. 15.
8. *The Arden Shakespeare, As You Like It*, p. 28n.
9. The 'openness' of the play has been argued by Mary Lascelles in John Garratt (ed.), *More Talking of Shakespeare* (1959). Norman Rabkin, *Shakespeare and the Common Understanding* (New York, 1967) deploys the concept of 'complementarity' from theoretical physics to establish the play's undecidability. Alexander Leggatt in *Mosaic* 5 (1971) comments on the play's 'instability'. A similar outlook underlies Helen Gardner's views, both in her essay on *As You Like It* in *More Talking of Shakespeare*, and, more recently, in her rebuff to critics whom she accuses of importing 'inappropriate seriousness' into the comedies, in 'Happy Endings: Literature, Misery, and Joy', *Encounter* 57 (1981).
10. Norbert Elias in *The Civilising Process* (1939) argued that courtiership resulted from a real loss of power, but established a courtly preserve of refinement, a theme taken up by Joan Kelly-Gadol's 'Did Women

Have a Renaissance?' in Renate Bridenthal and Claudia Koonz (eds), *Becoming Visible: Women in European History* (Boston, 1977), and Lauro Martines's 'The Gentleman in Renaissance Italy: Strains of Isolation in the Body Politic', in Robert S. Kinsman (ed.), *The Darker Vision of the Renaissance* (Berkeley, California, 1971).
11. Quoted in Robin Headlam Wells, *Shakespeare, Politics and the State* (1986), p. 12.
12. Ibid., pp. 29–30.
13. John Shaw, 'Fortune and Nature in *As You Like It*', *Shakespeare Survey* 6 (1955), argues that this distinction is the central theme of the play. Elliott Krieger, *A Marxist Study of Shakespeare's Comedies* (1979) gives no quarter: *As You Like It*

> articulates an ideological process, whereby the ruling class uses Nature, or its own translation and redefinition of *nature*, to justify its freedom from labour and the subordination of, or struggle against, other social classes (p. 96),

while in *Twelfth Night*

> the ruling-class ideology that 'all is fortune', that fortune creates and determines nature, is meant to keep people, especially servants, blind to the opposite proposition: that people create nature as they act within time, as they bring about changes in the social order. (p. 130)

My point is that 'nature' is not *used* by the play, but is raised in it and by it, as a teasing question. I will argue that Viola's 'fortune' in *Twelfth Night* is shown to be neither deserved nor preordained, which takes much of the sting out of the view that it might be being used to prop up a ruling class's right to rule, though I find the proposition lying behind Elliott Krieger's view, that is that ideology is a potent instrument for doing just that, an unexceptionable argument in principle. I think that its application here is misplaced.

14. See Brian Vickers, *The Artistry of Shakespeare's Prose* (1968), and Marion Trousdale, *Shakespeare and the Rhetoricians* (1982).
15. P. 41n.
16. Malcolm Evans, *Signifying Nothing: Truth's True Contents in Shakespeare's Text* (1986).
17. The 'dark' view of the comedies has been treated of by Clifford Leech, *Twelfth Night and Shakespearean Comedy* (1965); G. K. Hunter, *Shakespeare, the Late Comedies* (1962, rev. 1969); Anne Barton, in Bradbury and Palmer (eds), *Shakespearean Comedy* (1972); Alexander Leggatt, *Shakespeare's Comedy of Love* (1974); Ralph Berry, *Shakespeare's Comedies* (Princeton, N.J., 1972) and *Changing Styles in Shakespeare* (1981); Majorie Garber, in Charney (ed.), *Shakespearean Comedy* (New York, 1980).
18. Anne Barton recognizes this in her essay in Garratt (ed.), *More Talking of Shakespeare*.
19. See Helen Gardner in Garratt (ed.), *More Talking of Shakespeare*; John

Notes to pp. 104–110

Dover Wilson, *Shakespeare's Happy Comedies* (1962); John K. Hale, '"I'll Strive to Please You Every Day": Pleasure and Meaning in Shakespeare's Mature Comedies', *Studies in English Literature* 21 (1981). A. P. Riemer has argued interestingly that the 'dark' view of the comedies arises from criticism's own habits and procedures; see his *Antic Fables: Patterns of Evasion in Shakespeare's Comedies* (Manchester, 1980).

20. This perception accords well with M. M. Mahood's accurate remark that comedy is 'a communal and hence not totally unanimous event' ('Shakespeare's Middle Comedies: a Generation of Criticism', *Shakespeare Survey* 32, 1979).
21. *The Arden Shakespeare, Twelfth Night*, ed. J. M. Lothian and T. W. Craik (1975), p. 10n.
22. *The Crisis of Parliaments*, p. 17.
23. Disguise is well discussed by Nancy K. Hayles in 'Sexual Disguise in *Twelfth Night* and *As You Like It*', Shakespeare Survey 32 (1979). The question of gender definition in Shakespeare's comedies is well introduced by Catherine Belsey in Drakakis (ed.), *Alternative Shakespeares* (1985).
24. At this point the question of the discourse of pastoral as a whole is raised, but it is beyond the scope of this essay to consider it. Louis A. Montrose has discussed the relationship between pastoral and social mobility in 'Of Gentlemen and Shepherds: the Politics of Elizabethan Cultural Form', *ELH* 50:3 (Fall, 1983). His useful conclusion, that 'Elizabethan pastoral form is the symbolic equipment of gentlemen-shepherds who (as Puttenham slyly puts it) "do busily negotiat by coulor of otiation"', cannot be put to work directly for either of these plays, unless it is assumed that they were composed exclusively, or at least primarily, for performance at court (which is where they would participate in the deployment of such equipment).

    It is my assumption that they were not, and cannot be seen as part of the life of the gentry at court or on its fringes. The distance from courtly play, which Louis Montrose rightly calls 'courtly *work*', gives us a different view of 'play' in these plays. 'Play' is taken 'out of court' by these plays, and is offered to an audience whose relationship to Elizabeth's Court is imaginative in a spirit of rueful and ironic awareness of that distance and of its implications.
25. See William W. E. Slights, 'Maid and Man in *Twelfth Night*', *The Journal of English and Germanic Philology* 80 (1981) for a fascinating discussion of androgyny as a central image in Renaissance discussions of love. See also Leonard Tennenhouse, *Power on Display*, pp. 64–7. Tennenhouse raises the question of androgyny as well. It is interesting to note that Philip Stubbes took exception to women wearing men's clothes:

> Our Apparell was giuen vs as a signe distinctiue to discern betwixt sex and sex, and therfore one to weare the Apparel of another sex is to participate with the same, and to adulterate the veritie of his owne kinde. Wherefore these Women may not

improperly be called *Hermaphroditi*, that is, Monsters of bothe kindes, half women, half men. (*The Anatomy of Abuses*, 1583, repr. *New Shakespeare Society*, 1877–9, p. 73)

26. See *Carnival and Theater*, especially Part One.
27. Catherine Belsey comments:

    Fictional texts neither reflect a real world nor present an ideal one. But they do offer definitions and redefinitions which make it possible to reinterpret a world we have taken for granted .... New meanings release the possibility of new practices (*Alternative Shakespeares*, p. 190).

28. Geoffrey Hartman gleefully exploits word-play in *Twelfth Night* in his contribution to P. Parker and G. Hartman (eds), *Shakespeare and the Question of Theory* (1985).
29. Barbara Everett, 'What You Will', *Essays in Criticism* 35 (1985) is excellent on time in the play.
30. For a good exposition of Marcel's thought see Kenneth T. Gallagher, *The Philosophy of Gabriel Marcel* (New York, 1962).
31. The literature on revelry has now become too extensive to sample effectively: Enid Welsford's *The Court Masque* (1927) and *The Fool* (1935); B. Scribner's essay, 'Reformation, Carnival, and the World Turned Upside-Down', *Social History* 3 (1978); P. Burke, *Popular Culture in Early Modern Europe* (1978); B. Babcock (ed.), *The Reversible World: Symbolic Inversion in Art and Society* (New York, 1978); M. Bakhtin, *Rabelais and his World* (Bloomington, Indiana, 1984); M. Mullett, *Popular Culture and Popular Protest in Late Medieval and Early Modern Europe*, are all useful. I have already mentioned Michael Bristol, C. L. Barber, and J. M. Golby and A. W. Purdue.
32. Ralph Berry is surely right in *Changing Styles in Shakespeare* (1981), when he says that 'we know too much about the sadistic undercurrent of much practical joking to be at ease with it'. If Essex's fate is in the air, there may well be an echo of his imprisonment to add poignancy to Malvolio's. I would not go as far as Ralph Berry does in 'Twelfth Night: the Experience of the Audience', *Shakespeare Survey* 34 (1981), when he says that the play offers the audience 'theatre as blood-sport'. I think that we come close enough to see that his point about practical joking is right (and come to judge revelry in this light). I do not think the play is at ease with practical joking either.
33. See Keith Wrightson, *English Society, 1580–1680* (1982), for a fascinating account of popular responses to these events, especially the closing chapter for the speed with which the old 'pastimes' which had been suppressed during the Interregnum reappeared with the Restoration.
34. Though Roger Warren argues well for a cheerful view of the play ('"Smiling at Grief": Some Techniques of Comedy in *Twelfth Night* and *Cosi Fan Tutte*', *Shakespeare Survey* 32, 1979), I do not think that his view that Feste's closing song 'provides a perspective on the happiness achieved by the lovers, on their "golden time", without

## PART III: LATE ROMANCES: MAGIC, MAJESTY AND MASQUE

1. Robert Cecil in 1603; quoted in Neil Cuddy, 'The Revival of the Entourage: the Bedchamber of James I, 1603–1625', in David Starkey, ed., *The English Court* (Longman, 1987) p. 196.
2. See R. F. Leslie, ed., *The Wanderer* (Manchester University Press, 1966), p. 62: (my translation) 'Often when sleep and sorrow bind the wretched exile, he dreams of embracing his lord, of laying his hand and his head on the lord's knee, as in the days when he enjoyed the bounty of the treasure-throne. When the man without joy awakes again, he sees before him the yellow waves, sea-birds swimming and spreading their feathers; frost and snow fall mingled with hail'; and I. L. Gordon, ed., *The Seafarer* (Methuen, 1960) p. 35: (my translation) 'For my entertainment I had the song of the wild swan; in place of the laughter of men, the cry of the gannet and the scream of the curlew; instead of mead, my ears drank only the call of the sea-gull'.

    The extraordinary vitality of these rhetorical conventions can be illustrated by their re-appearance in the primary source for *The Winter's Tale*, Greene's *Pandosto: The Triumph of Time*, 1588, reprinted (from a 1595 edition) in J. H. P. Pafford, ed., *The Arden Shakespeare: 'The Winter's Tale'* (London, Methuen, 1963) as the king's daughter is consigned to the sea: 'And shalt thou, sweet babe, be committed to fortune, when thou art already spited by fortune? Shall thy tender mouth, instead of sweet kisses, be nipped with bitter storms? Shalt thou have the whistling winds for thy lullaby, and the salt-sea foam instead of sweet milk?' (p. 193).
3. James I, speech before Parliament at Whitehall, 21 March 1610; see J. R. Tanner, *Constitutional Documents of the Reign of James I* (Cambridge University Press, 1930) p. 15.
4. George Herbert, *The Bag* (c. 1630), l. 5.
5. HMC, *Portland MSS*, II, p. 126. The phrase describes one of the original tempest-quellers in *Matthew*, 8: 24–7.
6. 17 May 1603; see S. Schoenbaum, *Shakespeare: a compact documentary life*, (Oxford University Press, 1977).
7. Stephen Orgel commits a substantial error by promoting Shakespeare from Groom to Gentleman of the Chamber: see Orgel, ed., *The Oxford Shakespeare: 'The Tempest'*, (Oxford University Press, 1987). All my quotations from *The Tempest* are taken from this edition.
8. G. E. Bentley, 'Shakespeare and the Blackfriars Theatre', *Shakespeare Survey*, 1, 1948, p. 40.
9. Revels Accounts; see E. K. Chambers, *William Shakespeare*, vol. 2,

(Oxford University Press, 1936) p. 342.
10. Leonard Tennenhouse, 'Strategies of State and Political Plays', in Jonathan Dollimore and Alan Sinfield, eds, *Political Shakespeare* (Manchester University Press, 1985).
11. J. M. Nosworthy, 'The Narrative Sources of *The Tempest*', RES, 24, 1948; Jan Kott, '*The Aeneid* and *The Tempest*', Arion, 3 and 4, 1976, pp. 424–51; John Pitcher, 'A Theatre of the Future: *The Aeneid* and *The Tempest*', Essays in Criticism, xxxiv, 3, 1984, pp. 193–215.
12. This view is summarized approvingly by Frances Yates in *Shakespeare's Last Plays: a New Approach*, (Routledge and Kegan Paul, 1975).
13. Stuart Clark, 'The Theatre State: Spectacles of Disenchantment in Early Modern Europe', paper delivered at a University of Wales Staff Colloquium, *History and Literature*, May 1987. I am grateful to Stuart Clark for letting me have a copy.
14. Stuart Clark, quoted from the conference paper 'The Theatre State'.
15. Stephen Orgel, *The Illusion of Power: political theatre in the English Renaissance* (Berkeley: University of California Press, 1975) p. 38.
16. See Leah S. Marcus, *The Politics of Mirth* (University of Chicago Press, 1986); and Stephen Orgel, *The Jonsonian Masque* (Columbia University Press, 1965).
17. Muriel Bradbrook, *The Rise of the Common Player* (Chatto and Windus, 1962) (Cambridge University Press, 1979) pp. 39–40.
18. 'Preface' to *The Tempest, or the Enchanted Island*, 1670, in Maximilian E. Novak and George Robert Guffey, eds, *Works of John Dryden*, vol. x (*Plays*), (Berkeley: University of California Press, 1970) p. 3.
19. Simon Forman's *Bocke of Plaies*, Bodleian MS. Ashmole, 208, ff. 200–13; see Chambers, 1936, ii, pp. 337–41.
20. It may seem imprudent to hang part of an argument on J. C. Maxwell's emendation: the Folio text reads 'present', while in the Arden text Frank Kermode's editorial judgement, following Maxwell, condemns this as meaningless, and conjectures 'presence'. Stephen Orgel in the Oxford text restores the Folio reading, asserting 'present' to be a perfectly acceptable reading, and arguing (correctly) that there is no bibliographical parallel for the phrase.

    Actually 'the peace of the present' is clearly in context quite meaningless; where both 'peace' and 'presence', with their technical links to the language of royal authority – 'the king's peace', 'in the presence' – and their Christian overtones, belong in a dialogue about authority and the limits of power, which in turn extends the previous reference to Gonzalo's powers as a 'councillor'.
21. An instructive parallel is provided by Prospero himself as he apologises for the aborted masque, interrupted by the strange accession of his own ungovernable rage:

    > A turn or two I'll walk
    > To still my beating mind
    > (IV.i.162–3).
22. William Blake's maxim from *The Marriage of Heaven and Hell*: 'Energy

is Eternal Delight'; see Geoffrey Keynes, ed., *Blake: Complete Writings* (Oxford University Press, 1966) p. 149.

23. See Stephen Greenblatt, 'Martial Law in the Land of Cockaigne', in *Shakespearean Negotiations* (Oxford University Press, 1988); Terence Hawkes, 'Playhouse-Workhouse', in *That Shakespeherian Rag*, Methuen, 1986; Peter Hulme, 'Hurricanes in the Caribees: the constitution of the discourse of English colonialism', in Francis Barker, *et al.* eds, *1642: Literature and Power in the Seventeenth Century* (University of Essex, 1981); Paul Brown, '"This thing of darkness I acknowledge mine": *The Tempest* and the discourse of colonialism', in Dollimore and Sinfield, *Political Shakespeare* (1985); Francis Barker and Peter Hulme, 'Nymphs and reapers heavily vanish: the discursive contexts of *The Tempest*', in John Drakakis, ed., *Alternative Shakespeares* (Methuen, 1985).
24. Michel de Montaigne, 'Of the Cannibals', *The Essays*, translated by John Florio, 1603, Book 1, chapter 30. Printed in Orgel, *The Tempest* (1987).
25. E. M. Forster, *A Passage to India*, 1924; Howard Brenton, *The Romans in Britain*, (Methuen, 1981).
26. See Hawkes, *Shakespeherian Rag* (1986).
27. See Lawrence Stone, *The Crisis of the Aristocracy* (London: Oxford University Press, abridged edition, 1967) pp. 176–82.
28. See Greenblatt, *Shakespearean Negotiations* (1988).
29. Orgel notes resemblances to Ben Jonson, *Hymenaei* (1606) and *The Haddington Masque* (1608); to Campion's *Lord Hay's Masque* (1607), and to Samuel Daniel's *Vision of the Twelve Goddesses* (1604). See Orgel, *The Tempest* (1987) pp. 173–4n.
30. Enid Welsford, *The Court Masque* (1927) p. 3.
31. J. H. P. Pafford, ed., *The Arden Shakespeare: 'The Winter's Tale'* (London: Methuen, 1963) p. lv.
32. See John Drakakis, 'Introduction' to his edition, *Alternative Shakespeares* (London: Methuen, 1985) p. 10.
33. The obvious contrast between the climate of receptiveness and institutional hospitality currently afforded to feminist criticism, and the corresponding institutional resistance confronting gay criticism, seems to me a serious contemporary moral and ideological problem. For a corrective emphasis see Simon Shepherd, 'Shakespeare and Homosexuality' in Graham Holderness, ed., *The Shakespeare Myth* (Manchester: Manchester University Press, 1988).
34. See John Turner, 'Introduction' to Graham Holderness, Nick Potter and John Turner, *Shakespeare: The Play of History* (London: Macmillan, 1988) pp. 7–8.
35. Robert Greene, *Pandosto: the Triumph of Time*, 1588, reprinted (from a 1595 edition) in Pafford, ed., *The Winter's Tale*, p. 185.
36. See John Turner's discussion of this passage in Holderness, Potter and Turner, *Shakespeare: The Play of History* (1988) pp. 99–100.
37. See Judie Newman, 'Exit Pursued by a Bear', *Notes and Queries*, 35:4, December 1988, p. 484; drawing from Emmanual Le Roy Ladurie, *Carnival: A People's Uprising, 1579–1580* (Scolar Press, 1980).

38. Bryan Loughrey and Neil Taylor, 'Ferdinand and Miranda at Chess', *Shakespeare Survey*, 35, 1983.
39. Inga-Stina Ewbank, 'The Triumph of Time', in Kenneth Muir, ed., *'The Winter's Tale': a Selection of Critical Essays* (Macmillan, 1969).

## ENDGAMES

1. Norbert Elias, *The Court Society* (Oxford: Blackwell, 1983); Lawrence Stone, *The Crisis of the Aristocracy, 1558–1641* (Oxford: Clarendon Press, 1965); G. R. Elton, *The Tudor Revolution in Government* (Cambridge: Cambridge University Press, 1953). The results can be sampled in David Starkey *et al.*, *The English Court* (London: Longman, 1987).
2. Sir Walter Raleigh, 'The Lie', in *Selected Writings*, ed. Gerald Hammond (Manchester: Carcenet Press, 1984) p. 51.
3. Leonard Tennenhouse, *Power on Display: the Politics of Shakespeare's Genres* (London: Methuen, 1986); Stephen Orgel, *The Illusion of Power: Political Theatre in the Renaissance* (Berkeley: University of California Press, 1975).
4. Thomas M. Greene, 'Magic and Festivity at the Renaissance Court', *Renaissance Quarterly*, XL:4, Winter 1987, p. 643.
5. William Hudson, 'A Treatise of the Court of Star Chamber', c. 1633, in J. R. Tanner, ed., *Constitutional Documents of the Reign of James I* (Cambridge: Cambridge University Press, 1961) p. 142. The editor comments sourly: 'Hudson's courtly explanation can scarcely be taken seriously'.
6. As I write this the education ministry of the Conservative Thatcher government is about to launch an attack on the uses of 'empathy' in the teaching of history at GCSE level in our schools.
7. Augusto Boal, *Theatre of the Oppressed* (London: Pluto Press, 1979).
8. W. B. Yeats, 'Among School Children', *Collected Poems* (London: Macmillan, 1950) p. 245.
9. Malcolm Evans, *Signifying Nothing: Truth's True Contents in Shakespeare's Text* (Harvester, 1987).
10. See for example Graham Parry, *The Golden Age Restor'd: the culture of the Stuart court, 1603–42*, (Manchester University Press, 1981); and Roy Strong, *Henry, Prince of Wales, and England's Lost Renaissance* (Thames and Hudson, 1986).
11. R. Malcolm Smuts, *Court Culture and the Origins of a Royalist Tradition in Early Stuart England* (University of Pennsylvania Press, 1987).

# Index

Anderson, Perry, 5, 53
Aragon, Katherine of, 240

Babcock, B., 258n
Bacon, Francis, 15–18, 58, 73, 251n, 253n, 254n
Bakhtin, Mikhail, 258n
Barber, C. L., 9, 20, 44, 46, 252nn, 255n, 258n
Barker, Francis, 176, 178, 261n
Barton, Anne, 256nn
Beaumont, Francis, 138, 234
de Belleforest, François, 61
Belsey, Catherine, 257n, 258n
Bentley, G. E., 259n
Bernstein, Basil, 123
Berry, Ralph, 73, 256n, 258n
Blake, William, 167, 244, 260n
Boal, Augusto, 243
Bohannan, Laura, 253n
Bradbrook, Muriel, 88, 260n
Brecht, Bertolt, 38, 145, 154, 255n
Brenton, Howard, 178
Bridenthal, Renate, 256n
Bristol, Michael D., 8, 23, 39, 83, 110, 250n, 258nn
Brooke, Christopher, 180
Brown, Paul, 176, 261n
Browne, Robert, 116
Buckingham, Duke of (George Villiers), 130, 133
Burke, Peter, 253n, 258n

Campion, Edmund, 139, 234, 261n
Castiglione, Baldassare, 65, 254n
Cecil, Robert, 78, 83, 85, 106, 129–31, 259n
Chambers, E. K., 259n
Charles I, 120, 130, 145
Chaucer, Geoffrey, 27, 216
Clark, Stuart, 143–4, 250n, 260n
Coleridge, Samuel Taylor, 1
Colie, Rosalie L., 60, 253n
Congreve, William, 21

*The Way of the World*, 31
Conrad, Joseph, 62, 83
Cooper, David E., 251n
Corneille, Pierre,
  *Le Cid*, 91
Cuddy, Neil, 133–4, 259n

Danby, John, 4, 9, 77
Daniel, Samuel, 261n
David, Richard, 251n
Davies, John, 250n
Davies, Sir John, 1, 11, 243
  *Orchestra*, 10
Derrida, Jacques, 99
Devonshire, Countess of, 130
Dickens, Charles,
  *Bleak House*, 95
Digby, Sir John, 133
Digges, Dudley, 180
Dollimore, Jonathan, 251n, 255n, 260n, 261n
Donne, John, 11, 69
Douglas, Mary, 123
Drakakis, John, 257n, 261nn
Dryden, John, 147

Elias, Norbert, 3, 237, 255n, 262n
Eliot, George, 216
Eliot, T. S., 49, 57, 92
Elizabeth I, 1, 5, 6, 7, 29, 55, 78, 85, 92, 106, 123, 132, 255n
Elton, G. R., 238, 262n
Essex, Earl of (Robert Devereux), 5, 55, 60, 78, 83, 85, 88, 104, 106, 255n, 258n
Etherege, Sir George,
  *The Man of Mode*, 32, 35
Evans, Malcolm, 102, 262n
Everett, Barbara, 258n
Ewbank, Inga-Stina, 234, 254n

Fielding, John, 252n
Fletcher, John, 138
Foakes, R. A., 57, 65

## Index

Forman, Simon, 260n
Forster, E. M., 178
Freud, Sigmund, 50

Gallagher, Kenneth T., 258n
Garber, Marjorie, 256n
Gardner, Helen, 255n, 256n
Garratt, John, 255n
Gates, Sir Thomas, 180, 182–3
Geertz, Clifford, 11, 240, 242
Girard, René, 51, 73, 240
Golby, J. M., 84, 258n
Golding, William, 54
Gordon, I. L., 259n
da Granada, Luis, 73
Graves, Michael A. R., 250n
Greenblatt, Stephen, 176, 182–3, 249nn, 261n
Greene, Robert, 205–7, 216, 218, 259n, 261n
Greene, Thomas M., 240–42
Guffey, George Robert, 260n

Hale, John K., 257n
Hammond, Gerald, 262n
Hardy, Thomas, 259n
Hartman, Geoffrey, 254n, 258n
Hawkes, Terence, 261nn
Hayles, Nancy K., 257n
Heidegger, Martin, 113, 118
Heinemann, Margot, 255n
Henley, W. E., 53
Henry VII, 240
Henry VIII, 145
Herbert, George, 130
Hobbes, Thomas, 177
Hooker, Jeremy, 46
Hooker, Richard, 116
Horney, Karen, 75–6
Hudson, William, 241
Hulme, Peter, 176, 178, 261n
Hunter, G. K., 256n
Huysmans, J. K., 100

Ibsen, Henrik, 58

James I, 8, 46, 51, 85, 123, 125, 129–35, 139, 142–5, 153
James, Mervyn, 29, 58, 250n, 252n

Jones, Inigo, 146, 147
Jonson, Ben, 2, 11, 138, 139, 146
    *Fortunate Isles, The*, 179
    *Haddington Masque*, 261n
    *Hymenaei*, 261n
    *Masque of Oberon*, 139, 145, 223, 228
    *News from the New World*, 179

Kelly-Gadol, Joan, 255–6n
Kermode, Frank, 260n
Keynes, Geoffrey, 261n
Khan, M. M. R., 54
Kierkegaard, Søren, 124
Kinsman, Robert S., 256n
Kitto, H. D. F., 253n
Koonz, Claudia, 256n
Kott, Jan, 260n
Krieger, Elliott, 256n

La Bruyère, Jean de, 2, 11, 47–8
Lascelles, Mary, 255n
Latham, Agnes, 90, 98, 101
Lawrence, D. H., 59, 216
Leech, Clifford, 256n
Leggatt, Alexander, 255n, 256n
Leicester, Earl of (Robert Dudley), 87
Le Roy Ladurie, Emmanual, 261n
Leslie, R. F., 259n
Li Tai Po, 118
Loades, David, 8, 26, 35, 250n, 251n
Long, Michael, 72
Loughrey, Bryan, 230–1
Louis XIV, 2
Lupset, Thomas, 95–6
Lyly, John, 88

Machiavelli, Niccolò, 70, 71, 254n
Mack, Maynard, 74
Mahler, Gustav, 118
Mahood, M. M., 257n
Manningham, John, 88, 110
Marcel, Gabriel, 115, 118
Marcus, Leah S., 260n
Marston, John, 2, 11, 249n
Martines, Lauro, 256n
Marx, Karl, 239
Maxwell, J. C., 260n

# Index

Mercer, Peter, 252n, 254n
Montaigne, Michel de, 54, 96, 97, 172, 177, 181, 251n, 253n
Montrose, Louis A., 6, 21, 33, 34, 36, 37, 46–7, 257n
*Mucedorus*, 223
Muir, Kenneth, 262n
Mullett, M., 258n

Newman, Judie, 261n
Nietzsche, Friedrich, 84, 118, 120, 124
Nosworthy, J. M., 260n
Novak, Maximilian E., 260n

Orgel, Stephen, 139, 146, 147, 160, 170, 191, 243, 259n, 260nn, 261n, 262n
*The Illusion of Power*, 239
Overbury, Sir Thomas, 133
Ovid, 138

Pafford, J. H. P., 261n
Parker, Patricia, 254n, 258n
Parry, Graham, 262n
Pembroke, Earl of (William Herbert), 180
Pitcher, John, 260n
Plato,
*Gorgias*, 100
Pole, Reginald, 95–6, 97
de la Primaudaye, Peter, 22
*The French Academie*, 23
Prosser, Eleanor, 56, 254n
Purdue, A. W., 84, 258n
Puttenham, George, 99

Rabkin, Norman, 255n
Raleigh, Sir Walter, 1, 2, 29, 238
Riemer, A. P., 257n
Russell, Conrad, 109, 255n

Schoenbaum, S., 259n
*Seafarer, The*, 129, 259n
Scott, Paul, 178
Scribner, B., 258n
Shakespeare, William,
*Antony and Cleopatra*, 78
*As You Like It*, 7, 79, 83, 86–104, 110, 113, 116, 122, 123, 125, 246, 254–5n, 256n
*Coriolanus*, 78, 150
*Cymbeline*, 185–7
*Hamlet*, 3, 6, 8, 12, 16–17, 31, 35, 47, 49–79, 122, 140, 161, 206, 210
*Henry VIII*, 138, 246
*Julius Caesar*, 150
*King Lear*, 8, 71, 78, 97, 150, 161, 166, 215
*Love's Labour's Lost*, 4, 5, 6, 7, 16, 17, 19–48, 52, 54, 59, 63, 78, 110, 122, 137, 139, 160, 196, 203, 246
*Macbeth*, 8, 56, 57, 71, 78, 91
*Merchant of Venice, The*, 7, 86
*Midsummer Night's Dream, A*, 228
*Much Ado About Nothing*, 7, 233–4
*Othello*, 78, 142, 177
*Pericles*, 150
*Richard II*, 5
*Taming of the Shrew, The*, 43
*Tempest, The*, 7, 8, 122, 123, 125, 135, 136–94, 209, 221, 222, 230, 232, 234, 235, 246, 249n
*Timon of Athens*, 78, 161
*Twelfth Night*, 7, 39, 83, 88, 104, 105–21, 122, 123, 124, 125, 249n, 256n
*Winter's Tale, The*, 7, 8, 122, 125, 142, 150, 159, 195–235, 259n
Sharpe, R. B., 88, 106
Shaw, John, 256n
Shepherd, Simon, 261n
Showalter, Elaine, 254n
Sidney, Sir Philip, 8, 9, 11, 12, 64, 69, 88, 162, 252n
*Arcadia*, 70–1
Sinfield, Alan, 255n, 260n, 261n
Skelton, John, 249n
Slights, William, W. E., 257n
Smuts, R. Malcolm, 262n
Southampton, Earl of (Henry Wriothsley), 88, 180
Spenser, Edmund, 8, 64, 69, 124, 162
Starkey, David, 20, 250n, 251nn, 259n, 262n

# Index

Starkey, Thomas, 95–6
Stone, Lawrence, 21, 32, 181, 237–8, 261n, 262n
Strachey, William, 180–2
Strong, Roy, 262n
Stuart, Prince Henry, 132, 180
Stuart, Princess Elizabeth, 136
Stubbes, Philip, 9, 10, 11, 118, 257–8n

Tanner, J. R., 259n, 262n
Taylor, Gary, 255n
Taylor, Neil, 230–1
Tennenhouse, Leonard, 86, 87, 88, 110, 111, 112, 138, 239, 243, 257n, 262n
Terence, 55
Thatcher, Margaret, 262n
Trousdale, Marion, 256n
Turner, Victor, 110

Vernon, Elizabeth, 88

Vickers, Brian, 256n
Virgil, 138

Walter, J. H., 88, 106
*Wanderer, The*, 129, 259n
Warren, Roger, 258n
Weber, Max, 21
Wells, Robin Headlam, 256n
Wells, Stanley, 255n
Welsford, Enid, 258n, 261n
Wilson, John Dover, 256–7n
Winnicott, D. W., 63, 252nn
Wordsworth, William, 12, 46, 216
Wrightson, Keith, 258n
Wyatt, Sir Thomas, 2

Yates, Frances A., 251n, 260n
Yeats, W. B., 5, 53, 77, 119, 120, 262n
Young, Alan, 249n

Zitner, S. P., 60